Meditations on Various Subjects

BY

SAINT JOHN EUDES

Translated from the French

With an Introduction by

THE LATE REVEREND CHARLES LEBRUN, C.J.M., S.T.D.

FORMERLY PROVINCIAL OF THE CANADIAN PROVINCE
OF THE EUDIST FATHERS

Foreword by

THE MOST REVEREND P. A. BRAY, C.J.M., D.D.

BISHOP OF SAINT JOHN, N. B.

NEW YORK
P. J. KENEDY & SONS
1947

Imprimi Potest:

    A. D'Amours, C.J.M.
        Praepositus Provincialis

Laval-des-Rapides, P.Q.,
die 27 Martii 1946.

Nihil Obstat:

    John M. Fearns, S.T.D.
        Censor Librorum

Imprimatur:

    ✠ Francis Cardinal Spellman
        Archbishop of New York

  July 12, 1946

GENERAL PREFACE

St. John Eudes has been called "the wonder of his age." Missionary, founder, reformer of the clergy, he crowded into a life of seventy-nine years so many and such varied accomplishments that one marvels how a single man could achieve so much. In addition to the activities of an incessant and many-sided apostolate, he wrote a number of valuable books, which rank him among the most prolific ascetic writers of the seventeenth century.

For many years the devotional works of St. John Eudes were practically unknown.[1] Occasionally a volume was discovered in the library of some seminary or religious house. Many others preserved in manuscript form were lost in the chaos of the French Revolution.[2] At the beginning of the present century the sons of St. John Eudes united in a tribute of filial piety to bring out a complete edition of the works of their spiritual father, seeking them in public and private libraries throughout the world.[3] About twenty volumes were found and edited in 1905 by the late Fathers Charles Lebrun, C.J.M., and Joseph Dau-

---

[1] Before the French Revolution the works of St. John Eudes were popular in France. In 1792 the houses of the Congregation of Jesus and Mary were confiscated by the Government and its members were massacred or dispersed throughout Europe. With the suppression of the Eudists, their rich literary heritage was widely scattered and partially destroyed. It was not until the re-establishment of the Congregation of Jesus and Mary in 1826 that effort was made to recover the printed and manuscript works of St. John Eudes. The research was carried on until the latter part of the nineteenth century. In the "Préface Générale" to the Oeuvres Complètes (Vannes, 1905), Father Charles Lebrun points out that one of the purposes of the edition was "to unearth these works buried too long in oblivion," *exhumer ces ouvrages ensevelis depuis trop longtemps dans l'oubli* . . .

[2] The following manuscripts were not found: *The Christian Man, All Jesus, The Divine Office, The Admirable Sacrifice of the Mass, Meditations* (2 vols.), *Sermons of St. John Eudes* (3 vols.), *Favors Obtained by the Diocese of Coutances through the Blessed Virgin, The Divine Childhood of Jesus, The Devotion to the Sacred Heart of Jesus, The Admirable Life of Mary des Vallées* (incomplete copy found at Laval University Library, Quebec) and *Correspondence of St. John Eudes.*

[3] Cf. *Oeuvres Complètes*, p. xiv.

phin, C.J.M. The first edition in French, *Oeuvres Complètes du Vénérable Jean Eudes,* ran into twelve octavo volumes with introductions, explanatory notes, analytic and alphabetic indexes of great value. These writings constitute a complete summa of ascetic and pastoral theology. The list is as follows:

Volume I. The Life and Kingdom of Jesus in Christian Souls. In this work the Saint develops his spiritual teaching on the Christian life, namely, that the Christian life is simply the life of Jesus extended and continued in each one of us.

Volume II. This volume contains six short treatises on subjects relating to the Christian life:

1. *A Treatise on the Respect Due to Holy Places,* which is an echo of the fiery denunciations he pronounced during his missions against profaners of the temple of God.

2. *Meditations on Humility,* a series of meditations on the profession of humility as used daily in his order of priests, the Congregation of Jesus and Mary.

3. *Interior Colloquies of the Soul with God,* meditations on creation, the end of man and the grace of Baptism.

4. *Man's Contract with God in Holy Baptism,* a summary of the teachings of Sacred Scripture and Tradition on the Sacrament of Baptism.

5. *The Practice of Piety,* a brief explanation of what is necessary in order to live a Christian life.

6. *Catechism of the Mission,* an outline of the catechetical instructions given during a mission.

Volume III. Contains two important works on sacerdotal perfection:

1. *The Memorial of the Ecclesiastical Life,* an explanation of the dignity and duties of the priesthood.

2. *A Manual of Piety for Use in an Ecclesiastical Community,* in which the author explains how the means of sanctification he recommended to his priests should be practically applied in their daily lives.

Volume IV. Comprises significant works on the priestly ministry.

1. *The Apostolic Preacher* is one of the first treatises written on the ministry of the Word of God and is even yet one of the most practical.

2. *The Good Confessor* explains the qualities and obligations of the minister of the Sacrament of Penance.

3. *Counsels for Mission Confessors* suggests practical means of assisting penitents to make their examination of conscience and excite themselves to contrition.

4. *The Manner of Serving Mass* explains the dignity and holiness of this act and what one must do to perform it devoutly and worthily.

Volume V. The Admirable Childhood of the Most Holy Mother of God. This book treats of the holy childhood of Mary and the practical means of honoring the mysteries and virtues of her early life.

Volumes VI, VII, VIII contain the entire writings of the Saint on the Sacred Hearts of Jesus and Mary. The work is entitled: *The Admirable Heart of the Most Holy Mother of God.* It comprises twelve books covering the complete theology of the devotion to the Sacred Hearts. Eleven books discuss the theory, history, and practice of the devotion to the Immaculate Heart of Mary. The last book deals with the devotion to the Sacred Heart of Jesus. It is this work, together with the Offices of the Sacred Hearts, that merit for him the title of Father, Doctor and Apostle of the Devotion to the Sacred Hearts.

Volume IX. The Rules and Constitutions of the Congregation of Jesus and Mary.

Volume X. Contains *The Rules and Constitutions of the Order of Our Lady of Charity*, the *Directory* of the Order, and a collection of two hundred and forty letters.

Volumes XI and *XII* embrace the Saint's *Liturgical Works*, comprising twenty-five Offices and Masses for feasts to which he urged special devotion, the *Memorial of God's Blessings* and several other minor works.

The second French edition appeared in 1935, *Oeuvres Choisies de Saint Jean Eudes*, prepared under the direction of Father Lebrun, the leading authority on Eudistic research. It comprises nine volumes: *The Life and Kingdom of Jesus in Christian Souls, Meditations of Various Subjects, Regulae Vitae Christianae et Sacerdotalis, Man's Contract with God in Holy Baptism, Letters and Minor Works, Writings on the Priesthood, The Sacred Heart of Jesus, The Admirable Heart of Mary,* and *The Admirable Childhood of the Mother of God.* The format of these volumes is compact and more convenient than the 1905 edition, which is now out of print.

The publication of the works of St. John Eudes revealed the extent and depth of their spiritual doctrine. Cardinal Pitra, who was associated with the cause of Beatification, discovered in the writings of St. John Eudes a remarkable depth of thought and purity of doctrine. Cardinal Vivès has more recently expressed his admiration:

I was acquainted with the Doctors of the Order of Saint Francis; I was acquainted with Saint Teresa and Saint John of the Cross, the mystical writers of my own country, Spain; but I was completely ignorant of the writings of Father Eudes. As a member of the Sacred Congregation of Rites it was my duty to study his life and his works, and I am in admiration. Blessed John Eudes must be ranked with the great lights of the Church. His spiritual doctrine is profound and of wonderful exactitude. He is one of the writers who has best propounded the doctrine of the Gospel.[4]

The late Father Ange Le Doré, for fifty years Superior General of the Congregation of Jesus and Mary, wrote:

The works of Blessed John Eudes, although they do not bear the scientific touch of the professional theologian, are nevertheless proof of his remarkable theological, ascetic and scriptural knowledge. . . . He is not a Doctor after the fashion of the scholastics of the thirteenth century or of the great theologians of the sixteenth and seventeenth centuries. As they, he might have built up theses and composed books didactic in form; but he was before all a saver of souls. For him the science of theology found its chief field of usefulness in the practice of virtue and in the acquisition of sanctity of which it is the principle. . . . He was a Doctor after the manner of the Apostles, the Fathers of the Church, St. Francis de Sales and St. Alphonsus de Liguori. The science which shines in his works not only emits light; it engenders piety and sanctity.[5]

The spiritual doctrine expounded by St. John Eudes follows the teaching of Cardinal Pierre de Bérulle and Father Charles de Condren, two prominent members of the seventeenth-century French School of Spirituality. St. John Eudes applies this doctrine to the devotion to the

[4] Quoted by P. A. Bray, C.J.M., *Saint John Eudes* (Halifax, 1925), p. 116.
[5] Quoted by Bray, *op. cit.*, p. 117.

Sacred Hearts of Jesus and Mary, developing and rendering it more precise and practical. He has the rare gift of expressing the most sublime truths in simple, familiar language. He also excels in condensing into a few pages a complete scheme of Christian life and perfection.

The wish was repeatedly expressed that these inspirational writings could be made available to English-speaking readers. Excellent abridged editions of certain books were published in England and in Canada, but they did not do justice to the literary value of the Saint. Consequently, the Eudist Fathers commemorating their tercentenary in 1943 resolved to publish a complete translation of the principal works of their founder. Competent translators were secured and much time and effort were expended to produce readable volumes in modern English, faithful to the spirit and style of the original.

The first English edition, *Selected Works of Saint John Eudes,* is the result. In presenting it to the public the Eudist Fathers and the Religious of Our Lady of Charity of the Refuge, and of the Good Shepherd, wish to thank all those who contributed to the success of this comprehensive undertaking. They are especially grateful to the distinguished churchmen who have so graciously accepted to introduce these volumes to Catholic readers, because they consider that the works of St. John Eudes should be more widely known. The Saint in his apostolic work and in his writings ranks with the eminent figures who belong not to one country and to one religious order but to the universal Church. Three centuries have passed since he wrote the works now being printed in the new world, a striking illustration that he wrote for all time. He still speaks in accents that penetrate the mind and heart of the reader to enlighten, purify and sanctify so that Jesus Christ may live and reign in the Christian soul.

WILFRED E. MYATT, C.J.M.
PATRICK J. SKINNER, C.J.M.
Editors

Holy Heart Seminary
Halifax, N. S.
Feast of St. John Eudes, 1945

CONTENTS

I.

MEDITATIONS ON THE MYSTERIES OF JESUS

for

EACH DAY OF THE WEEK

II.

INTERIOR COLLOQUIES

of a

CHRISTIAN SOUL WITH GOD

III.

MEDITATIONS ON HUMILITY

IV.

MEDITATIONS

on

BIRTH AND BAPTISM

V.

MEDITATIONS

on

THE PREPARATION FOR DEATH

VI.

MEDITATIONS

on

THE ADMIRABLE CHILDHOOD

of

THE BLESSED VIRGIN MARY

VII.

MEDITATIONS

on

THE HOLY HEART OF MARY

MEDITATIONS FOR THE FEAST OF THE HOLY HEART

OF MARY

EIGHT OTHER MEDITATIONS

on

THE HOLY HEART OF MARY

VIII.

MEDITATIONS

on

THE SACRED HEART OF JESUS

MEDITATIONS FOR THE FEAST OF THE SACRED HEART OF JESUS

EIGHT OTHER MEDITATIONS

on

THE SACRED HEART OF JESUS

IX.

MEDITATIONS

for

SPECIAL DAYS OF THE YEAR

FOREWORD

It was indeed a happy inspiration which prompted the late Reverend Charles Lebrun, C.J.M., to gather into a single volume, and thus render easily accessible, the various meditations that Saint John Eudes scattered so profusely through his many spiritual writings. It was also a happy inspiration on his part to have enriched the volume with his own brilliant essay on prayer as practised and recommended by Saint John Eudes. No one has studied more carefully or understood more thoroughly the spiritual teaching of the Saint, and no one was more highly qualified to develop his thought on prayer—its nature, importance, form and the place it occupies in his concept of the Christian life.

It is a fundamental principle in the teaching of Saint John Eudes that the Christian life is nothing more than the reproduction, continuation and completion of the life of Jesus, the Head of the Mystical Body, in each one of us, the members. "When a Christian prays," he says, "he continues and accomplishes the prayers of Jesus Christ. When he works, he continues and accomplishes Christ's laborious life. When his relations with his neighbor are inspired by charity, he continues and accomplishes Christ's public life . . ."[1]

Now it was with the hope of aiding Christians to reproduce and continue in their lives the life of prayer of Jesus while on earth that Saint John Eudes composed his meditations. To facilitate the practice for those who find it difficult to concentrate and reflect, he frequently proposes an elevation or ready-made colloquy by means of which they can easily raise their minds and hearts to God and give expression to their sentiments of tenderest love and deepest devotion, as is evident the Saint himself was accustomed to do. We know that the entire life

[1] *The Kingdom of Jesus* (New York, 1946), Part I, p. 6.

xxi

of Jesus on earth was a life of continual prayer, and consequently that there can be nothing more important in the life of a Christian than the practice of prayer. *Oportet semper orare* (Luke 18, 1).

For the first time, this book of Meditations by Saint John Eudes, with the admirable Introduction of Father Lebrun clarifying the mind of the Saint on the whole subject of prayer, is offered to the public in English dress. With it go the hope and the prayer that it may prove serviceable to many souls in the world and in the cloister; that it may assist them in reproducing and continuing the life of prayer of Jesus; nay more, that it may help many to "put on Christ," become more perfectly "other Christs," and thereby greatly extend His kingship on earth.

P. A. Bray, C.J.M.
Bishop of Saint John

Saint John, N.B.
December 8, 1945

INTRODUCTION

THE wish has been expressed that the meditations scattered through the spiritual writings of St. John Eudes be gathered together in one separate volume. To comply with this request, the present work has been compiled. All the meditations in *The Kingdom of Jesus, The Sacred Heart of Jesus, The Admirable Heart of Mary, The Admirable Childhood of Mary,* and the *Manual of Piety,* will be found in this book. A brief note at the beginning of each series indicates the work from which the meditations are taken and adds explanatory material to make them more useful to the reader. The following general introduction outlines the teaching of St. John Eudes on prayer, especially on mental prayer or meditation.

I. PRAYER IN GENERAL

St. John Eudes did not write a special book on prayer, but the few pages devoted to the subject in *The Kingdom of Jesus*[1] enable us to give an account of his ideas on it. Moreover, that book is full of prayers and meditations that make it, in M. Joly's words, "a manual of prayer" and show us the theoretical ideas of the author reduced to practice.

In that volume the Saint uses the word "prayer" in its widest sense so that he applies it to every kind of prayer, no matter what acts it comprises or how it is offered. In his eyes spiritual meditation and the reading of good books are true prayers for they arouse in us devotional sentiments and acts of love of God.

Prayer is often defined as a request made to God for our necessities, and some Christians restrict prayer to petition. Such a prayer is certainly good, and the Divine Master recommends it in the Gospels: "Ask, and it shall be given you," He said to His apostles, "seek and

---

[1] In this Introduction and elsewhere all references to *The Kingdom of Jesus* and to *The Sacred Heart of Jesus* are to the new American translation published in the series *The Selected Works of St. John Eudes,* New York: P. J. Kenedy & Sons, 1946.

you shall find: knock, and it shall be opened to you" (Matt. 7, 7); and on another occasion He reproached them for having made no requests: "Hitherto, you have not asked any thing in my name. Ask, and you shall receive" (John 16, 24).

Excellent as the act of petition may be, it is not the main element of prayer. St. John Eudes unfolds a much wider idea of prayer which he draws from Catholic traditions. "Prayer," he says, "is a respectful and loving elevation of your mind and heart to God. It is a joyous meeting, a holy communication, a divine conversation between God and the Christian." [2]

As a rule, in actual fact, a Christian speaks to God in prayer in the style of the *Our Father*, and God replies by inspiring in his mind good thoughts, or acts of faith, confidence, love and the like. But it may happen in prayer that the mind and heart are raised to God with a more or less active feeling of adoration and love which finds no expression in either external or internal words; yet, this is most certainly prayer. That is why the Saint begins by telling us that prayer is "a respectful and loving elevation of your mind and heart to God."

After defining prayer, St. John Eudes goes on to describe in detail the elements that compose it. "In it," he says, "the soul considers and contemplates its Creator in His divine perfections, in His mysteries and in His works; it adores and blesses Him, loves and glorifies Him, gives itself to Him, is abased before Him at the sight of its sins and ingratitude. It implores Him to be merciful and learns to become like Him by imitating His divine virtues and perfections, and finally, asks for all the things necessary to serve and love Him." [3]

[2] cf. *The Kingdom of Jesus*, Part I, p. 24. St. Augustine, St. John Damascene, and many subsequent writers define prayer as *Ascensus mentis ad Deum*, but in adopting this definition St. John Eudes develops it in his own way. He remarks that it is a respectful and loving elevation of the heart as well as of the mind, and this indeed is how everyone considers it. The second part of his definition (an intercourse with God) is also classical, and is to be found in St. Francis de Sales' *Treatise of the Love of God*, as well as in the writings of St. Teresa and many others. On the idea of prayer, see Brémond, *Histoire du Sentiment Religieux*, VII, p. 5 ff.

[3] cf. *The Kingdom of Jesus*, Part I, pp. 24-25. The Saint is not here dealing exclusively with infused contemplation. He often uses the word contemplation in *The Kingdom of Jesus*, but in its widest sense, meaning the attentive consideration (apparently without reasoning) of the divine perfections or of the mysteries of our Lord and of His holy Mother.

These few lines, inserted almost accidentally in one of the chapters of
The Kingdom of Jesus, really contain the germ of a complete theory of
prayer, to which we will return when dealing with the subject of mental prayer. For the moment we may merely note that according to St.
John Eudes prayer is primarily an exercise, the object of which is to
render to God that tribute of adoration and love, of satisfaction and
thanksgiving, to which He has a right. It is only when he has duly
performed these duties that a Christian may turn to his own needs and
ask for their fulfilment, and he does so less from self-interest than from
a desire to be able to love and to serve God. As St. John Eudes (like
Cardinal de Bérulle and his followers) frequently reminds us: "the
interests of God must be dearer to us than our own." Accordingly
prayer in his view is profoundly theocentric.

Saint John Eudes next stresses the excellence of prayer so defined.
"Prayer," he says, "is a participation in the life of the angels and
saints, in the life of Jesus Christ and of His most holy Mother, even
of the life of God and of the Three Divine Persons. For the life of
the angels and saints, of Christ and of His most holy Mother is nothing else but a continual practice of p. ayer and contemplation, in
which their uninterrupted occupation is to look upon God, to praise
and love Him, to ask Him, on your behalf, for the things you need.
And the existence of the Three Divine Persons is a perpetual contemplation, praise and love of one another, which is accomplished first
and foremost by prayer." [4]

"Prayer," continues the Saint, "is perfect delight, supreme happiness,
a true earthly paradise. It is by this divine exercise of prayer that the
Christian soul is united to God, who is the centre of its being, its goal
and its supreme good. It is in prayer that God belongs to the soul and
the soul to God. It is by praying that the soul pays Him rightful
service, homage, adoration and love, and receives from Him His lights,
His blessings and a thousand tokens of His exceeding great love. It
is during your prayers that God takes His delight in you, according
to this word of His: 'My delights were to be with the children of men'
(Prov. 8, 31), and gives us an experimental knowledge of the fact
that our true joy and perfect satisfaction are to be found in God, and

[4] *The Kingdom of Jesus,* Part I, p. 25.

that a hundred, or even a thousand years of the false pleasures of this world are not worth one moment of the true delights which God allows those souls to taste, who seek all their contentment only in conversing with Him in holy prayer."[5]

Of course prayer has its difficulties and trials, as St. John Eudes well knew; he devoted a section of *The Kingdom of Jesus* to spiritual dryness and afflictions.[6] But whether it be easy or laborious, delightful or arid, prayer is always an exercise of praise and love of God, and even when we are deprived of the sweetness of sensible devotion, the Saint would have us find all our happiness in conversing with God in prayer.

He adds that prayer is "the one true and proper function of a man and of a Christian, since man is created for God and to be with God, and the Christian is on earth only for the purpose of continuing what Jesus Christ did during His life."[6a] Therefore prayer is the basis of a truly human life, and above all the foundation of a Christian life. It is true that if we are to be really Christian we must add to prayer the practice of virtue and the fulfilment of our daily duties; but it is prayer which makes us love and practise virtue and gives us the necessary courage to face the demands of duty however formidable these may be.

And the Saint concludes with this pressing admonition: "Therefore, with all my power, I urge every one of you who read these words, and in God's name I adjure you, since our dear Jesus condescends to take His delight in being with you and speaking to you through prayer, do not deprive Him of His satisfaction, but learn by your own experience that like holy wisdom 'His conversation hath no bitterness, nor His company any tediousness, but joy and gladness' (Wisd. 8, 16). Look upon prayer as the first, the principal, most necessary, most urgent and most important business of your life, and as far as possible, free yourself from all less necessary duties, to give as much time as you can to prayer . . ."[7]

[5] *The Kingdom of Jesus*, loc. cit.
[6] *Ibid.*, Part I, p. 83.
[6a] *Ibid.*, p. 25.
[7] *Ibid.*, p. 26.

II. MENTAL PRAYER

Mental prayer is inward prayer which consists, not in the recitation of a formula, but of interior acts in which language has a purely accidental part, as, for instance, when we make use of a formula to arouse our attention or to stimulate our devotion.

Mental prayer has always been held in high honor by devout souls in religious communities, but since the fifteenth century the custom has arisen in many institutes of devoting a fixed time every day to the regular practice of mental prayer.

St. John Eudes considered mental prayer of capital importance, and called it "the mother and nurse of true piety;" indeed, in his *A Memorial of the Ecclesiastical Life* he boldly declared it "as necessary for the soul of a Christian, and much more so for that of a priest and pastor, as is material bread for the body." So, too, in his *Good Confessor*, after showing that piety is indispensable to all who propose to hear confessions, he adds these strong words: "But what is piety? If you would be acquainted with it and possess it you must practise it. But I declare to you that so long as you do not know what true piety is, you will not be fit to hear confessions."

He is no less outspoken in *The Apostolic Preacher*: "It is in prayer," he says, "that God so enlightens our minds that we are able to see the importance and the beauty of Christian virtue; it is therein, too, that He takes possession of our hearts so that we may taste and love that virtue. And when we are fully persuaded of this and powerfully influenced by it, then we have a wonderful power of making it intelligible to others and of firmly impressing it in their hearts.

The truths with which God enlightens our minds, whose consideration moves us to serve and to love Him, have an incomparably greater power of inflaming our hearts than have those which we derive solely from books without having meditated and pondered upon them before God. There is almost as much difference between these two sets of truths as there is between well-cooked and well-seasoned dishes and those that are totally unprepared."

He considered that religious communities absolutely require mental prayer, and that without it they cannot survive: "Without prayer," he one day wrote to the superior of one of his houses, "it is impossible for a Congregation to subsist in the spirit of piety and virtue which is necessary if it is to be pleasing to God and useful to the Church." And he added: "There is little difference between making half an hour's prayer and not making it, yet nothing is more necessary for ecclesiastics, and I know of no seminary in which they do not make an hour's mental prayer." [8]

In *The Kingdom of Jesus* also the Saint strongly recommends pious souls to practise mental prayer. "This kind of prayer," he tells them, "is more holy, more useful and more filled with blessings than words can convey. For this reason, if God draws you to mental prayer and gives you the grace to practise it, you should indeed thank Him for this very great gift. If He has not yet given you this grace, pray that He may do so, and for your part exert all your efforts to correspond with His grace, and cultivate this holy practice. God Himself will instruct you in the ways of this prayer better than all the books and all the teachers in the world, if you cast yourself down at His feet with humility, confidence and purity of heart." [9]

III. NATURE OF MENTAL PRAYER

St. John Eudes does not dwell at any length on the nature of mental prayer, but the few lines given to the subject in *The Kingdom of Jesus* have a clarity and precision that leave nothing to be desired. "The first is called mental or interior prayer, in which the soul communes with God, taking as the subject of conversation one of His divine perfections, or some mystery, virtue or word of His Divine Son, whether something He accomplished in the past, or is doing now, in the order

---

[8] *Letters and Minor Works*, Letter 228.

[9] *The Kingdom of Jesus*, Part I, pp. 26-27. These words show that the Saint does not attach very much importance to treatises and rigid methods of prayer. Not that he despises them. He advises his priests to give retreatants and beginners in the spiritual life the guidance they require for commencing the practice of prayer, and he even suggests that they should give them the sixth volume of Louis of Grenada's *Memorial of the Christian Life*. He also advises that beginners should be assigned subjects of prayer suited to their capabilities, and he would have them give an account of their prayer. But in spite of all this he only attaches secondary importance to these means of training. For him, as for everyone else, the true master of prayer is the Holy Spirit, and it is for Him to teach us to pray well.

of glory, grace or nature, in His Mother, His saints, His Church or in the world. You begin the conversation of prayer by applying your understanding to consider with a determined, yet unstrained, attention and effort the truths to be found in the subjects chosen, truths which can arouse the soul to love God and hate sin. Then make your heart and will produce a few fervent acts of adoration, praise, love, humility, contrition and oblation, with the resolution to avoid evil and do good, according to the prompting of the Spirit of God." [10]

With all their brevity these few lines plainly show the Saint's mind on the subject of prayer; they tell us what should be its subject and of what acts it should be composed. The author's teaching on both these points is succinct. In the first place, he would have us take as the subject of our prayer one of the divine perfections, a mystery, a virtue, or a saying of the Incarnate Word, or else consider how our Divine Master operates in His saints, in His Church, or in the natural world. He seems to exclude purely moral subjects which, instead of drawing a soul to God and His love, throw it back upon itself and plunge it into preoccupation with its own personal interests.

Nor would he have us limit ourselves in our prayers to considering in themselves the Christian virtues, the evangelical truths or the example of the saints, but he wants us always to consider them in relation to the Incarnate Word. In his eyes the Christian virtues are a participation in the virtues of Jesus, the Gospel truths are words of instruction that have fallen from His lips, and the examples left by the saints are the fruits of Christ's sanctifying action in each of them; and thus he was accustomed to consider them in his views on prayer, in perfect harmony with his teaching on devotion to the Incarnate Word and the life of Christ within us.

As for the acts that comprise prayer, these are of two kinds, springing, respectively, from the intellect and the will. It is true that, strictly speaking, prayer consists of affections of the will acting under the influence of grace; but the will is a blind faculty, and, if it is to be attached to what is good, the intellect must present that good and make the will recognize it.

We, therefore, should begin our prayer with acts of the intellect,

[10] *The Kingdom of Jesus*, Part I, p. 26.

"applying our understanding," as the Saint says, "to consider with a determined, yet unrestrained, attention and efforts the truths to be found in the subjects chosen . . ." [10a] Thus, we should not dwell on purely speculative truths: to do so would be to make our meditation a study, whereas it ought to be an exercise of piety.

The only truths which should engage our attention are those which can move us to love and serve God, and these we should consider with gentle and insistent attention; gentle, because prayer should be made quietly, without striving or fatigue; and insistent, because otherwise the heart will remain cold and will soon stray off to distractions.

Later on we shall see what the Saint asks us to consider in the mysteries of the Incarnate Word, but for the present we may note that he does not ask of us wise and profound considerations, but very simple and easy reflections. Prayer, in fact, is within the grasp of all devout souls; provided they know enough of the mysteries and the teaching of the Incarnate Word to be able to achieve first-rate prayer. "O Jesus, my Saviour, Thou art all lovable, infinitely lovable and infinitely worthy of love. O my God, I need no other knowledge but this. What concern have I with so many studies and ideas and considerations? It suffices me to know that my Jesus is all lovable, and that there is nothing in Him that is not worthy of being loved beyond measure. Let my mind then be satisfied with this knowledge; but may the hunger of my heart to love Him Who can never be loved enough, never be sated." [11]

There are to be found in the Saint's works, and especially in *The Kingdom of Jesus,* some complete meditations which are models of mental prayer, and it is obvious at a glance that their "points" are extremely simple and well within the range of all minds. This is the case, for example, with the meditations for each day of the week and on the subject of baptism. Unfortunately, for want of understanding these principles, many souls are never trained to prayer, for they try to make use of learned reflections which are beyond their capacity and have nothing in common with prayer.

The acts of the will demanded by prayer may be reduced to three. The first is an act of adoration united to acts of praise, thanksgiving,

[10a] *Ibid.,* p. 26.   [11] *Ibid.,* Part V, p. 223.

reparation and especially love. We must adore Jesus in all His mysteries, in all His virtues and works because He is our God and, therefore, always has a right to the supreme worship owed by the creature to his Creator. We must praise and glorify Him because of His infinite perfections, we must thank Him for His benefits and above all for the glory that He procures for His Heavenly Father. We must beg His pardon for our ingratitude and our sins, and lastly affirm that we love Him with our whole heart, and seek to employ all that we are and all that we have for the purpose of loving Him.

The second act is what the Saint calls oblation, which means not only the giving and consecration of self to Jesus, but also and more particularly an act by which, renouncing all power of disposing of ourselves or acting of our own accord, we surrender ourselves to Him entirely, so that He can take possession of us, eradicate everything opposed to His influence, make us sharers in His mysteries and virtues, and guide us in everything as the head guides the members that it vivifies.

It is, in short, that "adherence" so strongly recommended by Bérulle and his school. To this oblation is naturally added an invitation to Jesus Christ to take possession of our hearts and to establish therein His life and virtues. It is true that this request is already virtually included in the oblation of which we speak, but St. John Eudes almost always makes it the subject of a formal act, as for instance in his salutation to the Sacred Heart, *Ave Cor Sanctissimum*,[12] and in many of the prayers in *The Kingdom of Jesus* and in the *Manual of Piety* that he composed for his congregation of priests.

The last act involved in prayer is a resolution to shun evil and to do good, imitating the example of the Divine Master and putting His holy teaching into practice. This shows us that the Saint had the same view of prayer as had Father de Condren, Father Olier and all the fol-

---

[12] In the *Ave Cor Sanctissimum*, a prayer written by St. John Eudes in honor of the Sacred Heart of Jesus, we find after acts of adoration, praise, thanksgiving and love, these words: "We offer Thee our heart. We give it to Thee. We consecrate it to Thee. We immolate it to Thee. Receive it and possess it wholly; purify it, enlighten it, sanctify it, that Thou mayest live and reign in it now, always and forever and ever. Amen."
Cf. *The Sacred Heart of Jesus* (New York, 1946), p. 173.
This is that oblation or adherence which we have just explained.

lowers of Cardinal de Bérulle.[13] Prayer, as taught by this school, is but the practical application in our relations with God of the principles that sum up St. John Eudes' spiritual teaching.

The various elements of prayer unite and interact throughout its whole course; therefore, St. John Eudes sees no necessity to make our considerations and our affective acts two distinct matters. The intellect and the will have to work together, as they do in the meditations given in *The Kingdom of Jesus*. Nor is it necessary to separate the various acts of the will so as to make them in the order we have just shown. They also combine and intermingle, and we may even say that in practice each of them calls up the other two, implicitly contains them and can suffice for the completion of a good prayer.

IV. MEDITATION ON THE MYSTERIES

St. John Eudes says that the mysteries of our holy religion must be "the subject of our contemplation and adoration," "the object of all our pious exercises," the "daily bread and nourishment of our spiritual life," consequently the ordinary subject-matter of our mental prayer. To help us in meditating on these mysteries the Saint points out seven elements which we have to consider and to honor in each mystery.

Of these the first is the body or external aspect of the mystery, which St. John Eudes explains as being "all its outward manifestations. For

[13] To grasp his concept of prayer, we must bear in mind the fact that St. John Eudes belongs to the Seventeenth-Century French School of Spirituality, also called "the Berullian School" from the name of its founder and most illustrious member, Cardinal Pierre de Bérulle, who in 1611 organized the French Congregation of the Oratory on the model of the one founded some years before by St. Philip Neri at Rome. In 1623, St. John Eudes entered the Oratory and received his spiritual training from Bérulle himself and from his saintly successor, Father Charles de Condren. These two holy men concentrated their devotion on Jesus Christ, the Incarnate Word, and on His most holy Mother; they looked upon the Christian life as a continuation and an extension of the life of Christ in each one of us; they stressed the virtue of religion and the supreme worship of adoration that we owe to God in union with His Divine Son. These ideas, so clear to de Bérulle and de Condren, constitute the basis of the spiritual teaching of St. John Eudes. To be sure, he sets them forth in his way; nevertheless, they are the essence of his spiritual doctrine. Other distinguished disciples of de Bérulle were Bossuet, St. Vincent de Paul and Father Jean Jacques Olier. In 1643, St. John Eudes left the Oratory to found the Congregation of Jesus and Mary for the training of priests and the preaching of missions.

cf. *The Spiritual Teaching of St. John Eudes* (London, 1934) pp. 49 ff.

instance, the visible exterior elements in the mystery of the birth of Jesus are the nakedness, poverty, cold and weakness of the newborn Infant, the little swaddling bands in which He was wrapped, His cradle in the crib and on the straw between the ox and the ass, His tears and baby cries, the tiny movements of His sacred feet and hands, the first gaze of His baby eyes, His slumber in the arms of His Blessed Mother, the nourishment He took from her most holy breasts, the sweet kisses He received from her and from St. Joseph, the visit of the shepherds, and all the other touching incidents that took place outwardly in the stable of Bethlehem, on the night of the birth of the Son of God." [14]

Saint John Eudes then adds, "Every detail deserves your consideration and honor, because there is nothing unimportant in the mysteries of Jesus, but, rather, each aspect is great, divine and worthy of adoration. If the Son of God, therefore, takes the trouble to concentrate His divine Spirit and Heart (which ought not, it seems, to be concerned about anything other than divinity itself), on the consideration of every step you take, even numbering the hairs of your head, as He Himself asserts, and writing and treasuring in His Heart the slightest actions you perform for Him, so that He may do honor and glorify them for all eternity in heaven, how much more should you centre your mind and heart on the consideration, adoration and glorification of the smallest details of the infinite mysteries of His life, seeing that there is not one thing about them which is not infinitely great and admirable, and deserving of infinite honor and adoration!" [15]

The second feature to be considered in each mystery is, in St. John Eudes' words, "the interior spirit of the mystery, that is, the particular virtue, power and grace which inhere in the mystery and are peculiar to it, since each mystery has its own proper virtue and spirit of grace. This includes the thoughts and intentions, the affections, sentiments, dispositions and interior activity accomplishing the mystery. In a word, it includes all that took place inwardly in the mind, Heart and holy soul of Christ, and in the minds and hearts of all those who participated directly in the mystery." [16]

[14] *The Kingdom of Jesus*, Part VI, p. 260.   [15] *Ibid.*, pp. 260-261.
[16] *Ibid.*, Part VI, p. 261.

"This spiritual aspect," the Saint proceeds, "ought to engage your principal attention and honor in the mysteries of the life of Our Lord; yet it actually receives the least attention and honor. Many Christians are satisfied to contemplate the body and the externals, without passing on to the inward features of these tremendous mysteries. Yet it is the spirit and the core that are most important, constituting the foundation, the substance, life and truth of the mystery, whereas the exterior is no more than a covering, an accessory, and the accidental being of the mystery. The exterior and body are passing and temporal, but the interior virtue and spirit of grace which dwell in each mystery are permanent and eternal." [17]

The third element to be honored in Our Lord's mysteries comprises the effects He has produced and still continually produces by each of them.

The fourth comprises the particular designs entertained by Jesus in each of His mysteries.

The fifth is the share and the special part taken by the Blessed Virgin in each mystery.

The sixth feature to consider in His mysteries is the part played by the angels and saints particularly connected with each mystery.

Lastly, the seventh matter to be considered and revered is our own participation in these mysteries. "You have a very particular part in each mystery of the Son of God, inasmuch as He had some thought, some plan, some special love for each one of you, and the design to impart to you special graces and special favors, both on earth and in heaven by every mystery of His perfect life." [18]

Obviously St. John Eudes does not attempt to persuade us to include all these considerations in our meditations. Every person is free to choose those which most attract him or correspond to his particular needs, and to concentrate his thoughts and his love on these. In due proportion, these principles apply equally to other possible subjects of prayer, especially to the mysteries of the Blessed Virgin, the Christian virtues, and the teachings of our Divine Master.

[17] Loc. cit.   [18] *Ibid.*, Part VI, p. 264.

V. HOW TO BEGIN AND END
MEDITATION

- In his *Manual of Piety*, St. John Eudes indicates four ways to begin and end the regular exercise of morning prayer. Fundamentally they are similar, but their difference purposely preserves us from the monotony which accompanies the constant repetition of any formula and diminishes its efficacy. The study of the first method will be sufficient for us.

- The Saint wishes us to commence our prayer by four preliminary acts:

The first is an act of adoration. "Let us adore God," he says, "and humiliate ourselves deeply before Him, recognizing the fact that we are infinitely unworthy of appearing before His face and of thinking of Him, and that we do not deserve that He think of us, nor that He suffer us in His presence." The greater number of spiritual authors invite us to place ourselves in the presence of God while beginning our prayer. The act of adoration recommended by St. John Eudes presupposes and implies this Divine presence. It is impossible to adore God and to humiliate ourselves before God without feeling that we are in His presence.

The Saint does not ask that we place ourselves by a formal act in the presence of God, because he desires the prayer to be said before the Blessed Sacrament and also because the Three Divine Persons of the Blessed Trinity are present everywhere and reside in a special way in the soul of a Christian who is in the state of grace.

The second preparatory act for prayer is an act of purity of intention or of pure love. "Let us humble our spirit and self-love at the feet of our Lord," the Saint tells us, "renouncing all curiosity of mind and all self-satisfaction, confessing to Him that we wish to do this action, by means of His grace, for His pure love and for His sole contentment."

Prayer is an act of faith and of love; therefore we must try to seek first the glory of God and then personal advantage. The Saint puts us on our guard against speculations in which the mind is merely pleased with itself, and against devotion which simply delights the heart. To

seek and enjoy these emotions would be to forget that prayer is fundamentally a religious act designed to render to God His due homage of
adoration, praise and love, and there is no prayer-value in extravagant
speculations nor the pleasantness of sensible devotions. St. John Eudes
invites us to renounce them and to resign ourselves in advance to dryness and aridity which, instead of vitiating prayer, renders it more
excellent, particularly when the dryness and aridity are involuntary.

The third preparatory act for prayer consists in our surrender to
Jesus and His divine spirit. "Let us give our mind and heart to Our
Lord, begging Him that He possess them and that He lead them into
prayer according to His Holy Will." This act is called the adherence.
It is required for every act of Christian life, since the Christian life is
the life of Jesus in us, since it emanates from Him, and since we can do
nothing without Him. We are like the branches which can produce
neither leaves nor fruit without the sap which comes from the trunk of
the tree. Here, as always, St. John Eudes invites us to join to the act of
oblation and adherence an act of request which follows in the natural
sequence.

In *The Kingdom of Jesus* the Saint strongly emphasizes this act of
oblation to Jesus: "Finally, to make all the other holy dispositions complete, at the beginning of your prayer, fervently give your mind and
heart to Jesus and to His divine spirit, praying Him to inspire in your
heart such thoughts and affections as' He may desire. Abandon yourself entirely to His holy guidance, that He may guide you as He pleases
in this divine activity. Trust in His great goodness to lead you in the
most fitting manner, and to give you all that you shall ask . . ." [19]

Finally, remembering that we are the members of the mystical body
of Jesus Christ, and that we are completely with Him, with His holy
Mother and all the saints, Saint John Eudes invites us to unite our
prayer to that of Jesus and to all those who pray with Him on earth
and in heaven. "Let us give ourselves to our Lord, Jesus Christ," he
says, "in order to enter into the holy dispositions of His continual
prayer before His Eternal Father, and to unite ourselves with the
prayer now being said by His holy Mother, by St. Joseph, by St.
Gabriel, and by our good angels."

[19] *Ibid.,* p. 32.

These preparatory acts are simply the fundamental application of the theory of the Seventeenth-Century School of Spirituality. They find their application everywhere, in the preparation for prayer as well as in the prayer itself.[20]

In finishing the prayer four things should be done.

The first is to give thanks to God and to ask His pardon. "Let us thank God," says St. John Eudes, "for the graces that He gave us in this prayer, let us ask pardon for the faults we have committed during it, and let us beg Our Lord Jesus Christ to amend them and that He Himself be our perpetual prayer before His Father."

Then comes an invitation to make what St. Francis de Sales calls "the spiritual bouquet or nosegay," but St. John Eudes never uses the expression. He prefers to call it an "ejaculatory prayer." "Let us make," he says, "a selection of the principal resolutions and suggestions that God has given us in daily prayer, and as an ejaculatory prayer we shall say: . . . ."

In the Congregation of Jesus and Mary founded by him, St. John Eudes requested that the ejaculatory prayer be recalled not only at the end of all the community prayers, but also after the Litany of the Blessed Virgin recited in the evening. The Saint desired that his children remain the whole day under the influence of their morning prayer.

In the third place, the Saint invites us to rely entirely on the assistance of Our Lord and His holy Mother for carrying out our resolutions. "Let us guard well," he said, "against depending on our own thoughts and resolutions, but rely on the pure mercy which our Divine Saviour imparts to us in prayer, begging Him to give us the grace to practise them. Let us also place ourselves with this same intention in the hands of the Blessed Virgin."

After that we must beg the angels and saints to continue our prayers. "Let us pray," said St. John Eudes, "to the Blessed Virgin, St. Joseph, St. Gabriel, our guardian angels, to all the angels to help us to overcome our faults, to help us continue our prayer for ourselves and to join our prayers with their unceasing chorus of praise and prayer before the face of God."

[20] See footnote 13.

Verbal prayers usually conclude with the expression of sentiments similar to those which we have just indicated, and have as their object to obtain from Our Lord, from His holy Mother, from the angels and from the saints, the grace to spend the day in a spirit of prayer.

CONCLUSION

Such is the idea of prayer given by St. John Eudes, and his understanding of its practice. We have already mentioned that his views on this point are those of the followers of the Seventeenth-Century French School of Spirituality for whom prayer is paramountly adoration and love and is deeply theocentric. It is, in addition, a way of increasing the life of Jesus in us, and that is why the offering of ourselves to the Incarnate Word occupies an important place in it. But, as participation in the life of Jesus demands upon our part the comprehending of His feelings and virtues, so it requires the resolutions which assure its efficacy.

We might add that prayer, as the followers of Cardinal de Bérulle understand it, leaves little room for the imagination or for human reasoning. It is based entirely upon the principles of faith, such as those furnished us by Holy Scripture; it does not contain anything arbitrary or factitious, and it demands of the intelligence only that it seeks to fathom the truths of Scripture in order that the heart, in its turn, find in them an increase of generosity and love.

We need not try to find out how this concept of prayer agrees with that of Louis of Grenada, of St. Ignatius, and of St. Francis de Sales. There are fewer differences than at first appears to be the case, because they are all only various applications of the Catholic doctrine.

Charles Lebrun, C.J.M.

PRAYERS BEFORE AND AFTER
MEDITATION

PRAYERS BEFORE AND AFTER MEDITATION[1]

To prepare your soul for meditation, recite the following vocal prayers:

Come, O Holy Ghost, fill the hearts of Thy faithful and enkindle in them the fire of Thy love.

V. Send forth Thy Spirit, and they shall be created.

R. And Thou shalt renew the face of the earth.

LET US PRAY.—O God, Who by the light of the Holy Spirit didst instruct the hearts of the faithful, grant us by the same Holy Spirit a love and relish of what is right and just, and a constant enjoyment of His consolations. Through Christ our Lord. Amen.

Our Father. Hail Mary. I Believe in God.

Hail, Heart most holy.
Hail, Heart most meek.
Hail, Heart most humble.
Hail, Heart most pure.
Hail, Heart most devout.
Hail, Heart most wise.
Hail, Heart most patient.
Hail, Heart most obedient.
Hail, Heart most vigilant.
Hail, Heart most faithful.
Hail, Heart most blessed.
Hail, Heart most merciful.
Hail, most loving Heart of Jesus and Mary.

We revere Thee.
We praise Thee.
We glorify Thee.
We give Thee thanks.
We love Thee,
With all our heart,
With all our soul,
And with all our strength.
We offer Thee our heart.
We give it to Thee.
We consecrate it to Thee.
We immolate it to Thee.
Receive it and possess it wholly;
Purify it, enlighten it, sanctify it,
That Thou mayest live and reign in it now, always and forever and ever. Amen.

[1] These vocal prayers and acts before and after meditation are taken from *A Manual of Piety* compiled by St. John Eudes.

O Angel of God, my guardian, enlighten and protect, direct and govern me.

All hail, ye Angels and Saints of the heavenly courts. Deign to intercede for our salvation and for the salvation of the world.

Select one of the methods to be used before meditation and read it, pausing after each paragraph to make the acts suggested.

FIRST METHOD[2]

ACTS BEFORE MEDITATION

I

Let us adore God and humble ourselves profoundly before Him, acknowledging that we are infinitely unworthy to appear before His face or think about His divine Majesty; and that we do not deserve to be thought of by Him or admitted into His presence.

II

Let us annihilate our self-love and our pride at the Saviour's feet, renouncing all intellectual curiosity and self-satisfaction, and assuring our Lord that we wish to perform this action, with the help of His grace, for the sake of His pure love and His sole satisfaction.

III

Let us give our minds and hearts to our Divine Lord, supplicating Him to take complete possession of them and guide them in this prayer, according to His holy will.

IV

Let us give ourselves to Our Lord Jesus Christ, that we may enter into the holy dispositions of His continual prayer before His Heavenly Father, and that we may also join in the prayer now being offered by all the holy souls in heaven and on earth, particularly by His Blessed Mother, Saint Joseph, Saint Gabriel and our guardian angels.

[2] To prevent routine in this most important act of the spiritual life, St. John Eudes gives four methods or ways of beginning and ending meditation. cf. "Introduction," p. xxxv.

3

ACTS AFTER MEDITATION

At the end of meditation, read the following paragraphs, pausing after each to make the acts.

I

Let us thank God for the inestimable graces He has given us and ask His divine pardon for the faults committed in the course of our prayer; let us implore our Lord Jesus Christ to make amends for them and to be Himself our perpetual prayer before His Father.

II

Let us consider the principal inspirations and resolutions which God has given us in the prayer, that we may recall them throughout the day; and as an ejaculatory prayer, let us say:

Here recall a brief and appealing invocation to God or the saints, taken from Sacred Scripture or the Divine Office, or from one of the Fathers, to serve as an ejaculatory prayer during the day.

III

Let us take care not to rely solely on our own thoughts and resolutions, but rather on the infinite mercy of God; let us place at Our Lord's disposal whatever blessing He has imparted to us in the prayer, supplicating Him to preserve it and grant us the grace to practise it. Let us also place the same intention in the hands of the Blessed Virgin Mary.

IV

Let us implore the Blessed Virgin, Saint Joseph, Saint Gabriel, our guardian angels and all the angels and saints, to make up our deficiencies, continue our prayer for us and admit us as partners in the prayer which they offer perpetually in God's presence.

V

Let each one make an examination of conscience in order to foresee customary faults and possible occasions of sin; let him likewise review the virtues he is especially obliged to practise, particularly humility, obedience, charity and meekness. Let him resolve to avoid any faults against these virtues and let him beg God for the grace to accomplish this end.

SECOND METHOD

ACTS BEFORE MEDITATION

I

Let us adore God, humble ourselves before Him and give Him our minds and hearts with the desire to perform this act well, for love of Him alone.

II

Let us make an act of self-renunciation, surrendering ourselves to Our Lord Jesus Christ, that we may offer our prayer in His loving Spirit.

III

Let us pray to the Most Holy Virgin, the angels and saints for assistance to help us to perform this action worthily.

ACTS AFTER MEDITATION

I

Let us thank God for the graces He has given us and ask pardon for our omissions.

II

Let us make a selection of the inspiring thoughts and sentiments God has given us; and as an ejaculatory prayer, let us say:

Here recall a brief and appealing invocation to God or the saints, taken from Sacred Scripture or the Divine Office, or from one of the Fathers, to serve as an ejaculatory prayer during the day.

III

Let us mistrust ourselves and our resolutions, placing all our confidence in Divine Mercy; and let us implore the Blessed Virgin Mary, the angels and saints to help us.

IV

Let each one make a brief examination of conscience to foresee the faults frequently committed in the course of the day.

THIRD METHOD

ACTS BEFORE MEDITATION

Let each one yield himself to the spirit of God, that he may cultivate the dispositions necessary to prepare his soul for the prayer; and that he may say, to that end, in his heart and with all his heart, what I am about to say.

I

O my God, prostrate at the feet of Thy infinite grandeur and engulfed in the abyss of my nothingness, I adore Thee as my Creator and the universal Lord of all things, acknowledging that I am infinitely unworthy to appear before Thy face and even to think of Thee. I do not deserve that Thou shouldst think of me nor suffer me to come within Thy presence. I ask pardon of Thee, my God, for all the sins which have rendered me so unworthy of Thee.

II

O my God, at Thy feet I place my self-love and my pride; deign to annihilate them. I desire to perform this prayer as well as possible, with the help of Thy holy grace, for Thy greater glory and my salvation.

III

My Divine Jesus, I give Thee my mind and my heart. I implore Thee to take possession of them and guide them throughout this prayer according to Thy holy will.

IV

O Jesus, in complete self-renunciation I give myself to Thee with all my heart, that I may enter into Thy spirit of prayer, uniting myself with the prayer Thou dost offer unceasingly before Thy Father and with that of all the holy souls in heaven and on earth.

V

O Mother of Jesus, O blessed Saint Joseph, O blessed Saint Gabriel, O my holy guardian angel, all ye angels and saints of Jesus, implore my God to give me the true spirit of prayer, and grant me fellowship in the unceasing prayer which you offer before the throne of His divine Majesty.

ACTS AFTER MEDITATION

Let each one give himself to the spirit of God, that he may finish his meditation in the dispositions suggested by the following words which everyone should repeat in his heart.

I

O my God, I thank Thee for the graces Thou hast given me in my prayer, and I ask pardon of Thee for the faults I have committed therein. I implore Thee, O my Jesus, to make reparation for them in my name and to be Thyself my perpetual prayer before Thy Father.

II

O my Saviour, I trust entirely in Thy boundless mercy, not in my weak and feeble self, nor in my resolutions. In Thy Heart and Thy hands I place the salutary thoughts and inspirations Thou hast given me in this prayer; deign to preserve them and grant me the grace to bring them to fruition. To that end, O Mother of my Jesus, I place them also in thy tender heart!

III

O Blessed Virgin Mary, O Saint Joseph, O Saint Gabriel, all ye angels and saints of Jesus, supply my deficiencies and deign to continue my prayer for me.

IV

Let each one make a selection of the inspiring thoughts and sentiments that God has given him. As an ejaculatory prayer, let us say:
*Here recall a brief and appealing invocation to God or the saints,
taken from Sacred Scripture or the Divine Office, or from one of the
Fathers, to serve as an ejaculatory prayer during the day.*

V

Let each one make the customary examination of conscience.

FOURTH METHOD

ACTS BEFORE MEDITATION

After the *Veni, Sancte Spiritus,* read the following words and then pause for the length of a *Miserere* to make the acts.

Let each one give himself to the spirit of God, that he may enter into the dispositions customary for beginning the prayer, that is, to adore God, to humble ourselves before Him, to renounce self, to consecrate our being to Our Lord's spirit of prayer, and to invoke the Blessed Virgin, the angels and saints.

ACTS AFTER MEDITATION

At the end of meditation, read the following words and then pause about the length of a *Miserere.*

Let each one finish the prayer in the usual way, that is, by thanking God, imploring His forgiveness, reviewing the principal thoughts and inclinations He has given us, placing them in the hands of Our Lord and His Holy Mother; by invoking the Blessed Virgin, the angels and saints, and by making the recommended spiritual preview of the day.

Conclude your meditation with the following vocal prayers:
We fly to thy patronage, O Holy Mother of God; despise not our petitions in our necessities, but deliver us from all dangers, O glorious and blessed Virgin.

Lord Jesus Christ, we are nothing, .
We can do nothing,
We are worth nothing,
We possess nothing but sin;

We are useless servants,
We are children of wrath,
The last of men and the first of sinners:
Upon us be confusion and shame,
To Thee be honor and glory forever and ever. Amen.

Blessed be forever the most loving Heart and the sweet Name of Our Lord Jesus Christ and of the most glorious Virgin Mary, His Mother.

In the name of the Father, and of the Son, and of the Holy Ghost. Amen.

I

MEDITATIONS FOR EACH DAY
OF THE WEEK

I

MEDITATIONS FOR EACH DAY OF THE WEEK[1]

FIRST MEDITATION

Sunday

The Divine Life of Jesus
in the Bosom of the Heavenly Father

FIRST POINT

THE LIFE OF JESUS IN THE BOSOM OF HIS FATHER
IS FILLED WITH GLORY AND DELIGHT

O JESUS, my Lord and my God, I contemplate, adore and glorify Thee in Thy divine life from all eternity in the bosom of the Eternal Father, before Thine Incarnation in the virginal womb of Thy Mother. What a holy life! How pure, divine, wonderful and filled with glory, greatness and delights! What joy to see Thee living, from all eternity, a life so filled with perfection, contentment and wonders! Blessed be Thou, O Father of Jesus, for having imparted such a life to Thy Well-beloved Son! O Jesus, I offer Thee all the glory, love and praise Thou dost derive from the Father and the Holy Spirit throughout the eternity of Thy divine life.

[1] "Meditations for Each Day of the Week" are taken from "Part Four" of *The Kingdom of Jesus.*

15

SECOND POINT

The Chief Function of Jesus from All Eternity Is To Contemplate and Love His Father

O Jesus, when I consider Thy divine and eternal life, I see that Thy chief function for all eternity is to contemplate, glorify and love Thy Father, to refer Thyself to Him as to Thy principle, to give Him Thy being, Thy life, Thy perfections and all that Thou shalt be forever, as gifts received from Him, to be employed in glorifying and loving Him, and to offer Him infinitely worthy praise and love. Blessed be Thou, O Jesus, for all these things. O Most Amiable Father, how I rejoice to behold Thee so loved and glorified by Thy Son! I offer Thee all love and glory that Thou dost receive from Him during all eternity, by His divine life in Thy fatherly bosom before His Incarnation.

THIRD POINT

From All Eternity Jesus Thinks of Me and Loves Me

O Good Jesus, Thou hast expended all Thy divine life for my benefit. From all eternity Thou dost think of me, love me and offer me to the Father, and Thou dost offer Thyself also to Him, to come one day upon earth to be made flesh, to suffer and die on earth for love of me. O Dearest Jesus, Thou hast loved me from all eternity, and I hardly know if I have yet begun to love Thee as I ought. Forgive me, my Saviour. From now on, and for all eternity, let me live but to love Thee!

Ejaculatory prayer:

"I have loved Thee with an everlasting love."
In caritate perpetua dilexi te (Jer. 31, 3).

SECOND MEDITATION

Monday

The Incarnation .

FIRST POINT

Jesus Shows His Love for His Father in His Incarnation

O Jesus, I adore Thee at the moment of Thy Incarnation, which is the first instant of Thy mortal life. I adore all the marvelous things that took place in Thee at that moment. What great accomplishments were effected in Thee and by Thee, in that blessed instant, in the eyes of the Father, the Holy Spirit, Thy sacred humanity, and Thy Blessed Mother! What thoughts, what affections, what love! How Thy holy soul in that instant devoted itself, before Thy Father's face, to adore and glorify Him and sacrifice Thee entirely to His glory, and to accomplish all that He willed!

O Good Jesus, I adore Thy first thoughts and Thy first acts of adoration, oblation, love and praise, which Thou didst offer to Thy Father at that time. How exalted and divine were the love and glory Thou gavest Him then! Truly Thou didst give Him infinitely more honor and love in that moment alone than all the angels and all men accorded Him in the five thousand years that preceded Thine Incarnation, or ever shall give Him for all eternity. O Father of Jesus, what satisfaction for my soul to behold Thee so loved and glorified by Thy Son! O Jesus, be Thou blessed, adored and glorified forever for the honor and love Thou didst give to Thy Father at the blessed moment of Thine Incarnation!

SECOND POINT

Jesus Shows His Love for Mary
in His Incarnation

O Jesus, when I consider Thee in this mystery, I see by the light of
faith that Thou dost entertain most exalted thoughts and great designs
upon her in whom the Incarnation was accomplished, and that Thou
dost indeed effect great and marvelous works in her. O Jesus, I adore
the first thoughts, the first acts of love and movements of grace, of
light and of eminent sanctity which Thou didst produce in Thy
Blessed Mother at the moment of Thine Incarnation. So, too, do I adore
the first acts of adoration, praise and-love of the most admirable
Mother for the Most Adorable Son. Blessed be Thou, O Jesus, Son of
Mary, for all the wonders Thou didst work in Thy divine Mother by
this stupendous mystery! Blessed be thou, O Mother of Jesus, for all
the glory thou hast given thy Son in this same mystery! Unite me, I
implore thee, to all the love and honor thou didst give thy Dear Son
in the first instant of His life, and grant that I may share in thy peerless love for Him and in thy zeal for His glory.

THIRD POINT

Jesus Shows His Love for Me
in His Incarnation

O Most Amiable Jesus, at the same instant that Thou didst look up
to the Father, after the Incarnation, Thou didst also look upon me.
Thou didst begin to think of Him, refer Thyself to Him and love Him
and Thou didst likewise begin to think of me, to give Thyself to me
and love me. At the very instant Thou didst begin to live, it was to live
for me, to prepare and acquire for me most extraordinary graces, and
to form plans for my salvation. From that very moment Thou didst
plan and desire to create in me an image of the mystery of the Incarnation and to become incarnate in me, that is, to unite me to Thyself,
and Thyself most intimately to me, both physically and spiritually by
Thy holy grace and Thy divine sacraments, and then to fill me with

Thyself, and establish Thyself in me to live and reign perfectly in me.

O what goodness! What boundless love! Infinitely blessed be Thou, O Good Jesus! May all Thy mercies and all Thy wonders for the children of men bless Thee forever! I most humbly beg Thy forgiveness for the obstacles which I have put in the way of the accomplishment of the great designs Thou hast deigned to have in my regard. Never allow me to impede Thy grace again. From now on I desire to annihilate, at all costs, everything in me that opposes Thy holy will. My Jesus, may it please Thee to grant me the grace and strength to do this.

Ejaculatory prayer:

"He came down from heaven for us men and our salvation."
Propter nos homines et propter nostram salutem descendit de caelis.

THIRD MEDITATION

Tuesday

The Holy Childhood of Jesus

FIRST POINT

JESUS BECAME A LITTLE CHILD
TO SANCTIFY HUMAN CHILDHOOD

O GREAT and Admirable Jesus, Thou wast not satisfied to become man for love of men, but Thou didst also will to become a child, subject to all the lowliness and weakness of infancy, in order to honor the Eternal Father in every condition of human life, and to sanctify all the states of our life. Blessed be Thou, Good Jesus, for these favors! May all Thy angels and saints bless Thee eternally! O most amiable Child, I offer Thee my own childhood, although it is past, imploring Thee most humbly that, by virtue of Thy divine Childhood, Thou mayest wipe out all that was bad or imperfect and cause my whole life as a child to render homage to Thy most adorable Childhood.

SECOND POINT

JESUS LOVED HIS FATHER AND HIS
MOTHER DURING HIS CHILDHOOD

O Divine Jesus, when I contemplate Thee in Thy holy Childhood, I see that Thou art never idle, but dost effect great things for Thy Eternal Father, contemplating, adoring and loving Him, and also for Thy Blessed Mother, heaping upon her a world of graces and blessings, also for St. Joseph, and little St. John the Baptist and the other saints with whom Thou didst associate as a child, accomplishing in them most wonderful works of illumination and sanctity. I adore Thee, love Thee and bless Thee in all Thy divine occupations and in the marvelous effects of Thy divine Childhood. I offer Thee all the honor and love Thou didst receive in Thy holy Childhood from Thy Father, Thy Blessed Mother, St. Joseph, St. John the Baptist, St. Gabriel, and from the other angels and saints who are in any special way associated with Thy divine Childhood.

THIRD POINT

JESUS LOVED ME DURING HIS CHILDHOOD

O most amiable Child, I adore all Thy thoughts and designs and Thy most burning love for me. Thou wast thinking of me, and didst love me without interruption in Thy Childhood. Thou didst cherish the plan and the strong desire to imprint upon my heart an image of Thy divine Childhood, that is, to make me enter upon a state of holy and sacred childhood, which should imitate and honor the meekness, simplicity, humility, purity of body and spirit, the obedience and innocence of Thy holy Childhood. O my Jesus, I give myself to Thee to accomplish Thy plan and desire and to enter into this state. I shall henceforth strive, with the help of Thy holy grace, which I invoke with my whole heart, to become meek, humble, simple, pure, obedient, free of all arrogance, bitterness and malice, like a child, so that I may render some small honor to Thy Childhood which so deserves to be honored.

Ejaculatory prayer:
"He was subject to them."
Erat subditus illis (Luke 2, 51).

FOURTH MEDITATION

Wednesday

The Hidden and Laborious Life of Jesus

FIRST POINT

During His Hidden Life, Jesus Teaches Us to Love Recollection and Solitude

O JESUS, although Thou didst have so many and such great acts to perform on earth, converting so many souls, working so many miracles, doing so much good by, Thy blessed example and holy preaching, if Thou hadst gone out among men, yet Thou didst not will to do this until the age of thirty, performing in the meantime no outward act that might make Thee known to men. Thou didst remain hidden and withdrawn into the Father, in Whom Thy mind, heart, thoughts, desires and affections were uninterruptedly enclosed. Thou didst choose this secluded life to honor Thy hidden life from all eternity in the bosom of Thy Father, and to teach us that solitude and recollection are pleasing to Thee. Of the thirty-four years of Thy life upon earth, no more than four were spent in active intercourse among men, while thirty were spent in seclusion and solitude. Blessed be Thou, O Good Jesus, for all the glory Thou didst give Thy Father during these thirty years of Thy hidden life! Grant that I in their honor may henceforth love recollection and solitude, both interior and exterior. Draw me apart and hide me in Thee. Absorb my mind into Thine, my heart into Thy Heart and my life into Thy life. I desire henceforth, with the help of Thy grace, to make every effort to withdraw my thoughts and affections from all things into Thee, O my Jesus, as into my place of refuge, my centre, my element and my paradise, outside of which all else is hell

and perdition. I wish to dwell ever in Thee, following Thy commandment: "Abide in me" (John 15, 4), that is, in Thy Spirit, Thy love, Thy
sentiments and inclinations, never to leave Thee again.

SECOND POINT

JESUS IN HIS LIFE OF LABOR
TEACHES US HUMILITY

O Most Great and Most Adorable Jesus, Thou didst will to lead
an unknown and despised life, a life lowly and abject in the eyes of
men, a life of poverty, labor and suffering, bearing the name and following the trade of carpenter, to teach us first by example what Thou
didst later teach us by words, namely, that "what is high to men is an
abomination before God;" *quod hominibus altum est, abominatio est
ante Deum* (Luke 16, 15). O Jesus, imprint this truth deeply in my
mind and firmly implant in my heart a great hatred and horror of all
fame, praise, greatness and vanity, and for all that catches and dazzles
the eyes of men, giving me a very strong love for all that involves lowliness, abjection and humiliation.

THIRD POINT

JESUS IN HIS HIDDEN LIFE RENDERS INFINITE
GLORY TO HIS HEAVENLY FATHER

O Jesus, Thou art God, even as Thy Heavenly Father and Thou art
but One God with Him; Thou dost share one power and operation,
and with Him Thou art the Creator, Preserver and Governor of our
vast universe. From all eternity Thou dost send forth with Him a
Divine Person, that is, the Holy Ghost, who is God even as the Father
and Thou. This and other exalted marvels worthy of Thy supreme
greatness, Thou dost accomplish. Yet in Thy hidden life of labor on
earth, I see that Thou dost lower Thyself to the commonest and most
lowly actions of human life, such as eating, drinking, sleeping, working, earning Thy living with the toil of Thy hands and in the sweat
of Thy brow. I am filled with wonder and consolation because Thou
art no less great and admirable in small things than in great. In these

lowly commonplace activities Thou didst render infinitely great glory to the Omnipotent Father because, O Jesus, Thou didst perform all actions, even the smallest and most ordinary, not with common or ordinary dispositions, but with an infinite love for the Father and for us. Thou didst merit and acquire, by the power of Thy holy actions, a special grace for all our acts, to enable us to perform them meritoriously. Hence we can and must do everything devoutly; otherwise we nullify and waste the graces Thou hast acquired for us in the performance of similar actions. Do not allow this to happen, O Good Jesus! Give me the grace Thou hast acquired for me by Thy holy actions, so that I may perform all my own acts with holiness. This is my desire and my resolve. Grant me grace to fulfil it purely for Thy glory, that in future I may offer up all my acts, even the smallest, in honor of Thine and that I may, as far as possible, perform my tasks with the dispositions and intentions that exalted the lowliness of all Thy most humble, human deeds.

Ejaculatory prayer:

"Your life is hid with Christ in God."
Vita vestra est abscondita cum Christo in Deo (Col. 3, 3).

FIFTH MEDITATION

Thursday

The Public Life of Jesus and His Life in the Blessed Eucharist

THERE ARE FIVE POTENT REASONS WHY JESUS LIVED HIS PUBLIC LIFE

O MOST Amiable Jesus, Thou dost live, reign and commune for all eternity with the Eternal Father and the Holy Spirit. How rich is this association and how delightful to Thee! What glory and praise Thou dost receive from the Father and Holy Spirit! Yet Thou didst will to come forth from the bosom of the Father to appear on earth, to associate, eat and drink in familiar visible companionship, not only with Thy Blessed Mother, St. Joseph and the holy apostles and disciples, but even with sinners, from whom Thou didst sustain all kinds of outrages and indignities. Thou didst will to do this: first, to give homage to Thy divine and holy association with the Father and the Holy Spirit from all eternity by association with Thy Blessed Mother, St. Joseph, the holy apostles and the disciples; secondly, to deliver us from the punishment, so rightly deserved by our sins, of being reduced forever to the wretched company of demons, and to make us worthy to dwell eternally in the company of the angels and saints, Thy Blessed Mother, and the Three Divine Persons; thirdly, to show us the vital truth of Thy words, "My delights were to be with the children of men" (Prov. 8, 31); fourthly, to acquire for us, by the merit of Thy active life, the grace we need to behave virtuously in our relations with one another; fifthly, in order that the perfection of Thy holy and divine conduct in Thy relations with other men might serve as a model and example of the way we should act towards our neighbor.

DISPOSITIONS WHICH CHARACTERIZED THE PUBLIC LIFE OF JESUS

I adore Thee, O Jesus, I bless Thee and love Thee for all these favors. I adore Thee in Thy public life and active ministry, which lasted from Thy thirtieth year to the day of Thy death. I adore and give Thee glory for everything in this period of Thy life, inward and outward, that is, all the actions, words, teachings, miracles, journeys, labors and weariness, and for all Thy thoughts, feelings, intentions, affections and inner dispositions. I bless Thee for all the glory Thou didst render to the Eternal Father. I offer Thee all the love and honor accorded during the time of Thine active life by all the holy souls who came in contact with Thee. I also offer Thee all my own associations and contacts, whether past or future, in homage to Thine own, and I implore Thee to cause all my actions relating to my neighbor to be consecrated to the glory of Thy public life.

O Jesus, I adore the thoroughly holy and divine dispositions which characterized Thy activity among men. With what dignity, charity, meekness, patience, modesty, detachment from creatures and attention to God didst Thou move and act in the world of men! O my Saviour, I desire that such dispositions may henceforth characterize all my relations with my neighbor. Alas! How far I am from such perfection and how many faults I have committed in the days gone by! For all these I beg Thy forgiveness, imploring Thee to implant in me all the dispositions I have requested.

JESUS STILL LIVES WITH US IN THE BLESSED EUCHARIST

O Lord, Thou wast not satisfied to live and associate with mankind during Thy mortal life. When Thou wast on the point of returning to heaven, Thy most insatiable love and exceeding great desire to prove the tremendous truth that Thy delight is to be with the children of men inspired Thee to devise a most admirable institution that would keep Thee ever with us, and give Thyself to us with all the essence of Thy riches and wonders. All this was accomplished by means of the Holy Eucharist, which is a compendium of all Thy wonders and the greatest of all the effects produced by Thy love for us. O love! O goodness! How is it that I am not utterly transformed into love and praise for Thee? O Jesus, forgive me my past abuse of so great a grace; grant that in the future I may make better use of this Divine Sacrament and that, as Thou dost find Thy delight in being with me, I may also find all my delight in Thy company, in thinking of Thee, in loving and glorifying Thee.

Ejaculatory prayer:

"My delights were to be with the children of men."
Deliciae meae esse cum filiis hominum (Prov. 8, 31).

SIXTH MEDITATION

Friday

The Passion and Death of Jesus

JESUS PRACTISES SUBMISSION AND PATIENCE THROUGHOUT HIS PASSION

O JESUS, Thou art the love and the delight of God and the angels, of heaven and earth. Thou art the God of consolation, the source of all joy and bliss, joy and blessedness itself. Yet, when I behold Thee on the final day of Thy mortal life, I see that Thou art the object of the wrath and persecution of heaven, earth, hell, of God, men and all creatures. I see the universe and the powers of evil leagued against Thee, expending all their energies to make Thee suffer. Thou art, as it were, a target exposed to every volley of contradiction and outrage. I behold Thee so filled with sorrow, anguish and torments in every part of Thy body and soul, that Thou dost seem to be transformed into pain and sufferings. Hence the Prophet Isaias calls Thee "the man of sorrows." *Virum dolorum* (Isa. 53, 3). O my Dearest Jesus, what has reduced Thee to so pitiable a state? It is Thy goodness, my Saviour, and the excess of Thy love. O my Sweet Jesus, let me adore, love and bless Thee in all Thy sufferings, both interior and exterior; let me adore in Thee the holy and divine dispositions of Thy suffering. With what submission to Thy Father's will, with what deep humiliation under the burden of all the sins of the world, with what charity for us, with what meekness and patience towards Thine enemies Thou didst endure the culmination of all sufferings! How ashamed I am to behold my Jesus suffering so extremely, with such dispositions, while I see how sensitive I am to the slightest pain, and so far from sharing His dispositions! O Good Jesus, I give myself to Thee to suffer all Thou dost will and

I offer Thee all that I have suffered and am yet to suffer in my whole life. May it please Thee to unite my works and trials with Thine; bless them through Thine; use them as Thine own, to glorify the Father and to honor Thy holy Passion. Grant that I may share in the love, humility and other dispositions with which Thou didst suffer!

SECOND POINT

Jesus Manifests His Love of the Eternal Father During His Passion

O Most Amiable Jesus, Thou didst bear the torments of the Cross and of death with so much love for the Father and for us that the Holy Spirit speaks of the day of Thy Passion as "the day of Thy Heart's joy" (Cant. 3, 11), to show that Thou didst find joy and satisfaction in suffering. O my Saviour, let me also find my joy and all my happiness in this world in trials and labors, in contempt and sufferings, if by them I can give Thee greater glory and love! Implant these dispositions in my soul, and imprint upon my heart intense hatred for the delights and pleasures of this earth, and a particular affection for hard work and suffering.

THIRD POINT

The Death of Jesus Is an Object of Love and a Model for Us

O Jesus, I contemplate and adore Thee agonizing and dying on the Cross. I adore Thy last thoughts, words, actions and sufferings, the last use of Thy bodily senses and of the faculties of Thy soul, the last graces Thou didst infuse into the soul of Thy Blessed Mother and the other watchers who remained at the foot of the Cross; Thy last acts of adoration and love for the Heavenly Father; the last sentiments and dispositions of Thy Heart and Soul and the last breath that yielded up Thy life. I offer Thee the last moment of my life together with my death, in honor of Thy holy death and the consummation of Thy life. Bless my death, O Jesus, my Saviour, and sanctify it by Thine own; unite it to Thine; grant that I may share the holy and divine dispositions with which Thou didst die. Grant that the last moments of my life and my last breath may be consecrated to Thee and that they may be acts of most pure and perfect love for Thee.

Ejaculatory prayer:

"Christ died for all."
Pro omnibus mortuus est Christus (2 Cor. 5, 15).

SEVENTH MEDITATION

Saturday

The Life of Jesus in Mary and of Mary in Jesus

JESUS LIVES IN MARY

O JESUS, Thou only Son of God, only Son of Mary, I contemplate and adore Thee, the Divine Author of her existence, living and reigning in Thy most holy Mother. Thou art all and dost all in all things, so surely Thou art and dost all in Thy most holy Mother. Thou art her life, her soul, her heart, her spirit, her riches. Thou art in her, sanctifying her on earth and glorifying her in heaven. Thou art in her, accomplishing greater works and giving to Thyself, in and by her, greater glory than through all the other creatures of heaven and earth. Thou art in her, clothing her with Thy qualities and perfections, inclinations and dispositions, imprinting in her being a most perfect image of Thyself, of all Thy states, mysteries, and virtues, and making her so like Thee, that whoever sees Jesus sees Mary, and he who sees Mary beholds Jesus. Blessed be Thou, O Jesus, for all that Thou art and all that Thou dost accomplish in Thy most holy Mother! I offer Thee all the delights, all the love and all the glory Thou didst ever have or ever shalt have in her perfections.

SECOND POINT

MARY LIVES IN JESUS

O Mother of Jesus, I honor and venerate thy most holy and admirable life in thy Son Jesus; a life which is resplendent with every kind of virtue and perfection; a life of which one single moment is more

31

dear to God than the lives of all angels and men; a life that imparts more honor and love to God than all other lives combined in heaven and on earth. This life is none other than the life of thy Son Jesus, which He communicates to thee from moment to moment by a most particular and ineffable favor. Blessed be thou, O holy Virgin, for the wealth of honor thou hast given to thy Well-beloved Son throughout thy life! I offer thee all my life, O Mother of being and grace, and I consecrate it completely to the honor of thy holy life, and with my whole heart I beg thy Son Jesus, the God of being and love, to grant by His great goodness that my whole existence may pay continual and eternal homage to His most holy life and to thine.

THIRD POINT

JESUS LIVES IN US

O Jesus, God of my life and of my heart, Thou hast a very great desire to dwell in me, and to make me live in Thee an entirely holy and heavenly life. Forgive me for having obstructed the fulfilment of Thy desire by my sins and infidelities. Eradicate the corrupt and depraved life of the old Adam in me, and in its place establish Thy holy and perfect life. Dwell in all Thy fulness in my spirit, heart and soul, and therein accomplish all the works Thou dost desire for Thy glory. Love Thyself in me, and in me glorify Thyself completely according to Thy most holy will. O Mother of Jesus, if it please thee, obtain from thy Son the accomplishment of these designs in me.

Ejaculatory prayer:

> "For to me, to live is Christ."
> *Mihi vivere Christus est* (Phil. 1, 21).

EIGHTH MEDITATION

Sunday

The Glorious Life of Jesus in Heaven

FIRST POINT

JESUS LIVES A GLORIOUS LIFE WITH THE ETERNAL FATHER

O JESUS, having considered and adored Thee in Thy mortal life, the agony of the Cross, the shadow of death and the chill of the Sepulchre, let me now adore and contemplate Thee in the exaltation, brightness and delights of the life of glory and blessedness Thou didst enter by the Resurrection, which Thou hast enjoyed in heaven in the bosom of the Father since the Ascension. O immortal and glorious life of my Jesus! O life entirely free from the sorrow and suffering of this earth! O life completely rapt and absorbed in God! O life of undiluted love, of love most pure and all-encompassing, because in His heavenly life Jesus finds no thought other than to love His Father, and to love us for His Father, to love, bless and glorify His Father for us, to offer us to His Father and to intercede for us with Him! O life most holy, most pure and most divine! O life replete with unutterable joy and exultation! O life that enjoys the fulness of glory, greatness and bliss which is God! O my Dear Jesus, what joy for my heart to behold Thee living such a radiant life! May Thy Most Lovable Father be blessed forever for having brought Thee into heaven.

SECOND POINT

JESUS LIVES IN GLORY WITH HIS SAINTS

O Jesus, most worthy of love, not only art Thou in Thyself living a life of glory and blessedness, but so also are all the angels and saints who are with Thee in heaven. Thou livest in them; Thou dost communicate to them Thy glorious and immortal life; Thou art glorious and blessed in them, as St. Paul testifies in the words: *omnia in omnibus* (1 Cor. 12, 6). It is Thou who dost adore, praise and love Thy Eternal Father in them and by them. Blessed be Thou for all these things, O Good Jesus! I refer and offer to Thee the glorified and blessed life of all the citizens of heaven, together with all the love and praise they give Thee now and shall give Thee forever, in homage to the life of bliss and glory which Thou hast in Thyself. I beg all Thy angels and saints to love and glorify Thee for me, and to associate me with all the love and glory they give Thee and shall render Thee forever.

THIRD POINT

JESUS WILL LIVE IN GLORY WITH ME IN HEAVEN

O Jesus, object of all desire, I know that Thy love for me is infinite, that Thy extreme zeal for Thy glory most ardently desires Thy Self to be perfectly loved and glorified in me, and also that Thou hast an infinite desire to draw me to Thee in heaven. I know that Thou mayest live perfectly in me and fully establish in me the kingdom of Thy glory and Thy love. Thou wilt not live and reign perfectly in me so long as I remain on earth. Therefore, O my Saviour, I no longer desire to live on earth except to long without ceasing for my heavenly home. Heaven! O heaven! How desirable art thou! How thou dost call to our love! O God of heaven, when will the time come for me to see Thy holy face? When wilt Thou live fully in me and when will I love Thee perfectly? O earthly life, how hard, how unbearable art thou! O God of my life and of my heart, how long and cruel is this life in which Thou art so little loved and so much offended!

Ejaculatory prayer:

> "Let us dwell in spirit in heaven."
> *Mente in coelestibus habitemus.*

Another Meditation for Sunday

The Mysteries of Christ's Life

FIRST POINT

WE SHOULD ADORE AND LOVE JESUS
IN HIS MYSTERIES

O JESUS my Lord, I cast myself down and efface myself at Thy feet; I surrender myself to the might of Thy divine spirit and Thy holy love, in their immense power and greatness; I adore, glorify and love Thee in Thyself and in all the mysteries and phases of Thy life. I adore Thee in Thy temporal life on earth for thirty-four years. I adore Thee in the first moment of that life, in Thy holy Childhood, in Thy hidden life of labor, in Thy public ministry among men, both when Thou didst live and walk on earth for all to see, and now that Thou art still among us in the Blessed Eucharist. I adore Thee in all Thy sufferings, interior and exterior, and in the last moment of Thy passible life. I adore Thee in Thy life of glory and bliss in heaven ever since the Ascension. I adore Thee in Thy life in the most Blessed Virgin and in all the angels and saints, whether in heaven or on earth. And, in general, I adore, love and glorify Thee in all the other mysteries and wonders that are embraced in the measureless expanse of Thy life, divine, temporal and glorified. I bless Thee and give Thee infinite thanks for all the glory Thou didst ever and ever shalt render to the Father in all the phases of Thy life.

I offer Thee all the love and honor Thou ever didst or shalt receive forever, in all Thy mysteries and states, from all the angels and all the saints, begging them most humbly to love and glorify Thee, for me, in every way possible and fitting to Thy glory.

WE SHOULD ASK JESUS TO GRANT US A PARTICIPATION IN HIS MYSTERIES

O Jesus, I give myself to Thee and beg Thee with my whole heart to enter into me, there to destroy all that is not Thee, and to imprint a perfect image of Thyself, the states and mysteries of Thy life, Thy qualities and Thy virtues. Come, Lord Jesus, enter into me to destroy all that is not Thee and establish Thyself perfectly, there to be all and do all, that thus my being and my life, in all aspects and ramifications, may be totally dedicated to the honor of Thy life and Thy sovereign being. May my birth in nature and in grace, my childhood, adolescence and my years of activity as a mature man, my agony, death and burial together with all the other phases of my temporal and eternal life, be consecrated to the honor of each successive part of Thy life, Thy birth, Thy childhood, Thy adolescence, Thy maturity, Thy passion, Thy death and Thy burial, and all the other states of Thy temporal and eternal life. May all my thoughts, words and actions give honor to Thine. May every step I take, all my works and sufferings give honor to every step Thou didst take on earth and all Thy works and sufferings. May all the powers of my soul and all the senses of my body be dedicated to the honor of Thy holy soul and senses of Thy deified body. Finally, may everything that ever was, is and shall be in me be transformed into ceaseless and eternal adoration, praise and love for Thee. Come, Lord Jesus, enter into me; live and reign over me perfectly, and there love and glorify Thyself as befits Thee, to carry out the designs of Thy goodness in my being, to accomplish the work of Thy grace and to establish forever in my heart the kingdom of Thy glory and Thy pure love. *Veni, Domine Jesu, veni in plenitudine virtutis tuae, in sanctitate Spiritus tui, in perfectione mysteriorum tuorum, et in puritate viarum tuarum. Veni, Domine Jesu.*

Come, Lord Jesus, enter into me in the fulness of Thy virtue, to destroy all that displeases Thee and execute all that Thou dost desire for Thy glory. Come in the sanctity of Thy Spirit to detach me entirely from all that is not Thyself, to unite me perfectly with Thee and to lead me in the path of holiness in all my actions. Come in the perfection of Thy mysteries, to perfect in me what Thou dost deign to operate by Thy mysteries. Come in the purity of Thy ways, to accomplish in me, no matter at what price, and without sparing me in any way, all the designs of Thy pure love, and lead me in the straight path of that pure love without permitting me to turn aside, without yielding anything to the inclinations and feelings of corrupt nature and self-love. Come, Lord Jesus!

Ejaculatory prayer:

> "Come, Lord Jesus."
> *Veni, Domine Jesu* (Apoc. 22, 20).

II

INTERIOR COLLOQUIES
OF
THE CHRISTIAN SOUL
WITH GOD

II

INTERIOR COLLOQUIES
OF THE CHRISTIAN SOUL WITH GOD[1]

FIRST COLLOQUY

God's Favors to Me Before My Creation
and My Consequent Debt to Him

FIRST POINT

GOD HAS LOVED ME WITH AN ETERNAL LOVE

WITH God there is neither past nor future, and everything has always
been before Him as present and visible in His eternal light. He cast
His divine gaze upon me from all eternity; He looked upon me with
the eye of mercy; He thought of me tenderly and ardently; He disposed and ordained, with wondrous kindness, everything that was to
happen to me in body and soul and in every circumstance, development
and event of my existence and life, even to the hairs of my head; He
formed great designs concerning me. He designed to create me with
all the natural advantages and perfections He has given me. He designed to preserve me as He does every moment of my life. He designed to create the world and to preserve it in existence for love of
me.

---

[1] The "Interior Colloquies" were first published with the "Meditations on Humility"
as Part Eight of *The Kingdom of Jesus*. In 1666 St. John Eudes published both series
in one separate volume. There are thirteen colloquies. The first eight deal with man as
a creature of God, Who is his principle, model and ultimate end. The last four consider
man's duties as a Christian, his relations with the Three Divine Persons of the Blessed
Trinity and his obligation to renounce Satan and follow Christ. The thirteenth colloquy
treats of the choice of a state of life.

The Eternal Father willed to send His Son and to deliver Him up to the death of the Cross to redeem me.

The Son willed to take human flesh and to do and suffer all that He did and suffered in this world for me.

The Holy Ghost willed to form the humanity which was united to the Son in the sacred womb of the Blessed Virgin for love of me and to come into this world Himself to be my light, my sanctification, the Spirit of my spirit and the Heart of my heart.

Lastly, the Most Holy Trinity willed to bestow upon me all the corporal and spiritual, temporal and eternal favors that He has since given me and will ever give me. And so God had great designs for me from all eternity. Thus, O my God, Thou didst bear me in Thy mind and in Thy heart from all eternity. Thus Thou didst think of me and love me an eternity before I was capable of knowing and loving Thee. There never was a time, O God of Love, when Thy mind and Thy heart were not concerned about me. "What is a man that thou shouldst magnify him? Or why dost thou set thy heart upon him?" (Job 7, 17). It would almost seem, O Eternal Goodness, that Thou hast no sooner thought of Thyself than Thou hast thought of me, no sooner loved Thyself than Thou hast loved me, since Thou hast thought of me and loved me from all eternity.

My God, what shall I do, what shall I render to Thee for Thy eternal love of me? Surely if I had existed from all eternity I should have given and consecrated to Thee my whole soul, my whole heart, all my thoughts, designs and affections. But not having existed from all eternity, I should at least have turned to Thee with my whole mind and will as soon as I was capable of doing so. Alas! I can truly say with St. Augustine; "Too late have I loved Thee, O Eternal Goodness." Forgive me, I beseech Thee, O my God. I wish to begin now to love, serve and honor Thee with all my heart, with all my soul and with all my strength; I beg Thee to grant me that grace by the infinite love Thou hast borne me from all eternity and give me grace to return Thy love.

SECOND POINT

GOD HAS LOVED ME WITH A CONSTANT LOVE

The love, wherewith God loved me before I existed, is not only eternal; it is also continual, immutable and constant. God began to think of me and love me without beginning and He has not ceased. There has been no interruption in His thought or love for me; His mind and His heart have always been turned to me. In spite of the fact that He foresaw all my offenses and ingratitude, it made no change in His invariable and permanent love for me; He never ceased to wish me an infinity of good. It may truly be said that during the time of His eternal duration, not a single moment elapsed (if there are moments in eternity) without His thinking of me.

O excessive goodness! O eternal and immutable love! May eternal thanks be offered to Thee by all Thy creatures! O my God, too late have I known Thee, too late have I loved Thee! Perhaps I have not even yet begun to do so as I ought; but if I have begun, how many interruptions have there been since? How many infidelities have there been? What coldness and remissness! Have mercy, O my God, have mercy on this ungrateful and perfidious sinner! Henceforth, I wish with the aid of Thy grace to spend every moment of my life in Thy love and service. To this end, I intend to regulate and arrange my time and my occupation so that everything may be consecrated to Thy glory.

THIRD POINT

GOD HAS LOVED ME WITH AN INFINITE AND PURE LOVE

God has not only loved me from all eternity with a constant and invariable love, but He has also loved me with all that He is, that is to say, He loved me with a most pure love, for nothing obliged Him to love me before I existed except His pure goodness. Thus the love of God for me before my creation has four qualities: it is eternal, immutable, infinite and most pure. I will return thanks for all these blessings; I will humble myself before Him and ask forgiveness for all my ingratitude. I will excite a great desire to begin in good earnest, and henceforth to employ my whole life, all my time and all my strength, in loving and honoring Him and causing Him to be loved and honored by others as far as lies in my power; and I will do so purely for love of Him and for His glory. I will beg Him to destroy in me everything that might oppose these resolutions and to give me the grace requisite for their accomplishment. I will beseech the Blessed Virgin Mary, all the angels and the saints to obtain this great grace for me.

Ejaculatory prayer:

> "To Thee be praise, glory and love, O Blessed Trinity."
> *Tibi laus, tibi gloria, tibi amor, O beata Trinitas.*

SECOND COLLOQUY

God's Favors to Me by My Creation and Preservation and My Obligations Towards Him

FIRST POINT

GOD CREATED ME BY HIS INFINITE POWER, WISDOM AND GOODNESS

Who has created me and given me being and life? Not the world, not the evil spirit, nor myself, but God, by the exercise of infinite power, wisdom and goodness. "He made us, and not we ourselves" (Ps. 99, 3). His infinite power drew me from the nothingness from which I could not emerge save by the power of an Almighty hand. His immense wisdom appears in the wondrous order and arrangement of every faculty of my soul and every part of my body. His ineffable goodness is manifested in the fact that He drew me out of nothingness to give me not the nature of a stone, not the vegetative life of a plant or a tree, nor the sensitive life of an animal. This He might have done without wronging me and without my having any reason to complain. He willed instead to create me to His own image and likeness, to give me the many advantages of the time and place of my birth, my parentage, the perfections of body and mind and other favorable circumstances accompanying my birth which I should carefully weigh and consider.

"What shall I render to the Lord, for all the things that He hath rendered to me?" (Ps. 115, 12) I will thank Him, bless Him and love Him with all my heart. I will endeavor to realize that, as God is the author and eternal principle of my being and life, I must, therefore, devote my existence entirely, not to my own interests and inclinations, but to God, to His glory and the accomplishment of His holy will. As God is not only the source whence I came, but also the prototype whose living image I am, I am obliged to imitate Him in His sanctity,

His charity, His patience, His meekness, His vigilance, His justice and His mercy.

I will examine myself to see if I have spent my past life for Him or for others, and whether I have studied to imitate Him, and show forth in my life His likeness rather than that of His enemy. If I find myself guilty, I will humble myself and ask pardon of God for my past infidelity. I will resolve to live in future solely for the Author of my life; to refer myself wholly to Him as to my Principle, I will study the life and perfections of my Divine Exemplar, so as to imitate them and bear His living image in me, with the help of His grace, which I will earnestly beseech of Him for that intention, humbly desiring Him to destroy in me everything that might oppose His admirable designs, and to imprint a perfect likeness of Himself in my soul.

SECOND POINT

GOD CREATED US FOR HIMSELF

Why did God create me? For Himself, to think of Him, to love Him, to speak of Him, to work for Him and to sacrifice myself for His glory. He is not only my principle and prototype but also my sole end. Hence, as God made me for Himself alone, I should consider attentively, weigh carefully and engrave deeply upon my mind the truth that I am in this world only to serve and honor Him. This is my only care and affection. All my thoughts, words and actions, all my time, all I have, all I know, all I can do, should tend towards this purpose of life. God is my last end, and consequently in Him I will find my sovereign good, my centre, my treasure, my glory, my felicity, my repose, and my true paradise; likewise, outside of Him I will find only trouble, anxiety, bitterness, anguish, malediction and hell.

Have I paid attention in the past to this great and important truth? Have I been one of those whom St. Bernard castigates when he says: "Foolish persons who take greatest care of the least things and least care of the greatest." If such is the case with me, I will ask pardon of God and consecrate myself wholly to Him. I will devote myself solely to this work, which is of such consequence that it entails nothing less than an eternity of bliss or misery.

THIRD POINT

PRESERVATION IS A CONTINUOUS CREATION WHICH INCREASES OUR OBLIGATIONS TO GOD

God created me not only once, but as many times as there are moments in my life. From the moment of my creation until now, He has borne me in His arms, in His bosom and in His Heart, with more care and love than a mother carries her child, and not a single moment has passed without His thinking of me, loving and preserving me. The most wonderful fact is that He preserved me even when I was offending Him, when He might justly have crushed me and cast me into hell. Now, preservation is continual creation, so much so that if God were to withdraw His Almighty Hand which sustains me, and were to cease for a single moment to preserve me, I would at that very instant return to the nothingness from which He drew me. Therefore, He gives me at each successive moment the identical being He conferred at the first instant of my life and with the selfsame power and goodness with which He gave it to me then. I belong to Him, therefore, by as many ties as there have been moments in my life and I am deeply indebted to Him for each succeeding moment as for the first.

O my God, since I am Thine by so many claims, and have so many obligations to serve Thee, do not permit sin, the devil, nor the world to have any share in what is Thine, but do Thou take full and entire possession of my being and life. O world, O prince of the world, O detestable sin, I renounce you forever. O my God, I consecrate myself to Thee and I declare that I wish to live, act, speak, think and suffer for love of Thee alone.

Ejaculatory prayer:

"Thou hast made me for Thyself, O Lord, and my heart can find no rest except it reposeth in Thee."
Fecisti me, Domine, ad te, et inquietum est cor meum, donec revertatur in te. St. Augustine, *Confessions* I, I.

THIRD COLLOQUY

The Dignity and Sanctity of Our Ultimate End

FIRST POINT

OUR ULTIMATE END IS THE SAME AS THAT OF THE ANGELS

For what end did God make us? For the same end as the angels. God placed us in this world to do what the angels constantly accomplish in heaven. Wherefore, being associated with the angels and created for the same duties, namely, to adore, praise, love and serve God and to follow His most holy Will always and everywhere, we should live angelic lives and delight in the fulfilment of these duties. Alas, if we examine our life, we will find that instead of imitating the angels in their purity, sanctity, humility, charity, love, submission to the Will of God and fidelity in His service, we have frequently imitated the demons in their malignity, pride, envy, disobedience, treachery and rebellion against God. In fact, instead of devoting ourselves to the functions of angels, we have actually performed the work of demons.

Let us humble ourselves; let us detest our malice; let us forever renounce the prince of darkness. Let us cultivate a great desire to imitate the angels, and to begin to perform on earth what we shall do in union with them for all eternity in heaven. Let us beg them to associate us in the praise they continually offer to God and to make us share in their love and fidelity.

SECOND POINT

OUR ULTIMATE END IS THE SAME AS THAT OF THE SAINTS

God placed us in this world for the same end as the holy patriarchs, prophets, apostles and martyrs, the holy bishops, priests and all the other saints who formerly lived upon earth and are now in heaven.

48

They were men such as we are, men of flesh and blood, frail, mortal, exposed to the same temptations as ourselves. We belong to the same Church as they, we adore the same God, we have the same Saviour and Mediator, Jesus Christ, Our Lord. We share the same Holy Gospel, the same Sacraments, the same faith, the same hope, the same promises. He who sanctified the saints has an infinite desire to sanctify us, too, provided we do not oppose His holy Will. Yet they are saints and they served God "in holiness and justice before Him," all the days of their life (Luke 1, 75).

As for us, who are we and what are we doing? What good reason we have to humble ourselves! What shall we say to the Son of God when, on the day of judgment, He will show us all the saints who were like us, and will reveal to us how much easier it was for us to serve Him with them rather than to follow those who are now forced to cry out in hell: "We have erred from the way of truth . . . and have walked through hard ways" (Wisd. 5, 6-7).

Let us, therefore, make a firm resolution to walk in the way of the saints, to read and study their lives, especially the lives of those who have been of our saintly calling, so as to imitate them. Let us beg them to obtain this grace for us.

THIRD POINT

OUR ULTIMATE END IS THE SAME AS THAT OF THE
BLESSED VIRGIN, OF OUR LORD AND
OF THE THREE DIVINE PERSONS

Not only have we the same destiny as the angels, archangels, cherubim, seraphim and all the saints, but we have also the same end as Mary, the Queen of the angels and saints, as Jesus, the Saint of saints, and as the Three Divine Persons of the Holy Trinity. Why did the Blessed Virgin and our Lord Jesus Christ come upon earth, except to honor and glorify God, and to make Him known and adored? What is the end of the Three Divine Persons but their Divinity? What is their greatest and continuous activity but to praise, bless, love and glorify each other perpetually? God created us for the same end, that is, to honor and glorify Him, to make others know and serve Him, in every possible way. Thus, we have one and the same end as the angels, the seraphim, all the saints, the Blessed Virgin, the God-man and the Most Holy Trinity.

How noble, how worthy, how holy is our destiny! How elevated is our status in having so high an end! How happy we are in being created for such exaltation! How miserable we are when we let our minds and hearts, our thoughts and affections, revel in the mud and filth, in the smoke and folly of the base, terrestrial affairs of the children of this world! How deeply we are indebted to our Creator, for having created us for so admirable an end, for having given us such a wondrous alliance with His angels, His saints, His Blessed Mother and Himself! What holy lives we should lead! How pure should be our intentions in every thought, word and action! Yet the majority of men live as if they were only made for earth, honor, wealth, pleasure, self, the world, the devil and hell.

And what have we done so far? Let us stir up a horror of ourselves and our sinful lives. "For in many things we all offend" (James 3, 2). Let us earnestly desire and resolve to be perfectly converted to God, and to live only to tend to our ultimate end and to direct other souls to their eternal destiny.

Ejaculatory prayer:

"What have I in heaven? And besides thee what do I desire upon
    earth?"
Quid mihi est in caelo, et a te quid volui super terram (Ps. 72, 25).

FOURTH COLLOQUY

Our Obligations to God for the Creation and Preservation of the World

FIRST POINT

GOD CREATED THE WORLD FOR US AND GAVE IT TO US WITH AN INFINITE LOVE

THE origin and end of the world is God, its Author and Creator, Who made it for Himself and for His own glory: "The Lord hath made all things for Himself" (Prov. 16, 4). All creatures bless, glorify and magnify God, each in its own way: "Full of the glory of the Lord is His work" (Ecclus. 42, 16). "His work is praise and magnificence" (Ps. 110, 3). "All the earth is full of his glory" (Isa. 6, 3). All irrational and inanimate creatures do the will of God, following the instincts He has given them, and never swerve from the laws he has prescribed for them: "He hath made a decree, and it shall not pass away" (Ps. 148, 6). "All things serve thee" (Ps. 118, 91). All creatures serve God for the accomplishment of His designs and the manifestation of His power, His wisdom and His infinite goodness. What power is manifest in creating such a multitude and a variety of beings out of nothing! What divine wisdom has established such a wonderful order, harmony and proportion in nature! What goodness has wrought so many wonders for all men in general and for each in particular, even for ungrateful and perfidious men who do not appreciate them, but use these creatures to wage war against their Creator and to dishonor Him.

Let us adore God, inviting all creatures to bless and praise with us His incomprehensible power, wisdom and goodness. "All ye works of the Lord, bless the Lord: praise and exalt him above all for ever" (Dan. 3, 57). This they do incessantly and invite us to do so with them. "For all creatures," says St. Augustine, "are so many tongues and voices

51

which cry out incessantly: 'Love, love Him who made us for you.' " O
my God, how strange it is that inanimate and irrational creatures
glorify Thee, while man, a rational creature who is infinitely more
indebted, dishonors Thee!

The ineffable goodness with which God created all things in the
universe appears not only in His having created them for our well-
being and given them to us, but also in His having given them to us
with infinite love; so much so, that if every morsel of bread we eat and
every drop of water we drink were of infinite value, He would give
them to us as lovingly as He does now. Thus it is with everything we
use. If we numbered all the creatures in the world, we would count
as many obligations to their Creator who gives them to us with infinite
love.

O my God, what shall I do for Thee and what return shall I make
for so many manifestations of Thy infinite goodness? Let me at least
learn from irrational and inanimate creatures to serve and glorify
Thee and to submit to Thy laws and orders, if I do not wish to be
numbered among those fools against whom Thy creatures will fight
in the day of judgment to avenge the wrongs Thou hast endured from
ungrateful men: "The whole world shall fight with him against the
unwise" (Wisd. 5, 21).

SECOND POINT

GOD PRESERVES THE WORLD FOR US
WITH AN INFINITE LOVE

God created the world, not only once, but an infinite number of
times, that is, as many times as there have been moments of time in
the thousands of years since the world was created. At every successive
moment, He has prevented it from falling back into the nothingness
from which He drew it and He continually preserves it, which preservation is a perpetual creation. If anyone could count the moments
which have elapsed from the creation of the world until now, he would
count so many infinite obligations on our part to the infinite goodness
of our adorable Preserver. For each one of us was present to Him from
the beginning of the world and throughout eternity before material

creation. He created the world for love of each one of us in particular, and likewise He has preserved it ever since for each one of us with infinite love. Be Thou blessed, O Great God, be Thou infinitely blessed! "Let the mercies of the Lord give glory to him: and his wonderful works to the children of men" (Ps. 106, 21).

THIRD POINT

Our Lord, at the Price of His Precious Blood, Has Purchased for Us the Right to Use Created Things

It is true that the world and everything in it was made for man. But man, having been condemned to death on account of his rebellion against God, lost his right to their employment when he sinned, so the sinner has no more right to make use of any creature. If the Son of God had not died to free us from our guilt of sin, all creatures, instead of serving our needs, would rise up against us as they will against the wicked on the day of judgment. But Our Lord Jesus Christ, by virtue of His Precious Blood and Redeeming Death, has restored to us the right to use the things of this world for our necessities, although not to the full and copious use man would have enjoyed if he had not sinned. Man is permitted to employ God's creatures as God Himself used them, according to the words of the Holy Ghost: "They that use this world, as if they used it not" (1 Cor. 7, 31), that is to say, without excess, without being attached to it or taking any undue pleasure in it, but simply according to necessity and insofar as is requisite for the service and glory of God, with thanksgiving to the Creator who made the creatures of the world, and to the Redeemer who acquired for us with His Precious Blood the right to their use which we had lost by our sins.

We would have no right to live a moment, to set foot upon the ground, to breathe the air, to receive light from the sun, warmth from the fire, to be cleansed by water, to be covered by the clothes we wear, to be protected from the inclemency of the weather by the houses in which we live, to rest in our beds, to eat a morsel of food, to drink a drop of water, nor to make use of any creature, if the Son of God had not shed His Precious Life-Blood to deliver us from the punishment of privation which we merited by our sins. Having employed the being and life God gave us to offend Him, we deserve to be deprived of existence and consequently of all our rights. If we now retain some measure of these rights, it is because the Son of God purchased them for us by His Death on the Cross. So we have not a moment of time, we do not eat a morsel of food, nor use anything in this world that has not cost the Blood of Jesus Christ. Wherefore, we are infinitely indebted to Him. If we could count all the service and assistance received from creatures at every moment of our life and our continual use of them, we would count so many infinite obligations to Jesus Christ, who purchased that privilege for us at the infinite cost of His Precious Blood.

Let us beg God to engrave these truths upon our hearts, Let us acknowledge our indebtedness and return thanks to Jesus Christ. Let us think of them frequently and raise our hearts to Him from Whom we receive so many favors every moment. Let us resolve to spend all our time in the honor and service of our most amiable Saviour Who purchased every moment of life so dearly for us. Let us declare to Him that we will never employ anything created except for His glory and in the way He used it while on earth. Let us ask Him to give us this grace for love of Himself.

Ejaculatory prayer:

"Let all thy works, O Lord, praise thee."
Confiteantur tibi, Domine, omnia opera tua (Ps. 144, 10).

FIFTH COLLOQUY

The Divine Claims upon Our Allegiance
Because of Our Creation

FIRST POINT

THE CLAIMS OF GOD TO OUR ALLEGIANCE

As A result of our creation, God assumes certain all-important claims to our allegiance. He is our origin; He is our last end; he is our centre and our element; He is our supreme good, our monarch and our absolute sovereign; He is our ruler, our protector and our defender; He is our judge.

Let us adore and praise God in all these divine aspects. Let us rejoice that He is so great, that He possesses countless perfections, and has so much power over all His creatures who are dependent upon Him in so many varied ways. Let us also rejoice that we belong to Him by so many claims to our allegiance and that He vouchsafes to exercise all these rights in our regard. It is a marvelous advantage, a great glory and a singular honor for us to have an origin so noble, an end so exalted, a centre so divine, a supreme good so bountiful and provident, a prototype so perfect, a king so powerful, a ruler and protector so prudent and strong, a judge so just and equitable, and a God so great, so admirable and so good.

SECOND POINT

THESE DIVINE CLAIMS ARE ALWAYS EFFECTUAL

All these claims which God wishes to extend to us are not vain, idle or ineffectual. He exercises them continually over us and over all creatures. He produces wondrous effects through them and would operate even more lavishly if we did not prevent Him.

55

As our origin, He not only gave us being at the moment of our creation, but He imparts it to us continually and produces us incessantly and more incomparably than the fountain produces its gushing waters, the tree its foliage and the sun its rays. Wherefore, we are more dependent upon God than the rivers upon their source, the leaves upon the tree trunk, or the rays upon the sun.

As our end, centre, element and supreme good, He calls and attracts us to Himself continually, saying: "Come to me all you who labour and are burdened: and I will refresh you" (Matt. 11, 28). If there is a secret virtue in the centre of a stone, in the element of the fish and in the sphere of fire, which so strongly attracts them, how much stronger is the virtue of our true centre, our true element and our real sphere, which is God? How is it, then, that we allow ourselves to be so little attracted to Him? Certainly, we must believe that we offer very great resistance and that there must be a terrible weight of sin within us to resist such powerful attraction. O my Sovereign End, my Divine Centre, attract me, draw me completely to Thee, and do not allow me to oppose Thy power in any way.

THIRD POINT

The Recognition of These Divine Claims Is the Means of Happiness

Moreover, as our last end, our centre, our element, our sphere and supreme good, God alone is capable of giving us true peace, perfect rest, and of filling and satiating the immense capacity of our soul: *Anima rationalis ita facta est capax majestatis tuae, quod a te solo et a nullo alio impleri possit,* says St. Augustine. When our soul renounces everything earthly to give itself entirely to its Creator, He fills it with ineffable repose, with a peace surpassing all understanding and the reward of infinite blessings.

As prototype, He gives us the model and example of admirable perfection and sanctity, saying: "Be holy because I am holy" (Lev. 11, 44). "Be you therefore perfect, as also your heavenly Father is perfect" (Matt. 5, 48). "Be ye therefore merciful, as your Father also is merciful" (Luke 6, 36). "Be ye therefore followers of God, as most dear children" (Eph. 5, 1). Furthermore, He Himself imprints His divine image upon souls who give themselves entirely to Him. O my God, I surrender myself to Thee; engrave in my soul a perfect image of Thy sanctity and Thy divine perfections.

As king, ruler and protector, God rules us by the holiest laws, and He is ceaselessly vigilant in governing and protecting us.

As judge, He continually exercises His justice and His judgment in the world, giving to everyone according to his works, punishing some and rewarding others.

Let us adore and bless God in all the effects He has produced and will produce in creatures by His claims upon man. Let us thank Him for the blessings He has produced in us or would have produced if we had not prevented Him. Let us ask pardon for our resistance. Let us give ourselves to Him, that He may exercise all His divine powers over us as He pleases and make them as fruitful in us as He desires.

Ejaculatory prayer:

"Thou art the God of my heart, and the God that is my portion for ever."

Deus cordis mei, et pars mea Deus in aeternum (Ps. 72, 26).

SIXTH COLLOQUY

The Rights of God Over Man as a Result of Creation

FIRST POINT

THE RIGHTS OF GOD BECAUSE HE IS OUR PRINCIPLE, OUR END AND OUR SOVEREIGN GOOD

BY REASON of the preceding aspects, God has many claims upon us which we should study in order not to violate them. If we are so careful to study and maintain our petty rights over our dependents, how much greater reason have we to consider the great and important rights God has over us, that we may fulfil the obligations towards Him that those rights entail. Therefore, let us see what they are.

By every quality of His Infinite Perfection, God has the right to be acknowledged, adored, praised and glorified by us as God, to whom we must sacrifice ourselves and all things.

As our origin, our last end and our supreme good, He is entitled to possess us entirely, as wholly His own, made only for Him and infinitely dependent upon Him.

As He is the origin and end of our being and life, God maintains a right to be the origin and end of all our thoughts, words and actions and of all the customs and functions of our life, that is, we should think, say or do nothing except through Him or for Him, by his command and for His glory.

As the origin who produces us continually and always bears us in His Hand and in His Heart, so that, should He cease to sustain us, we would at that very instant fall back into nothingness, He has the right to exact that, as we always necessarily live in Him, according to the words of St. Paul: "In Him we live, and move, and are" (Acts 17, 28), we should voluntarily abide in Him by means of love in charity: "God

58

is charity: and he that abideth in charity, abideth in God" (1 John 4, 16).

O my God, let me always abide in Thy love and in love of my neighbor so as to be always in Thee.

OTHER RIGHTS OF GOD OVER US IN VIRTUE OF HIS ALLEGIANCE

As our origin God imparts to us a being and life that are a participation in His being and life, as St. Paul tells us, "We are also his offspring" (Acts 17, 28). He has the right to exact that we lead a life conformable to His, that is, a life all holy and divine, so as not to degenerate from the nobility of our fountainhead, and dishonor the source and origin whence we have sprung.

As our end, centre, element and divine sphere, God has the right to expect that we should aspire unceasingly to Him, and seek our rest and contentment in Him alone.

As our supreme good, He is entitled to be loved above all things and to have entire possession of our hearts and all our affections.

O my God, in Thee are true good, honor and content and out of Thee, there is no good. Grant that I may love Thee with whole heart! Mayest Thou be henceforth the sole object of all my desires and affections.

RIGHTS OF GOD OVER US IN CONSEQUENCE OF HIS OTHER CLAIMS

As our prototype, God possesses the right to require us always to walk before Him and in His presence, continually and fixedly watching our Divine Exemplar so as to pattern our life and model our behaviour and actions on the perfection of His life and the sanctity of His principles and actions.

As king, He has the right to legislate and to reign over us.

As ruler, He possesses the right to direct our every act.

As protector, He has the right to our acknowledgment of the truth that He alone can assist and defend us, and that we should have recourse to Him in all our needs, both corporal and spiritual.

As judge, He has the right to watch over all our actions, examine them, demand an account of even every idle word and reward or punish us according to our merits.

Such are God's rights over us in consequence of these aspects of His divine claims to our allegiance.

O my God, I adore and glorify Thee in all Thy just and lawful rights over all creatures and over me in particular. I rejoice with all my heart and testify that if Thou didst not possess them, I would give them to Thee. How frequently I have prevented Thy enjoyment of those rights over me! I humbly ask Thy pardon. Henceforth, I will endeavor to avoid opposing Thy divine rights any more and to fulfil, with the aid of Thy grace the obligations they entail.

Ejaculatory prayer:

"My God and my All."
Deus meus et omnia.

SEVENTH COLLOQUY

Man's Obligations to God by Reason of the Preceding Rights

MAN'S OBLIGATIONS TO GOD

AFTER considering and studying God's divine claims and His rights over us as a result of creation, it is easy to see our consequent obligations.

1. As He is our origin, we should abide in Him, live a life worthy of our origin, continually refer to His authority all that we are and all that we do, sacrificing ourselves unceasingly to Him so that He may possess us entirely. "Look unto the rock whence you are hewn" (Isa. 51, 1).

2. Since He is our end, centre and supreme good, we should continually aspire and long for Him, choose and seek Him always and in all things, never desiring any rest or content save in Him alone.

3. Since He is our prototype, we should constantly study His life and perfections in order to imitate them and form in ourselves a living image of our adorable exemplar: "Look and make it according to the pattern, that was shewn thee on the mount" (Exod. 25, 40).

4. Since He is our king, ruler and protector, we owe Him honor, obedience and confidence.

5. Since He is our sovereign possessing more power over us than the potter over his clay, as holy Job says: "Multiply my wounds even without cause" (Job 9, 17), we should abandon ourselves wholly to Him.

6. As He is our sovereign judge, we should submit to His power to judge us. We should adore, bless and glorify Him in all the judgments, known and unknown, manifest and secret, that He daily exercises over all creatures and especially over us. Above all, we should adore and praise Him in the judgment He exercises every moment over

the souls that appear before His tribunal and in the judgment that He will exercise over us at the hour of death and in the day of judgment. Lastly, we should fear His justice, remembering that "it is a fearful thing to fall into the hands of the living God" (Heb. 10, 31). We should resolve to live as persons who will shortly have to appear before His dread tribunal, to render an account of each idle word.

Such are our obligations. Let us humble ourselves for neglecting them in the past. Let us plead for mercy, begging our Lord Jesus Christ, who came upon earth to satisfy for our sins, to repair our faults. Let us resolve to live henceforth in accordance with these obligations, invoking the aid of divine grace for that purpose.

SECOND POINT

Mortal Sin Is a Violation of All the Rights of God Over Us

Anyone who offends God mortally not only deprives God of all the homage he owes Him, but also robs Him, so far as possible, of all His claims upon him. He denies Him and disavows all allegiance to God's supreme authority. He usurps and appropriates those essential rights, thus denying God by his works, because the sinner destroys God so far as lies in his power and makes himself his own god. What is God? He is our Supreme Good, who should be loved and esteemed above all things. His glory, pleasure, interest and will should be preferred to every other glory, pleasure, interest and will. He is the beginning, end, centre, exemplar, king, master and ruler of all things. Consequently, all things should be referred to Him, tend to Him, take their pleasure in Him, follow Him as their rule and obey Him. What does the sinner do? He makes more account of himself than of God; he prefers his own will, interest, pleasure and glory to the will, interest, pleasure and glory of God. He desires to be master and dispose of himself as if he were his own instead of God's possession, as if he were his own beginning, holding his being and life from himself. He wishes to find his pleasure and happiness not in God, but in himself. He wishes to follow no rule but his passion and desires, no laws but his inclinations. He wants no ruler save his own blinded intellect and disordered will.

What is all this? Is it not to usurp God's rights and to rob Him of all His authority to appropriate them to ourselves? Is it not to deny God by our works? Do we not say to God by our depraved actions: "Lord, I am told that Thou art my beginning, end, centre, supreme good, exemplar, guide, king, and ruler, and that Thou hast manifold claims upon me; but I renounce Thee and disavow all these claims, I am my own beginning, end, rule and guide." Actually, we destroy and annihilate God by our defiance and make a god of self. This is what we do when we commit mortal sin.

O sin how terrible you are! How deeply I detest you! Forgive, my God, pray, forgive all my offenses.

THIRD POINT

By Inducing Others to Sin and Abusing Created Things, Man Robs God of His Rights and Makes Himself the God of Creatures

Anyone who induces others to do anything contrary to the will of God either by word, deed or example, anyone who makes improper use of the things God has put into this world for our necessity, who uses them to excess and to satisfy his own pleasure, ambition, avarice or other passions, instead of using them for God's glory, robs God, so far as lies in his power, of His rights over created things. He appropriates them to himself and makes himself the god of those things. When he encourages other people to do anything contrary to the law of God, he desires them to prefer his will and interest to that of God; and thus he seeks to be put in God's place in their regard. When he abuses the things God has made, he is not ruled by the will and glory of God but by his passions and corrupt inclinations, and he manifestly robs God of His rights over creatures and attributes them to himself. As God is the beginning and end of all things, His will and glory should be the measure and rule of our employment of creatures. Whoever uses anything otherwise, annihilates God in so far as he may, to put himself in His place and make himself god of creatures.

But how does God desire us to use the things of the world? He has declared His Will by the use His Son Jesus Christ made of them, for

He sent Him upon earth to be our model in that as in everything else.

O my God, I have followed this Divine Model most miserably! I am profoundly guilty of abusing the gifts Thou hast given me! Too often I have despoiled Thee of Thy supreme rights Thou hast over creatures to appropriate them to myself! Forgive me, O my God. I will no longer use anything save for Thy greater glory and in accordance with Thy holy will, in imitation of Thy Son our Lord Jesus Christ.

O my God, I have turned away from Thee in the past, from Thee who art my origin, my end and my supreme good. I have turned to myself, to the world and to Satan, preferring their will and mine to Thine. I affirm sincerely that I now desire to renounce entirely Satan, the world and myself, to be converted and turn to Thee completely and forever.

O my God, I give myself to Thee as my origin; possess me wholly. May I ever remain in Thee; may I avoid all that may not be worthy of my origin. Mayest Thou be the beginning and the end of all my actions.

O my God, I give myself to Thee as my end, my centre and my supreme good. Draw me to Thee. Grant that I may continually tend towards Thee. Be Thou alone my pleasure, my glory, my treasure and my all.

O my God, I give myself to Thee as my king. "Give me the grace to do what Thou commandest and command what Thou dost please" (St. Augustine, *Conf.* 10, 29).

O my God, I give myself to Thee as my prototype. Imprint upon my soul a perfect likeness of Thyself.

I give myself to Thee as my ruler and my protector. Direct me according to Thy holy will and preserve me from sin.

I give and abandon myself to Thee as my sovereign. Do with me what Thou wilt.

I give myself to Thee as my judge. Willingly I submit to all the judgments Thou hast exercised and ever wilt exercise upon me, in time and in eternity, saying with all respect and submission: "Thou art just, O Lord; and thy judgment is right" (Ps. 118, 137). "Yea, O Lord God Almighty, true and just are thy judgments" (Apoc. 16, 7).

Lastly, I give, consecrate and sacrifice myself wholly to Thee as my

God. If I contained within myself every created being and all the lives of men and angels, and if I had a thousand worlds in my hands, I would sacrifice them all to Thy supreme honor for the accomplishment of Thy most holy will.

O my God, do Thou employ Thy almighty power, Thy most infinite goodness, to take possession of me, to consecrate me to Thee, and to immolate me completely and forever to Thy pure glory.

Ejaculatory prayer:

"Satan, I renounce thee: My God, I cling to Thee."
Abrenuntio tibi, Satana: adhaereo tibi, Deus meus.

EIGHTH COLLOQUY

Our Obligation to Love, Honor, Imitate and Serve
God Because of All That He Is in Himself

GREATNESS OF GOD'S PERFECTIONS

SUPPOSE that we had never received any favors from God and were not obliged to serve Him by reason of our creation, our preservation, the creation and preservation of the world and all His consequent attributes and claims upon us. Even so we should still have infinite obligations, much more pressing than the preceding, simply because of the nature of God as He exists in Himself. Let us, therefore, adore God's divine essence and let us open the eyes of our faith, to behold and consider, with all possible respect and humility, His infinite being, His incomprehensible essence, His ineffable divinity, His supreme and adorable majesty, as follows:

"O divine Essence Who art a fathomless and unlimited abyss of marvels! O immense ocean of grandeur! O incomprehensible world of miracles! O unity of my God! O simplicity! O eternity without beginning and without end, to Whom all things are ever present! O immensity who dost fill and encompass all things and couldst fill a countless number of worlds if they existed! O infinity, who dost contain all perfections! O immutability! O immortality! O invisibility! O inaccessible light! O incomprehensible truth! O abyss of knowledge and wisdom! O truth! O sanctity of God, wholly detached fom all things and wholly centered in Himself!

"O sanctity that suffers the destruction of His works in His presence, that will destroy this world by fire, that has even delivered to the death of the Cross the most excellent of His works, the God-Man! O divine strength which bearest all and dost all! O omnipotence! O

66

divine providence governing and ordaining things! O justice! O bounty! O plenitude of good, joy, peace and honor! O divine will accomplishing all that Thou dost please in heaven and on earth! O love! O charity! O divine sufficiency, by which God is so sufficient to Himself that Sacred Scripture says: "I have said to the Lord: thou art my God for thou hast no need of my goods" (Ps. 15, 2). O divine vigilance, all-seeing eye of the power, justice and mercy' of God! O thoughts, designs, affections! O divine operations of God in Himself! O infinitely happy and glorious life of my God! O divine sovereignty which can dispose of all things, without anyone being permitted to question Thy decisions!

O my God, I adore Thee, with and through Jesus Christ Thy Son, in union with all the adoration, praise and benediction of His members. I adore all these infinite grandeurs and perfections, and all innumerable and inconceivable attributes that are unknown to me. I adore, praise, glorify and love Thee according to all Thou art. What joy it gives my heart to behold Thee so great and so replete with myriad excellences! Truly, my God, if all this greatness were mine instead of Thine, I would willingly renounce it to give it to Thee!

SECOND POINT

THE MUTUAL RELATIONSHIP OF THE THREE DIVINE PERSONS

Who are the Three Divine Persons and what do they accomplish for each one of us? The Father is continually communicating to His Eternal Son His being, His life, all His perfections, His glory, His felicity, all His goods and treasures. The Son is constantly referring to His Father as His origin, all that He has received from Him, and enjoys a perpetual state of glory and praise of His Heavenly Father.

The Father and Son give and communicate to the Holy Ghost all that They are, have and know. The Holy Ghost is continually referring to the Father and the Son, as to His source, all that He derives from Them. These divine communications, processions and relations, communications of the Father to the Son, of the Father and Son to the Holy Ghost, processions of the Son proceeding from His Father, and of the Holy Ghost proceeding from the Father and the Son, relations of the Father to the Son, of the Son to the Father, of the Father and Son to the Holy Ghost, of the Holy Ghost to the Father and the Son are eternal, continual and immense, filling heaven and earth.

With these divine communications and processions, the Father, Son and Holy Ghost have but one and the same essence and divinity, live one and the same existence, possess one and the same power, wisdom, goodness and sanctity, and abide in the most perfect Unity.

The three Divine Persons are continually and mutually considering and perpetually praising, loving and glorifying one another.

O Most Holy Trinity, I adore, bless and glorify Thee in this stupendous mystery. I unite with all the love and praise that the Divine Persons give one another. I offer Thee all the glory Thou hast in Thyself, for which I render infinite thanks with the Holy Church: "I give Thee infinite thanks, O Eternal Father, for the divine generation of the Eternal Son. I give thanks exceedingly, O divine Father and Only-begotten Son of the Father, for the procession of the Holy Spirit in unity of Source. I offer infinite thanks, O Father, Son and Holy Ghost, for the mutual love, glory and praise of the Trinity. O my God, Heavenly Father, how I rejoice to behold that Thy Son and Holy Spirit love and praise Thee from all eternity and to all eternity, with a love and praise befitting Thy greatness!

O Only-begotten Son of God, how my soul rejoices in contemplating the infinite love and glory Thou dost receive from the Heavenly Father and from the Holy Spirit! O Holy Spirit, what joy for my heart, to contemplate the love and blessings which are continually given Thee by the Father and the Son! O divine community, O unity, O society, love and life of the Three Eternal Persons! What rejoicing, what jubilation, what felicity for me to know that Thou art filled with ineffable glory, with inconceivable beatitude and infinity of good, and to know that Thou art God, the one only God living and reigning forever. "Sing joyfully to God, all the earth: serve ye the Lord with gladness. Come in before his presence with exceeding great joy. Know ye that the Lord he is God." (Ps. 99, 2-3).

OUR OBLIGATION TO HONOR THE DIVINE PERFECTIONS AND THE DIVINE PERSONS

All the perfections of the divine essence and the marvelous mysteries of the Three Eternal Persons constitute so many innumerable obligations for us to serve, honor and love the Blessed Trinity. God is so great and so admirable that His least perfection, if there be any less glorious than the others, merits infinite adoration, service and obedience. What honor does His supreme greatness and majesty demand of us? What love does His goodness and His incomprehensible charity merit? What fear does His dread justice inspire? What obedience is due His sovereignty? What purity of heart and life is required by His sanctity in those who serve Him?

What is our obligation to the Eternal Father for the being and life He imparts to His Divine Son by His Eternal generation, and to the Father and Son for all They impart to the Holy Ghost in his continual procession? Our debt is incomparably greater for this triune mystery than for the creation of a hundred thousand worlds.

What do we owe the Eternal Father for the infinite love of His Only-begotten Son, the Son for the love of His Father, and the Father and Son for their love of the Holy Ghost, and the Holy Ghost for the love of the Father and the Son? What do we owe to the Three Divine Persons for the praise and glory they give one another for all eternity and to all eternity? Certainly we owe them more service and obedience for all these mysteries than for all the graces we have received or can receive from Their divine liberality. The glory of the Three Divine Persons must be dearer to us than our own welfare, for we should love them more than ourselves. Let us, therefore, give ourselves to God to serve and honor Him according to His most holy will.

What God most desires of us is that we imitate Him for He is our Exemplar, as Jesus Christ says: "Be you therefore perfect, as also your heavenly Father is perfect" (Matt. 5, 48), and St. Paul enjoins: "Be ye therefore followers of God" (Eph. 5, 1). Let us give ourselves to

Him with a great desire to imitate His sanctity, his purity, charity, mercy, patience, vigilance, meekness and all His other perfections. Let us beg Him to imprint in our soul a perfect image and likeness of His sanctity and His divine virtues.

Ejaculatory prayer:

> "We give Thee thanks for Thy great glory."
> *Gratias agimus tibi propter magnam gloriam tuam.*

NINTH COLLOQUY

Our Obligations to God as Christians, and What It Means to Be a Christian

OUR OBLIGATIONS AS CHILDREN OF GOD, BROTHERS, AND CO-HEIRS OF CHRIST

To BE a Christian is to be a child of God, sharing one and the same Father with Jesus Christ His Only Son. "He gave them power to be made the sons of God" (John 1, 12). "I ascend to my Father and to your Father," says our Saviour (John 20, 17). "Behold what manner of Charity the Father hath bestowed upon us, that we should be called, and should be the sons of God," says St. John (1 John 3, 1). By creation, God is our creator, our origin, our efficient cause, our king, our sovereign; and we are His creatures, His handiwork, His subjects and His servants. By our regeneration and the new birth given us in baptism, in which we receive new being and a new and divine life, God becomes Our Father, and we His children, so that we can and must say: "Our Father who art in Heaven."

The consequences of this divine adoption are as follows:

1. By the new birth of baptism we emanated from the bosom of the Father, so we shall always remain there and be borne continually in His bosom. Otherwise, if He ceased to bear us for a single moment, we would lose the new being and life we received in baptism. He also says: "Hearken unto me, O house of Jacob, all the remnant of the house of Israel, who are carried by my bowels, are borne up by my womb" (Isa. 46, 3).

2. We are brothers of Jesus Christ, of His royal and divine race, sharers in His heritage. Whence it follows that the Christian, the new man and the new creature who is born only of God, knows no other

71

genealogy than that of Jesus Christ, no other Father but God: "And call none your father upon earth" (Matt. 23, 9). "Wherefore henceforth, we know no man according to the flesh," (2 Cor. 5, 16), says St. Paul. "That which is born of the Spirit, is spirit," says our Lord (John 3, 6).

3. We are co-heirs with Jesus Christ, and heirs of God. O marvels! O dignity! O nobility! O greatness of the Christian! "Behold what manner of charity the Father hath bestowed upon us, that we should be called, and should be the sons of God" (1 John 3, 1). What a tremendous favor of God to have made us Christians! How deeply we are indebted to His goodness! How miserable is the wretched creature who denies God for his Father and wishes to be a child of the devil! This is what those do who commit mortal sin. To them our Lord says: "You are of your father the devil, and the desires of your father you will do" (John 8, 44). Let us humble ourselves at sight of our sins. Let us renounce Satan and give ourselves to God, firmly resolving to live henceforth as true children of God, not to degenerate from the nobility of our birth, not to sully our race, and not to dishonor our Father. The wise son is the glory of his father; he who does not act wisely is the ignominy of his father.

SECOND POINT

OUR OBLIGATIONS AS MEMBERS OF JESUS CHRIST

A Christian is a member of Jesus Christ. "Know you not that your bodies are the members of Christ?" (1 Cor. 6, 15). Our alliance and union with Jesus Christ is consequently much more noble, more intimate and perfect than the members of a human and natural body with their head. Hence it follows that we belong to Jesus Christ as members to their head; that we are dependent upon Him and under His direction as members are upon their head; that we are one with Him as members are one with their head.

We must not be amazed when He assures us that His Father loves us as He loved Him: "Thou hast loved them, as thou hast also loved me" (John 17, 23); that He will write His name upon us: "I will write upon him the name of my God" (Apoc. 3, 12); that we will share one abode with Him, namely, His Father's bosom: "Where I am, there also shall my minister be" (John 12, 26); and He will let us sit with Him upon His throne (Apoc. 3, 21). What goodness! God is not content to call us His friends, His brothers, His children; He wishes us to be His members.

Let us love and bless Him and consider that this membership obliges us to live the life of our Head, to perpetuate His life upon earth, and to continue àll the virtues He practised. How far removed we are from that holy life! How horribly guilty is he who commits a mortal sin! He dismembers Jesus Christ; he tears one of His members from Him to make it a member of Satan. Let us give ourselves to Jesus Christ as His members, and profess to live His life henceforth. It would be an outrage to see a member live any other life than that of its head. Wherefore, St. Gregory of Nyssa says: "Christianity is the profession of the life of Christ" (*Ad Harmonium, De professione Christiana*).

THIRD POINT

OUR OBLIGATIONS AS TEMPLES OF THE HOLY GHOST

A Christian is a temple of the Holy Ghost. "Know you not," says St. Paul, "that your members are the temple of the Holy Ghost?" (1 Cor. 6, 19). Being children of God and one with the Son of God as members with their Head, it necessarily follows that we must be animated by the same spirit. St. Paul says: "And because you are sons, God hath sent the Spirit of his Son into your hearts" (Gal. 4, 6); and "if any man have not the Spirit of Christ, he is none of his" (Rom. 8, 9). Hence the Holy Spirit has been given us to be the Spirit of our spirit, the Heart of our heart and the Soul of our soul, to be always with us and within us, not only as if dwelling in His temple, but actually as part of the mystical body of Jesus Christ, which should be animated by His Spirit, for the members and every part of the body should be animated by the spirit of their Head.

This being so, who can tell or even imagine the excellence of the Christian religion, the dignity of a Christian who is a child of God, a member of Jesus Christ and animated by His Spirit? How great is our obligation to God, what should be the sanctity of our life, and how guilty he is who commits mortal sin? For he drives the Holy Ghost from His temple to give entrance to the evil spirit; he crucifies Jesus Christ in himself, stifling His indwelling spirit to establish His enemy, Satan, in his soul.

All these truths are essentially solid and infallible. Let us consider them attentively, weigh them carefully and engrave them deeply upon our hearts, to excite ourselves to bless and love God because of our infinite obligations to Him for having made us Christians. We must resolve to detest our ingratitude and our past sins, and henceforth to lead a life worthy of the perfection of the Father whose children we are, and of the purity of the Spirit whose body we share.

Ejaculatory prayer:

"Our Father Who art in Heaven, Thy Will be done on earth as it is in Heaven."

Pater noster qui es in caelis, fiat voluntas tua sicut in caelo et in terra.

TENTH COLLOQUY

Admirable Accomplishments of the Father, Son and Holy Ghost in Making Us Christians

To Make Us Christians God the Father Gave Us His Divine Son

Two great achievements, which include many others, were necessary to make us Christians. The first was to break and destroy the unhappy and detestable alliance we had contracted by sin, with Satan, whose slaves, children and members we had become. The second was to reconcile us with God, whose enemies we were, and establish us in a new alliance with Him, nobler and more intimate than the bond we enjoyed before sin. To accomplish those two things, it was necessary to blot out our sins, to deliver us from the power of Satan, to purify and cleanse our souls from the guilt of their crimes, and clothe them with the graces and gifts befitting the title of children of God and members of the Son of God.

Here is what the Eternal Father accomplished for this purpose. He sent His Only Beloved Son, His Heart, His love, His delight, His treasure, His glory, and His life. He sent Him, I say, and gave Him. But where, to whom and why did He send and give Him?

1. He sent Him into this world, to this land of misery and malediction, a place of darkness, horror, sin and tribulation.

2. He gave His Divine Son to us, that is, to His enemies, to ingrates and perfidious creatures, to Jews, Herods, Judases and executioners who have outraged, persecuted, sold and crucified Him, and who still outrage, persecute, sell and crucify Him every day. By giving His Divine Son to us, He delivered Him up to the torments

and death of the Cross. "God so loved the world, as to give his only begotten Son" (John 3, 16).

3. Why did He send and give His Only Son in this way? To deliver us from the tyranny of sin and the devil; to wash our souls in His Precious Blood, to adorn us with His sanctifying grace; to be our redemption, our reparation, our purification, our justification, our sanctification, and to raise us from the horrible position of slaves, children and members of Satan, to the admirable dignity of friends and children of God, brothers and members of Jesus Christ. "O ineffable goodness!" exclaims St. Augustine. "O incomparable mercy! We were not worthy to be slaves of God, and lo! we are numbered among His children!" O Good and Amiable Father, what shall we render to Thee for the infinite gift Thou hast bestowed upon us, in giving us that which Thou dost hold most dear and precious, Thy Only Son? We offer Thee Thy same Dearly Beloved Son in thanksgiving, and in union with our obligation, we offer, give, consecrate and sacrifice ourselves to Thee wholly and irrevocably. Take us and possess us perfectly and forever.

SECOND POINT

To Make Us Christians God the Son Assumed Human
Nature and Died on the Cross for Us

To make us Christians, the Son of God left the bosom of the Eternal Father and came into this world, was made man and lived thirty-four years upon earth, counting from the time of His Incarnation. How many mysteries and great works He accomplished during those thirty-four years! How many painful things He suffered! What confusion, opprobrium and torments He endured! What bitter tears and Precious Blood He shed! How many fasts, vigils, labors, fatigues and torments and how much weariness, bitterness and anguish He bore! All this He did to make us Christians, children of God and His members.

O my God, Thou didst employ only six days in creating the world, and a moment in making man; but to make him a Christian, Thou didst devote thirty-four years, and thirty-four years of a life of incessant labor and unspeakable suffering. It cost Thee only a few words for the creation, and it cost Thee all Thy Blood and Thy life with infinite sufferings for the Redemption. Since I have so many obligations to serve Thee because Thou hast created me, how much more am I obligated to Thee for having redeemed me? If I owe myself wholly to Thee for the gifts of being and life by creation, what do I owe Thee for having given Thyself to me by the Incarnation, and for having sacrificed Thyself for me on the Cross? O my Saviour, insignificant as I am, let me at least be wholly Thine! May I live only to love, serve and honor Thee, and to make Thee loved and honored in every possible way!

THIRD POINT

Role of the Holy Ghost in the Incarnation and the Sanctification of Our Souls

The Holy Ghost also helped to make us Christians. He formed our Saviour, our Redeemer and our Head in the sacred womb of the Blessed Virgin. He animated and directed God the Son in all He thought, said, did and suffered, His consummate Sacrifice on the Cross: "Who by the Holy Ghost offered himself unspotted unto God" (Heb. 9, 14). After our Lord ascended into heaven, the Holy Ghost came into this world, to form and establish the body of Jesus Christ, His Church, and to apply to it the fruits of His life, His Precious Blood, His passion and death; otherwise, our Lord would have suffered and died in vain.

Moreover, the Holy Ghost comes in baptism to form Jesus Christ in our souls, to incorporate us, to give us birth and make us live in Christ, to apply to us the infinite merits of His Precious Blood and His death, and to animate, inspire and direct us in all we think, say, do and suffer as Christians and for God; therefore we cannot pronounce the name of Jesus except by the power of the Holy Ghost, and we are not sufficient to think a holy thought without the grace of God. What great and wondrous marvels have been wrought by the Father, Son and Holy Ghost to make us Christians! O blessed St. John, you were indeed right to say in the name of all Christians: "The world

78 MEDITATIONS ON VARIOUS SUBJECTS

knoweth not us" (1 John 3, 1). How we should bless and love the
Father, Son and Holy Ghost for having called and exalted us to the
dignity of Christians! What should be our life! It should be all holy,
all divine, all spiritual for our Lord tells us: "That which is born of
the Spirit, is spirit" (John 3, 6). O Divine Spirit, I give myself wholly
to Thee: take possession of me and direct me in all things. Grant that
I may live as a child of God, as a member of Jesus Christ, and as one
born of Thee: "That which is born of the Spirit," who is consequently
Thine, and should be possessed, animated and directed by Thy vivi-
fying grace.

Ejaculatory prayer:

"Let the mercies of the Lord give glory to him: and his wonderful
works to the children of men."
*Confiteantur Domino misericordiae ejus: et mirabilia ejus filiis ho-
minum* (Ps. 106, 8).

ELEVENTH COLLOQUY

By Baptism We Were Made Christians

BAPTISM IS A NEW CREATION

BAPTISM is a new creation; therefore Sacred Scripture calls the Christian a new creature. Baptism is a second creation of man of which the first is merely a shadow and a figure.

By the first creation, God drew us from utter nothingness; by the second, He drew us from the nothingness of sin which is a much deeper abyss. The former void is not opposed to the power of God; but the latter infinitely resists Him by its infinite malice. When God created us in Jesus Christ, as St. Paul says, when He gave us new being and new life in Jesus Christ by baptism, He found us in the nothingness of sin, in a state of enmity, opposition and contradiction towards Him. But He overcame our malice by His goodness and by His infinite power.

By the first creation God gave us a human, frail and mortal being; by the second He imparted to us heavenly and divine being.

By the first creation He made us to His own image and likeness; by the second He restored His image which sin had effaced, and imprinted it more nobly and more excellently than the original pattern, making us partakers of His divine nature in a much more eminent degree.

By the first creation God placed man in the visible world made at the beginning of time. By the second He placed the Christian in a new world. What is this new world? What is the Christian's world? It is God with all His perfections, the very bosom of God. It is Jesus Christ the God-Man, considered in Himself, in His life, in His mysteries, and considered also in His body which is His Church. This is the world of the new creature, quite different from the first world of the first creature.

The original world is a world of darkness, sin and malediction: "The whole world is seated in wickedness" (1 John 5, 19); but the second is a world of peace, sanctity and benediction, in which there is an infinite number of infinitely beautiful, delightful and agreeable treasures. What ravishing and wonderful delights there are in God, in the perfections of God, in the sanctity of God, in the eternity of God, in the immensity of God, in His glory, in His felicity, in His riches, in the earthly life of Jesus Christ and in all His mysteries, actions, sufferings and virtues; in His glorious and immortal life, in His Church and in the lives of all His saints!

In the world of Adam there are heavens, stars and elements. In the world of the Christian the heaven is God and the bosom of God; the sun is Jesus; the moon is Mary; the planets and the stars are the saints; the earth is the sacred humanity of Jesus Christ; the water is Christian grace; the air is the spirit of the Holy Ghost; the fire is love and charity; the bread is the Body of Jesus Christ; our wine is His Precious Blood; we are clothed with Jesus Christ: "For as many of you as have been baptized in Christ, have put on Christ" (Gal. 3, 27). There are no poor, nor mendicants, in the world of the Christian, because all true Christians are infinitely rich: "All things are yours" (1 Cor. 3, 22). We are all magnates, princes and rulers.

Woe to the world of Adam, wholly corrupted by sin! Let us leave it to the children of this world and give our hearts to our Christian world. Let us forsake the world of Adam to enter the world of Jesus Christ. All who belong to Jesus Christ are apart from the world of the old man, as Jesus Christ is not of it: "They are not of the world, as I also am not of the world" (John 17, 16).

We Christians find true riches, honors and pleasures in our regenerated world. The children of darkness find pleasure in seeing the things of their world, in speaking of them and hearing of them: "They are of the world. Therefore of the world they speak" (1 John 4, 5). So we should find our happiness in studying, describing and learning the wonders and news of our world, which are infinitely more delectable than the news of the sinner's world: "The wicked have told me fables: but not as thy law" (Ps. 118, 85).

Finally, we should die to the world of Adam, to live in our world and the life of our world which is God and Jesus Christ our Lord. We inhere in Him as a part of Himself, consequently to be animated by His spirit and live His life. This death and this life are expressed in St. Paul's words: "You are dead: and your life is hid with Christ in God" (Col. 3, 3). Let us give ourselves to God that He may fill us with His lofty sentiments. Let us earnestly entreat Him to render His gifts fruitful in us, and to imprint in our hearts great contempt and aversion for the world of Adam, with a new, profound esteem and love for our own Christian world.

SECOND POINT

BAPTISM IS A REGENERATION

Sacred Scripture calls baptism a regeneration and a rebirth: "By the laver of regeneration" (Tit. 3, 5). "Unless a man be born again of water and the Holy Ghost" (John 3, 5). Baptism is a generation and birth, having for exemplar and prototype the eternal generation and birth of the Son of God in His Father's bosom, and His temporal generation and birth in the virginal womb of His Mother.

In His eternal generation, the Heavenly Father communicates to His Divine Son His being, His life and all His divine perfections; so, too, in our baptism, the Father gives us, through His Son and in His Son, a being and life all holy and divine.

In the temporal generation of the Son of God, the Eternal Father gives Him a new being and a new life, a life all holy and divine, yet none the less clothed with mortality, passibility, and all the wretchedness of human life; similarly, the new life which God gives us in baptism is wholly environed and beset by frailty, weakness, mortality and all the infirmities of human life to which it is united.

The Holy Ghost was sent to form the Son of God in the sacred womb of the Blessed Virgin. He is likewise sent to form our Lord and to make Him live by baptism in the depths of our soul, to incorporate and unite us with Him and to give us birth and life in Him: "Unless a man be born again of water and the Holy Ghost, he cannot enter into the kingdom of God" (John 3, 5).

The Three Divine Persons of the Blessed Trinity have cooperated by the same power and goodness in the admirable work of the Incarnation, are present in our baptism, cooperating to give us the new being and new life in Jesus Christ which is conferred upon each neophyte.

Thus baptism is an ineffable generation. "Of his own will hath he begotten us" (James 1, 18), and an admirable birth, a living image of the eternal and temporal generation and birth of the Son of God. Therefore our life should be a perfect image of His life. "We are created in Christ Jesus" (Eph. 2, 10); We are "born of God" (John 1, 13). We should live only by God, in God and for God; we must live no life but that of Jesus Christ, directed solely by His spirit, which should animate and possess us completely.

Let us be very humbled to find ourselves so removed from this life which should exist in all Christians. Let us give ourselves to God with a great desire to live the real life. Let us implore Him to destroy in us the life of the world and sin, and to establish His admirable life in us, that we may not be like those unhappy beings whom St. Paul says are "alienated from the life of God" (Eph. 4, 18).

THIRD POINT

BAPTISM IS A DEATH AND RESURRECTION

Baptism is a death and a resurrection. It is death. "If one died for all, then all were dead" (2 Cor. 5, 14), says St. Paul, that is, all who are incorporated in Jesus Christ as His members in baptism, are become members of a dead and crucified Head, and must be crucified and dead to the world, to sin and to self.

It is also a resurrection for by baptism we leave the death of sin to enter the life of grace.

Baptism is a death and a resurrection, having for its prototype the Death and Resurrection of Jesus Christ. Christians who are baptized in Christ Jesus are baptized in His death. "We are buried together with him," says St. Paul, "by baptism unto death" (Rom. 6, 4). The Christian likewise participates in His Resurrection: "for, as Christ is risen from the dead by the glory of the Father, so we also may walk in newness of life" (Rom. 6, 4). By baptism we are obliged to die to everything, to live with Jesus Christ an all-heavenly life, as if we are persons no longer of earth, but of heaven, whose mind and heart dwell in heaven, according to the words of the first Christians speaking by St. Paul: "Our conversation is in heaven" (Phil. 3, 20), and his own exhortation: "If you be risen with Christ, seek the things that are above, not the things that are upon the earth" (Col. 3, 1-2).

Finally, by baptism we are obliged to verify in ourselves the following words: "You are dead: and your life is hid with Christ in God" (Col. 3, 3). We must be dead to all that is not God, to live only in God and abide with Jesus Christ: "as those that are alive from the dead" (Rom. 6, 13), says St. Paul. We must consequently lead a heavenly life upon earth, that is, a holy life adorned with all kinds of virtue, a continual exercise of love, adoration and praise of God, and of charity to our neighbor.

Such should be the life of all baptized persons. Those who, instead of living this holy Christian life, follow the life of the world which is, as St. Ambrose says, the body of the dragon, the life of pagans, of beasts, of demons, renounce their baptism, and render themselves far more guilty than pagans and demons. How dreadful is sin which extinguishes a life so noble and precious as the Christian life we have received by baptism, the life of God, the life of Jesus Christ in our souls, and establishes instead the horrible life of sin, a diabolical and detestable existence! Let us detest our sins. Let us renounce with all our heart the life of the world and of the old Adam. Let us give ourselves to Jesus Christ, begging Him to destroy the old life in us, and to establish His own all-glorious life in our regenerated souls.

Ejaculatory prayer:

"I live, now not I; but Christ liveth in me."
Vivo autem, jam non ego; vivit vero in me Christus (Gal. 2, 20).

TWELFTH COLLOQUY

Baptism Is a Divine Contract Between Man and God

BY BAPTISM WE ENTERED INTO A SUPERNATURAL FELLOWSHIP WITH GOD

BAPTISM is a divine contract of man with God, containing three great provisos.

First, God by His incomprehensible goodness and mercy delivers us from our cursed alliance with Satan, whose children and members we have become by sin, and permits us to enter into a wonderful fellowship with Him. "By whom you are called unto the fellowship of His Son Jesus Christ our Lord" (1 Cor. 1, 9), says St. Paul. "That which we have seen and have heard, we declare unto you," says St. John, "that you also may have fellowship with us, and our fellowship may be with the Father and with his Son Jesus Christ" (1 John 1, 3).

What is this supernatural fellowship? It is the noblest and most perfect fellowship that can exist. It is not merely the alliance of friend with friend, of brother with brother, of children with their father, of bride with bridegroom, but of member with Head, which is the most intimate of all fellowships.

The natural and corporal union of the branches of a vine with the stalk, and of the members of the human body with the head, although the most intimate of all imaginable unions in nature, is only a figure and a reflection of our spiritual and supernatural union with Jesus Christ by baptism. Corporal and natural things are mere shadows of spiritual and supernatural life.

Furthermore, the union of the branches with the stalk of the vine, and of the members of the body with their corporal head, is in con-

84

formity with the quality, and the material nature of the things it joins together. But the union of the members of Jesus Christ with their Head is in conformity with the excellent holy and divine nature of the participants. Consequently, the more that divine Head and those sacred members are exalted above the natural head and its members, the more the alliance of Christians with Jesus Christ excels the union existing between the head and the members of the human body.

The friendship we contract with Jesus Christ by baptism, and through Him with the Eternal Father, is so lofty and so divine, that it merits comparison by Jesus Christ Himself to the unity that exists between the Father and the Son in the words: "That they may be one, as we also are one. I in them, and thou in me: that they may be made perfect in one" (John 17, 22-23). So the unity of the Father and Son is the ideal of the union with God by baptism; and this union is the living image of that adorable unity.

Moreover, the wondrous alliance we enjoy with God by baptism is exalted and ennobled by being founded, so to speak, on the Precious Blood of Jesus Christ and constituted by the Holy Ghost. Thus the Holy Ghost, who is the unity of the Father and the Son, is the sacred bond of our fellowship and union with Jesus Christ, and through Jesus Christ with the Eternal Father, a union indicated by the divine words: "That they may be made perfect in one" (John 17, 23).

Thus we see that, by baptism, we become one with Jesus Christ, and through Jesus Christ with God, in the most exalted and most perfect concordance possible, next to the hypostatic union of the human nature with the Eternal Word. O incomparable alliance! O ineffable fellowship! How deeply indebted we are to the infinite goodness of God for a contract so great! What praise and thanksgiving we should offer Him! "Thanks be to God for his unspeakable gift" (2 Cor. 9, 15).

Since we are thus associated with the Saint of saints in so intimate a union, what should be the sanctity of our life? Surely, as we are one with God, we should have but one heart, one mind, one will, one affection: "He who is joined to the Lord, is one spirit" (1 Cor. 6, 17). We should love only what He loves and hate what He hates. How deserving of hatred is sin! For what is it to sin mortally? It is to violate and break that divine alliance we formed with God by baptism, to return to our contract with Satan, His enemy. It is to dishonor the unity of the Father and the Son by destroying its image.

Sin profanes and renders fruitless the adorable Blood of Jesus Christ which is the foundation of our fellowship. It extinguishes the Spirit of God who is its sacred bond, according to the prohibitive: "Extinguish not the spirit" (1 Thess. 5, 19). What a horror we should have for our past sins! What fear of relapsing into them! And what care we should exert to preserve the rich and precious alliance we have contracted with God, and to associate with it our entire life and activity.

SECOND POINT

BY BAPTISM GOD BOUND HIMSELF TO TREAT US AS HIS CHILDREN AND MEMBERS OF HIS SON

The second proviso of our baptismal contract with God is that having received us into fellowship with Him, as His children and as members of His Son, He is bound to consider, love and treat us as His own children, and to regard and love our souls as His spouses. He has faithfully treated us in this way, and bestowed upon us inestimable gifts in conformity with the dignity and sanctity of our alliance with Him. He has endowed, enriched and adorned us with ineffable gifts and treasures. He has given us His grace of which the least degree is worth more than all the empires of earth. He has given us the gift of faith, hope, and charity, three priceless gifts and sources of inestimable blessings.

He has given us also the other virtues, which are all joined to charity, the seven gifts of the Holy Ghost and the eight beatitudes. Since our baptism, He has always kept His paternal eyes fixed on us, and His Heart loving us. He gives us everything necessary and suitable for body and soul, and is faithful in fulfilling all His promises to us. And after all that, He again assures us that we are to be His heirs in heaven, and that we will there possess benefits that eye has never seen, the ear heard, nor the human heart conceived! Oh, what graces! Oh, what mercies! "Let the mercies of the Lord give glory to him, and his wonderful works to the children of men" (Ps. 106, 31).

By Baptism We Consecrated Ourselves to God and Promised to Adhere to Jesus Christ

The third proviso in our baptismal contract is that we offered and consecrated ourselves to God through our godfather and godmother. We promised to renounce Satan and his works, that is, all kinds of sin, and his pomps, meaning the world, and to adhere to Jesus Christ. According to the ancient form observed in baptism, the person to be baptized, turning to the West, said: *Abrenuntio tibi Satana:* "I renounce thee, Satan." Then turning to the East, he said: *Adhaereo tibi Christe:* "I adhere to Thee, Jesus Christ." And the same thing is still said to-day in different but equivalent words. Such is our solemn promise to God in baptism, a promise made before the Church, a promise hidden and included in a great Sacrament, a promise so binding that no one can ever dispense us from it, a promise, says St. Augustine, recorded by the angels, according to which we shall be judged at the hour of our death.

Let us judge ourselves now that we may not be judged then, and let us condemn ourselves that we may not be condemned. Let us rigorously examine our life and see if we have lived in accordance with this promise. We shall find that we have frequently acted as if we had promised just the opposite, and instead of renouncing Satan, sin and the world, and following Jesus Christ, we have turned our backs upon Him and denied Him by our works, and chosen the side of His enemies. What treacherous perfidy! What base ingratitude after so many favors! Oh, what shame for us! How we should mark our infidelity and renew the promise and profession of our baptism with greater fervor!

This I now wish to do, O my God. For this end I renounce thee, cursed Satan, with all my heart and with all my strength. I renounce abominable sin. I renounce the detestable world. I renounce its false honors and vain pleasure, its deceitful riches, its diabolical spirit, its pernicious maxims and all its corruption and malignity.

I give myself to Thee, O Lord Jesus, wholly and forever. I will adhere to Thy holy doctrine by faith, to Thy holy promises by hope, to Thy divine commandments and counsels by love and charity. I will follow Thee in the practice of every virtue, and I will follow Thee as my Head, as one of Thy members. I will continue Thy life on earth as far as possible, with the aid of Thy holy grace, which I most earnestly entreat for this intention.

Ejaculatory prayer:

"But it is good for me to adhere to my God, to put my hope in the Lord God."

Mihi autem adhaerere Deo bonum est, ponere in Domino Deo spem meam (Ps. 72, 28).

MEDITATION

The Choice of a State of Life

CONFORMITY TO THE HOLY WILL OF GOD IN THE CHOICE OF YOUR STATE OF LIFE

You are not permitted to choose any state of life but the one God has designed for you from all eternity. You must not take up any work except that to which He is pleased to call you. You are not your own, but His, by an infinity of rights: by the claim of creation, preservation, redemption, justification, His complete sovereignty over all creatures, and by as many claims as there were thoughts entertained, words spoken, actions performed, sufferings endured, and drops of blood shed by the Son of God, to redeem you from the slavery of the devil and of sin.

Therefore, it is His divine right to dispose of you, of your life and works, for you belong to Him infinitely more than a subject to his king, a slave to his master, a house to its purchaser, or a child to his father. Hence, renounce yourself, affirm that you desire not only to be His and to serve Him, but to serve Him in the way that will be most pleasing to Him, and in the state to which He deigns to call you. Ask Him to make known His holy will on this point, and resolve to dispose yourself as best you can to know and follow His providential plan.

SECOND POINT

MEANS OF KNOWING THE WILL OF GOD

You have seven things to do in order to dispose yourself to learn the divine will concerning your vocation.

The first is to humble yourself profoundly, acknowledging that you

89

are infinitely unworthy to serve God in any state or condition whatever. Being involved in darkness, you cannot of yourself know God's will on this point, and you do not deserve that He should communicate His divine light to you.

The second step is to purify your soul from all sin and affection for sin, by means of sincere repentance and an extraordinary confession, to remove everything that might prove an obstacle to the heavenly light and graces you require for this decision.

The third step is to declare to God that you desire to be absolutely His, to serve Him with all your heart, for love of Him, in the kind of life to which He deigns to call you.

Fourthly, you must attain complete neutrality towards the professions in which you might please God, and rid yourself of all sorts of designs and aspirations, placing your ideas, tastes, desires and inclinations at the feet of our Lord, that He may clothe you with His own, fully resigning your liberty that He may dispose of you as He pleases, placing your heart in His hands like soft wax or like a blank page, for Him to engrave or write on it the message of His adorable will.

Fifthly, you must pray earnestly, with greatest confidence, that by His infinite mercy, He may place you in the state He has deigned to choose for you from all eternity, although you are infinitely unworthy of it; and that He may give you the light and grace you need to embrace this state and to serve Him faithfully therein.

Sixthly, you should fortify your prayers with mortification, alms, or other works of mercy, corporal or spiritual.

The seventh and last step is to implore the help of the Blessed Virgin, of St. Joseph, of your guardian angel and of all the other angels and saints, that they may obtain for you the grace to know and follow what God asks of you.

These are the seven things you have to do to dispose yourself to know your vocation. Ask Almighty God to give you the grace to follow them; and, on your part, endeavor to dispose yourself with the aid of His holy grace.

THIRD POINT

Signs Whereby You May Know the Will of God

If after following the preceding steps, and entering into the dispositions indicated, you feel an inclination to a particular kind of life, you must not immediately follow this desire. First, you must examine it thoroughly, for fear of following the attractions of your own will, or of self-love, or of the evil spirit, in place of the inspirations of the Spirit of God. In order not to be deceived, consider carefully: 1. whether the state to which you feel drawn is one in which you can readily serve God and work out your salvation; 2. whether God has given you the necessary physical and mental qualities and the requisite conditions to enter that state; 3. whether your desire is stable and permanent; 4. whether your motive is pure and disinterested, having no other intention but to honor God and accomplish His most holy will; 5. whether your desire is approved and confirmed by the advice of God's earthly representatives, capable of directing you in a matter of such importance.

These are the five marks of a true vocation from God. If they are to be found in your desire for any state, there is nothing left but for you to resolve firmly to embrace it, to seek the means leading to this end, to ask God to give you all the graces necessary to attain it, to serve and honor Him in it in accordance with His omnipotent designs, and to invoke the intercession of the Blessed Virgin, of the angels and saints.

Ejaculatory prayer:

"Make the way known to me, wherein I should walk: for I have lifted up my soul to thee."
Notam fac mihi viam in qua ambulem, quia ad te levavi animam meam (Ps. 142, 8).

III
MEDITATIONS ON HUMILITY

III

MEDITATIONS ON HUMILITY [1]

It is a daily practice in many religious communities to make a profession of humility. After the morning meditation, one of the members, inclining profoundly, recites it aloud, and at the end, the others, also bowing down, answer: "Lord Jesus Christ, have mercy on us."

But, if the truths contained in the words of this profession are to make a deeper impression, and produce greater fruits in souls, it is necessary to study carefully and meditate seriously upon them. This is why I have selected them as material for these meditations.

Protestation of Humility

Domine Jesu Christe, nihil sumus,	Lord Jesus Christ, we are nothing,
Nihil possumus,	We can do nothing,
Nihil valemus,	We are worth nothing,
Nihil habemus, praeter peccatum,	We possess nothing but sin,
Servi inutiles sumus,	We are useless servants,
Natura filii irae,	We are children of wrath,
Novissimi virorum et primi peccatorum,	The last of men and the first of sinners,
Nobis igitur confusio et ignominia,	Upon us be confusion and shame,
Tibi autem honor et gloria in saecula saeculorum. Amen.	To Thee be honor and glory forever and ever. Amen.
Domine Jesu Christe, miserere nobis.	Lord Jesus Christ, have mercy on us.

[1] See footnote, p. 41.

95

FIRST MEDITATION

On the Words: Nihil Sumus—"We Are Nothing."

GOD IS THE SOVEREIGN BEING

LET us adore God, pronouncing the divine words *Ego sum Qui sum:* "I Am Who Am" (Exod. 3, 14). Let us beg Him to make us realize their truth and render them fruitful in us, for all God's words are filled with light and power; light to illumine our minds and power to effect in our hearts the work of grace and sanctification in conformity with their significance.

Let us consider that God alone is worthy to exist and that He alone exists, properly speaking: "See ye that I alone am" (Deut. 32, 39). Any other creature whatsoever not only does not deserve to exist, but does not even exist before God. "All nations are before him as if they had no being at all, and are counted to him as nothing, and vanity" (Isa. 40, 17). His being is eternal, without beginning and without end, immense, filling all space, immutable, infinite, changeless, replete with admirable perfections, infinitely happy, rich and glorious, sovereign and independent, the source of all being, to whom every creature in heaven, on earth and in hell should be referred as to its source, should pay honor, homage, adoration and sacrifice as to the Sovereign Being of all Creation.

Let us rejoice that God is "He Who is." "Come in before his presence with exceeding great joy" (Ps. 99, 2).

Let us adore, bless and glorify Him. Let us offer and sacrifice to Him our being and the existence of all angels, men, irrational creatures and even the demons and damned.

HOMAGE DUE TO GOD

Since God alone is He who is, and all that is not God is as nothing before Him, God alone is worthy to be considered, esteemed, loved, desired and honored. We should, therefore, have neither mind nor heart, nor thought nor affection, nor eye, nor tongue, nor hand for anything else. Yet, there is nothing less esteemed, loved, desired, and sought after, nothing of which we think less, of which we speak so little, and for Whom we do so little, as God. What is not, that is, the nothingness of created things, is much more esteemed, desired and sought after than He who is, and we think, speak and do a great deal more for nothing than for our Supreme All.

Let us humble ourselves for having been among those who have preferred the nothing to the All. Let us ask pardon of this great All. Let us protest that, henceforth, we desire to see and love Him alone in all things, beseeching Him to annihilate all things and ourselves in our own eyes, so that He may be All in all to us.

SCORN OF SINNERS FOR GOD

Let us consider how sinners annihilate "Him Who is." First, the atheists in belief annihilate Him, saying there is no God: "The fool hath said in his heart: There is no God" (Ps. 13, 1). Secondly, the atheists in life and morals annihilate Him by living and acting as if they did not believe in Him. Thirdly, all those who commit mortal sin annihilate Him because they annihilate His sovereignty, by refusing to depend upon Him. They destroy His will, desiring the accomplishment of their own whims to the detriment of His eternal will. They impugn His wisdom, desiring that He should have no will to punish them, His power in wishing that He should have no power, His providence in persuading themselves that He has no thought of things here on earth. We have annihilated God in this way if we have sinned mortally.

Let us beseech Him to forgive us. In reparation, let us annihilate ourselves in every possible manner, in our own opinion and in that of
others. Let us seek all sorts of opportunities to annihilate ourselves by
various practices of humility, begging Him to employ His power and
His goodness in extinguishing us and impressing upon our hearts a
great affection for nothingness so that our highest ambition may be to
become nothing in this world, that God may be All in all things:
Omnia in Omnibus (1 Cor. 15, 28).

Ejaculatory prayer:

> Lord Jesus Christ, we are nothing.
> *Domine Jesu Christe, nihil sumus.*

SECOND MEDITATION

Annihilation of Our Lord Jesus Christ

OUR LORD ANNIHILATED HIMSELF IN HIS HUMANITY

LET us adore our Lord Jesus Christ in the annihilation revealed in these words: "He emptied himself" (Phil. 2, 7), and consider that He annihilated Himself in His humanity and even in His divinity.

In His humanity, He annihilated Himself in thought, interior dispositions, words and actions.

He annihilated Himself in His thoughts and interior dispositions. His sacred humanity clearly realized that of itself it was nothing and His holy soul dwelt in a continual disposition of annihilation before the greatness and supreme Majesty of God.

He annihilated Himself in His words for it was He who said: "My substance is as nothing before thee" (Ps. 38, 6). Whenever He spoke of Himself, He always referred to Himself as "the son of man" that is, the son of nothingness and consequently "nothing."

He annihilated Himself in His actions: during the whole course of His life He abased and humbled Himself as a man of no account. Everything that He did was for His Heavenly Father and nothing for Himself as man, no more than if He had not existed. "Christ is God's" (1 Cor. 3, 23).

He also annihilated His will, His intellect and His love of Himself.

Let us, therefore, exalt Jesus as much as He humbled Himself, and, imitating His example, let us endeavor to annihilate ourselves in thought, word and deed. Beg Him to give us a share in His divine knowledge, that we may realize our nothingness; to imprint upon our souls a lively perception of our nothingness; and to grant us the grace to think, say and do nothing for ourselves, but all for Him, our Supreme All.

OUR LORD JESUS CHRIST ANNIHILATED HIMSELF IN HIS DIVINITY

Our Lord annihilated Himself even in His divinity. He extinguished in a manner His supreme being in the nothingness of our nature, His divine life in our mortality, His eternity in time, His immensity and infinity in the littleness of childhood, His omnipotence in weakness and importance, His wisdom in the folly of the crib and the Cross, His sanctity in His likeness to sinners, His glory in ignominy, His joy in suffering, His plenitude in poverty, His sovereignty in dependence and subjection.

Adore and glorify Him in this annihilation. Thank Him for the glory rendered to His Eternal Father. He has annihilated such great, holy and divine privileges for us; therefore let us annihilate for Him things base, abject, evil and corrupt, such as is everything found in us.

OUR LORD JESUS CHRIST WILLED TO BE TREATED AS NOTHING

Consider that while He was on earth, our Divine Saviour willed to be treated as a non-entity, or rather, as if He were less than nothing, for He permitted mankind to treat Him with less respect and humanity, and with more ignominy and cruelty than they would have done if He had been only a nonentity. Consider, too, that even in our day, He is annihilated in His divinity and humanity in the Blessed Sacrament of the Altar; and is treated there even by the majority of Christians as a nothing, for they behave in His presence with less fear and reverence than if He were nothing.

Let us give ourselves to Him, to honor and imitate Him in this annihilation. Beg Him to blot out our vanity and give us a share in His spirit of humility, so that henceforth we may regard and treat ourselves and be glad to be esteemed and treated as nothings who deserve only contempt and humiliation.

Ejaculatory prayer:

"Lord Jesus Christ, we are nothing."
·Domine Jesu Christe, nihil sumus.

THIRD MEDITATION

Annihilation of the Blessed Virgin and of Holy Church

The Blessed Virgin Annihilated Herself in Her Own Eyes

THE Blessed Virgin resembled her Divine Son in His self-annihilation and imitated perfectly His thoughts, His interior dispositions, His words and actions in the manner we have indicated, and all proportions being observed, she also extinguished her own will, her intellect and her self-love, although all these things were sanctified in her. Let us honor her in this self-effacement and ask her to obtain for us the grace to imitate her profound humility.

SECOND POINT

Our Lady Was Treated by Others as if She Were Nothing

Let us consider that the Blessed Virgin treated herself and was treated by others in this world as if she were nothing. Offer to God all the glory that she rendered Him by this self-abnegation. Let us strive to exalt her in reward for her abasement and endeavor to imitate her.

THIRD POINT

Our Lord Willed that His Church Should Be Small and Humble

Let us consider that the Son of God compares His Church to a grain of mustard seed, "which is the least indeed of all seeds" (Matt. 13, 32), and that He willed that it should be small, humble and persecuted in this world. It was small in its foundation, being founded on a crucified

God-Man and twelve poor, weak and ignorant fishermen, all of whom died by the hands of executioners. It was small in its first members. "For see your vocation, brethren," says St. Paul, "that there are not many wise according to the flesh, not many mighty, not many noble. But the foolish things of the world hath God chosen, that he may confound the wise; and the weak things of the world hath God chosen, that he may confound the strong. And the base things of the world, and the things that are contemptible, hath God chosen: and things that are not, that he might bring to nought things that are" (1 Cor. 1, 26-28). The Church is even unpretentious in its tremendous sacraments, which are symbolized by very minor objects: Baptism by water, the Blessed Eucharist by bread and wine.

The Son of God has ordained this for three reasons:

1. To confound human pride which always desires its work to be conspicuous, while He wills that His greatest work, namely, His Church, should be concealed under these apparently insignificant things.

2. To teach us not to be guided by human judgment and reason which esteem and regard only sensible and apparent things, but by the spirit of faith which considers only things invisible and eternal according to the sacred words: "While we look not at the things which are seen, but at the things which are not seen. For the things which are seen, are temporal; but the things which are not seen, are eternal" (2 Cor. 4, 18).

3. To teach us to despise the ideas and opinions of the world and refrain from efforts to win its acclaim. If our Lord had wished to please the world, He would have founded His Church on the emperors, on the great and the wise of the earth, and would have followed a much more elaborate course with regard to His doctrine and Sacraments. He wished to teach us to despise fame and worldliness and to employ all our efforts in pleasing God alone in all we do and to serve Him by humbling and abasing ourselves everywhere and always.

Ejaculatory prayer:

> "Lord Jesus Christ, we are nothing."
> *Domine Jesu Christe, nihil sumus.*

FOURTH MEDITATION

We Are Nothing from Every Point of View

OUR ORIGIN IS NOTHINGNESS

LET us adore the Holy Ghost pronouncing these words by the mouth of St. Paul: "If any man think himself to be something, whereas he is nothing, he deceiveth himself" (Gal. 6, 3). Let us give ourselves to the Holy Spirit and earnestly beseech Him to make us realize this truth and give us grace to draw therefrom the fruit He wishes.

Let us consider that we are nothing in body or in soul, since both have been created out of nothing, so that our origin is nothingness. Worldly men may glory in the status of their ancestors. Let us Christians remember that we descended from nothing from which God draws us forth. What should humble us still more is that we did not deserve that He should draw us from it any more than an infinite number of other creatures who will remain in nothingness forever. God in His pure goodness withdrew us from the void.

Another truth which should confound our pride is that if God did not preserve us every moment, if He were to leave us to ourselves, we would fall back into the nothingness whence we came, so true is it that of ourselves and by ourselves we are nothing. By counting every moment that has elapsed since you came into the world, you may know how many times you would have been annihilated if God had not performed as great a miracle to preserve you as He did to create you. Hence, let us acknowledge that nothingness is our portion and our inheritance. We may glory in this and in nothing else. Let us adore and praise the divine power and goodness for having drawn forth and sustained us at every moment. Let us beg God to engrave these truths profoundly upon our mind, so that they may serve to destroy our vanity and to keep us humble.

Because of Our Sins We Have Deserved to Be Annihilated

Let us consider that as often as we have offended God in any way whatever, we have deserved to lose the being He has given us, and that if He willed to punish us as we deserve, He would have annihilated us, according to these words: "Correct me, O Lord, but yet with judgment: and not in thy fury, lest thou bring me to nothing" (Jer. 10, 24).

Now, if we have so often deserved to be annihilated, have we not also deserved all the humiliations, abjections and trials of this life? What would we think of a man who had merited not only death, but extinction, thousands of times? How unbearable are vanity and self-esteem in one who has been drawn from nothing, without any merit on his part, who has been preserved from annihilation as many times as there are moments in his life! How can man be vain when he has justly merited to be returned to nothingness as often as he has offended his Creator and Deliverer!

The Great Evil of Pride

The truth of our nothingness being conceded, let us consider how great an evil is pride, and how very wrong it is to attribute any vanity to oneself in thought, word and action or to seek honor and praise. Pride is an illusion, a lie and a theft. It is a truth of faith that we are nothing; therefore he who esteems himself and thinks himself to be something is a seducer who deceives himself: "he deceiveth himself" (Gal. 6, 3). He who speaks well of himself is a liar. "For I know that there dwelleth not in me, that is to say, in my flesh, that which is good" (Rom. 7, 18), says St. Paul. He who attributes anything to himself and seeks honor and glory, is a thief who robs of His property God who is All, to appropriate it to him who is nothing.

How often have we committed these faults? Let us ask pardon of God and beg Him to preserve us from them in future. To prevent our relapse, let us frequently reflect on and what we are of ourselves, and where we would be if God did not continually exercise His mercy on our behalf.

Ejaculatory prayer:

"Correct me, O Lord, . . . and not in thy fury, lest thou bring me to nothing."

Corrige me, Domine, . . . verumtamen non in furore tuo, ne forte ad nihilum redigas me (Jer. 10, 24).

FIFTH MEDITATION

On the Words: Nihil Possumus—"We Can Do Nothing."

GOD ALONE IS MIGHTY

LET us consider that God alone is mighty: (1 Tim. 6, 15). His power is eternal, infinite, immense, immutable and essential; that is, everything in Him is omnipotent, His goodness, His justice, His mercy and all His other divine perfections. He could, in a moment, annihilate all things. Heaven and earth cannot resist His power for an instant. "Almighty is his name" (Exod. 15, 3). Sin is the only thing He cannot enact; for ability to sin is not power, it is merely impotence.

Let us adore this divine power. Let us rejoice that we belong to a Master and Father Who is omnipotent. Let us give and consecrate ourselves to His divine power and beg Him to extinguish in us all power to do evil and make us powerful to do good: "Mighty in work and word" (Luke 24, 19).

SECOND POINT

OUR LORD ACKNOWLEDGED HIS IMPOTENCE

Let us consider and adore our Lord Jesus Christ uttering these words: "I cannot of myself do any thing" (John 5, 30), not only as man but even as the Son of God. As He received being and life from His Heavenly Father, He likewise received all power from Him and He acknowledged this in His public profession: "I cannot of myself do any thing." This profession He willed to be written in His Gospel in order to confound our pride and to teach us not to appropriate any part of our performance to ourselves; for even the Son of God acknowledged that of Himself and without His Father, He could do nothing, and thus referred to His Heavenly Father everything that He accomplished.

Let us consider also that the Blessed Virgin has perfectly imitated her Son in this humility; and that as a reward the Eternal Father has given all power to the Son, and to the Mother in relative proportion: "All power is given to me in heaven and in earth," says our Lord (Matt. 28, 18). And the Blessed Virgin can say the same in due proportion. Let us rejoice over this magnificent reward of humility and surrender ourselves to the Son and His Blessed Mother, begging them to employ their vast power in crushing our pride and making us share in their humility.

THIRD POINT

OF OURSELVES WE CAN DO NOTHING

Let us consider attentively the truth of these words: *Nihil possumus.* First, of ourselves we can do nothing pleasing to God. "Without me you can do nothing" (John 15, 5). Secondly, we cannot speak a good word: "O generation of vipers, how can you speak good things, whereas you are evil?" (Matt. 12, 34). "No man can say the Lord Jesus, but by the Holy Ghost" (1 Cor. 12, 3). Thirdly, of ourselves we cannot entertain a good desire. "It is God who worketh in you, both to will and to accomplish" (Phil. 2, 13). Fourthly, we cannot have a good thought without the grace of God. "Not that we are sufficient to think any thing of ourselves, as of ourselves: but our sufficiency is from God" (2 Cor. 3, 5). Lastly, we cannot perform the least act of Christian virtue, nor resist the slightest temptation in the world, even for a moment. What a source of humiliation for us! Let us rejoice in this abjection and engrave these truths deeply upon our minds, so that everywhere and always we may acknowledge our futility and our great need of God. This will compel us to have recourse to Him continually, saying frequently: "O God, come to my assistance; O Lord, make haste to help me" (Ps. 69, 2).

Ejaculatory prayer:

"Gladly therefore will I glory in my infirmities, that the power of Christ may dwell in me."

Libenter igitur gloriabor in infirmitatibus meis, ut inhabitet in me virtus Christi (2 Cor. 12, 9).

SIXTH MEDITATION

On the Words: Nihil Valemus—"We Are Worth Nothing."

FIRST POINT

OUR LORD WISHED TO BE TREATED AS IF HE WERE WORTHLESS

LET us consider that every detail concerning our Lord Jesus Christ is of infinite value. Every aspect of His divinity, His humanity, His body and soul, His thoughts, words and actions, is of infinite value. Let us rejoice in His sublime worth. Let us thank the Eternal Father for having made everything in His Beloved Son Jesus Christ so noble and so precious.

Let us consider that our Lord Jesus Christ, although He is infinitely adorable in all things, willed to be treated as though He were of no account. People despised His words, His works, His sacred humanity, His Precious Blood and His life as if they were of no value. Even in our own day He is similarly treated by Jews, infidels and heretics in the Blessed Sacrament and by many Christians who blaspheme, crucify and trample Him underfoot.

SECOND POINT

IN CONSEQUENCE OF SIN WE ARE THE MOST WRETCHED OF ALL CREATURES

Let us consider the essential truth of these words: "We are worth nothing." There is no creature, however wretched it may be, among insensible and inanimate things, that cannot be said to be better and more precious than we are, on account of our corruption from sin. So we should humble ourselves below the mire, the dust, and the most abject things, and make more account of the most contemptible objects in the world. We may regard ourselves like Jonathan, speaking to

David: "Who am I thy servant, that thou shouldst look upon such a dead dog as I am?" (2 Kings 9, 8) and say with Solomon: "What shall we be able to do to glorify him?" (Ecclus. 43, 30).

THIRD POINT

As Children of Adam We Deserved Eternal Death

Let us consider these words of our Divine Lord: "You are the salt of the earth. But if the salt lose its savour, wherewith shall it be salted? It is good for nothing any more but to be cast out, and to be trodden on by men" (Matt. 5, 13). Consider that as often as we have offended God, we have fallen into the state signified by these words: "Salt that has lost its savour." Hence, we are good for nothing any more but to be cast out of the house of God and to be trodden underfoot by men. Not only that; but we are fit only to be cast into eternal fire, according to the words which our Lord addressed to Ezechiel the prophet: "What shall be made of the wood of the vine? . . . Shall it be useful for any work?" (Ezech. 15, 2-4). No. As our Lord says in the Gospel, it is only fit for the fire of hell: to be "cast into the fire" (Matt. 3, 10).

This is our fitting destiny as children of Adam. Hence we are good for nothing but to be cast into eternal fire. And what is worse, we do not deserve even that the justice of God should take the trouble to cast us into hell, nor that God should ascend His mighty throne to judge us. We should cultivate the sentiments of Job, when, after considering the baseness and corruption of man, he exclaims: "And dost thou think it meet to open thy eyes upon such a one, and to bring him into judgment with thee?" (Job 14, 3).

Ejaculatory prayer:

> "Lord Jesus Christ, we are worth nothing."
> *Domine Jesu Christe, nihil valemus.*

SEVENTH MEDITATION

On the Words: Nihil Habemus Praeter Peccatum—
"We Possess Nothing Except Sin."

ALTHOUGH OUR LORD WAS FILLED WITH VIRTUE AND GRACE HE CONSTANTLY HUMILIATED HIMSELF

LET us consider and rejoice that God possesses in Himself the infinity of good. Let us consider also that there existed not the least shadow of evil in our Lord; yet He humbled Himself as if there had been all kinds of evil and no good within Him. He appropriated nothing to Himself, but referred everything to His Almighty Father, being regarded and treated as if He were destitute of all good, according to the words of Sacred Scripture: "I am the man that see my poverty" (Lam. 3, 1). Yet we who are full of evil and void of all good cannot humble ourselves! We even strive to rob God of what belongs to Him, and to attribute it to ourselves!

SECOND POINT

OF OURSELVES WE ARE NOTHING

Let us consider and weigh the truth of these words: "We have nothing." This means actually that we have nothing in the order of nature nor of grace, neither in heaven nor on earth, neither in body nor in soul. St. Paul said: "I know that there dwelleth not in me, that is to say, in my flesh, that which is good" (Rom. 7, 18). How much more truly may we say it? If we possess any good, any quality, or any advantage, either natural or supernatural, it is not our own. "What hast thou that thou hast not received? And if thou hast received, why dost thou glory, as if thou hadst not received it?" (1 Cor. 4, 7). So far

from being able to glory in the natural or supernatural gifts that God
has bestowed upon us, we should derive from them a sense of humiliation, confusion and fear. The more we have received from God, the
more we are obliged to render to Him. Yet if we examine ourselves
carefully, we will find that we are making very poor use of the graces
of God, and that we have more reason to humble ourselves before His
Providence than if we had received no blessings whatsoever.

THIRD POINT

VICE IS DEEPLY ROOTED WITHIN US

Let us consider how destitute we are of every virtue: faith, hope,
charity, fortitude, justice, temperance, prudence, humility, obedience,
patience, meekness; and how every vice lies deeply rooted within us.
Yet we esteem ourselves and wish others to have a good opinion of us.
Let us be profoundly humble; let us learn to know ourselves, to treat
ourselves and wish others to treat us as persons destitute of all good
and filled with every evil.

Ejaculatory prayer:

> "Lord Jesus Christ, we have nothing except sin."
> *Domine Jesu Christe, nihil habemus praeter peccatum.*

EIGHTH MEDITATION

On the Words: Servi Inutiles Sumus—"We Are Unprofitable Servants."

GOD IS SUFFICIENT TO HIMSELF AND DOES NOT NEED ANY CREATURE

LET us consider that the first reason why we are useless servants arises from the greatness, sufficiency and plenitude of God, Who calls Himself *Sadai*, that is, "sufficient to Himself," because He is so sufficient to Himself and replete with good, that He has no need of us nor of any creature of heaven or earth. Even the God-Man, Jesus Christ our Lord, says: "I have said to the Lord: Thou art my God, for thou hast no need of my goods" (Ps. 15, 2).

The fact that God has no need of our goods is an infallible mark of His divinity. That is why, when we offer or give anything to God, we sacrifice it to Him, that is, annihilate it before Him, to testify thereby that He has no need of anything. If anyone presented a valuable horse to a governor and were to kill the animal when offering it, the governor would not be pleased because the gift would be useless to him. But the greatest service we can render to God is to sacrifice and annihilate our offerings, to testify thereby that He has no need of them. This is why Jesus Christ sacrifices Himself on the Cross. Now, if Jesus Christ is not necessary to God, and if all the angels and saints and the Blessed Virgin can say: "We are unprofitable servants," with how much greater truth can we say it?

Let us rejoice that God is so replete with every conceivable good; let us be glad to be useless because He is quite sufficient to Himself.

SECOND POINT

WE ARE NOTHINGNESS IN THE ORDER BOTH OF NATURE AND OF GRACE

The second reason for our uselessness arises from our extreme poverty and our twofold nothingness in the way of nature and grace. Our first portion is the nothingness from which God created us: and the second is the nothingness into which we have fallen by sin, which deprives us of the ability to entertain even a single good thought. Nothing can come from nothing; consequently we are utterly useless and worthless.

Let us ask God to engrave these truths deeply upon our hearts and to preserve us from thinking that we are necessary or useful in any way whatever. God alone is necessary.

THIRD POINT

BY SERVING GOD PERFECTLY WE GIVE HIM ONLY WHAT COMES FROM HIM

The third cause of our uselessness is implied in the comparison drawn by our Lord in the Gospel. A servant who accompanies his master on a journey does not rest when he reaches home, but must prepare refreshments for his master and then serve him at table; yet even so his master does not thank him, for he has only done the duty he is paid to do. So, our Lord says: "When you have done all these things that are commanded you, say: 'We are unprofitable servants; we have done that which we ought to do'" (Luke 17, 10).

Now, besides this, there are three considerations which should make us deeply humble: 1. When we have done our utmost in the service of our Master, we have done only what we ought to do. 2. We never do all we could, nor practise all the virtues we might. 3. We accomplish nothing as perfectly as we might, but always with many faults. Even if we were to do everything possible as perfectly as we could, we would still do nothing: for it is God who operates in us. Even in our virtuous actions, we actually give nothing to God, but are continually receiving from Him. Therefore, if we were to perform the good works of all the angels and saints and were to practise every virtue to an eminent degree, we should still say: "We are unprofitable servants."

Let us ask God to imprint all these truths deeply upon our souls and make them fruitful, destroying our pride and giving us true humility.

Ejaculatory prayer:

> "Lord Jesus Christ, we are unprofitable servants."
> *Domine Jesu Christe, servi inutiles sumus.*

NINTH MEDITATION

Natura Filii Irae—"We Were Born Children of Wrath."

FIRST POINT

WE ARE CHILDREN OF WRATH BECAUSE OF ORIGINAL SIN

BY OUR ôwn corrupt and depraved nature we are children of wrath, because we are children of sin and iniquity. This is our second portion, our first being nothingness. We are children of sin and perdition for we were born in sin and in damnation. "We were damned before we were born," says St. Bernard. We have within us the source of every sin. Let everyone examine himself and he will find that he has within him the source of pride, avarice, envy and every other vice. So much so that if God left us to ourselves, we would be as proud as Lucifer, as avaricious as Judas, as envious as Cain, as gluttonous as the rich glutton, who "feasted sumptuously every day" (Luke 16, 19), as choleric and cruel as Herod, as lewd as Anti-Christ, as idle as the unprofitable servant in the Gospel, "the unprofitable servant cast ye out into the exterior darkness" (Matt. 25, 30).

Let us humble ourselves, contemplating the sins of earth and hell as if they were our own. When any one speaks evil of us, or offends us, let us not complain, but take his part against ourselves, remembering that we bear within us seeds of every evil. When we hear of impious and wicked men, let us consider that we have similar taints of sin in our own person, by reason of which the Church obliges the priest celebrating the Holy Mass to strike his breast and say: *Nobis quoque peccatorbus.* "Also to us sinners."

SECOND POINT

WE HAVE A STRONG INCLINATION TO EVIL

We have such a strong inclination to evil that if God did not continually bear us up, we would fall into a hell of every kind of sin with more impetuosity than a mill-stone hurled into the sky would fall if it were not restrained by a miracle. This weight which drags us down to sin is our self-love. "Self-love is my weight. I am carried by it wherever I go" (St. Augustine, *Conf.* 1, 13, c. 9). "It almost overcomes the weight of my actions" (*Breviar. rom. Comm. un. Mart., Oratio, Infirmitatem*). Our own enterprise is the work of sinners. Let us not be surprised when we see anyone fall, but thank the mercy of God which sustains us. Let us have compassion on the errors and lapses of others and never prefer ourselves to anyone. Let us reflect that if God were to give other men the same grace that He has given us, they would be far better than we and derive more profit.

THIRD POINT

WE ARE SLAVES OF SIN

We are slaves of sin: "Whosoever committeth sin, is the servant of sin" (John 8, 34). Wherefore, if God left us to ourselves, sin would tyrannize over us as it does over the damned, so that we could not think, speak or do anything but sin. We should be wholly transformed into sin as saints in heaven are transformed into sanctity. And so, of ourselves, we are nothing but sin, and we deserve to be treated as sin itself by God and His creatures.

This is how we should esteem ourselves; and we should be glad that others have the same low esteem for us and treat us as sinful men. Let us ask this grace of God.

Ejaculatory prayer:

"O Lord, rebuke me not in thy indignation, nor chastise me in thy wrath."

Domine, ne in furore tuo arguas me neque in ira tua corripias me (Ps. 6, 2).

TENTH MEDITATION

On the Same Words: "We Were Born Children of Wrath."

Not only are we the source of every sin, not only have we an original inclination to sin, but we are an abyss of every sin for four reasons. The first is that our sins annihilate God, which is the extreme malice of sin and of the sinner. The three reasons which prove this malice will form the three points of this meditation.

FIRST POINT

THE SINNER USURPS WHAT BELONGS TO GOD AND MAKES HIMSELF HIS OWN GOD

We are an abyss of sin because sin and the sinner, so far as possible, drag God from His throne and annihilate Him, and what is still worse, the sinner elevates himself to the throne of God, usurping the dignity belonging only to God. In order to understand this, we must remember that, when God created man and all things, He created them only for Himself: "The Lord hath made all things for himself" (Prov. 16, 4).

Being the principle, the exemplar and the end of man and of all creatures, God wishes men to return to Him as to their origin, to imitate Him, to model their life and their actions on Him as their exemplar, to follow Him as their rule, to work towards Him with all their strength, by every thought, word and action, as to their last end. To render him capable of doing this, God has given man a mind, a heart and a will to know and love Him, to return to Him, to imitate Him and to tend unceasingly to Him as to his center. And in order that man may do so with joy and facility, God has enlightened his mind with the light of faith, has poured divine grace into his soul and enkindled love in his heart.

But what has ungrateful man done? He has become separated from God and devoted his interests to self. Instead of employing his love for God, he has devoted it to himself and developed self-love. Instead of returning to God as to his principle, he has turned away from Him. Instead of referring to God all the blessings of nature and grace, man appropriates them to himself by complacency and self-esteem, as if they came from himself, who is only nothingness. Instead of following God as his exemplar and his rule, he follows the rule of his passions. Instead of allowing himself to be led by the spirit of God, he desires no other guidance than that of his own inclination. Instead of tending to God as to his end, taking his repose in Him and doing everything for Him, man wishes to tend wholly to himself, and to do everything for self.

Who is God? God is He whose will, interest, pleasure and honor should be preferred before every other will, interest, pleasure and honor. What does the sinner do? He prefers his own will, interest, pleasure and honor to the will, interest, pleasure and honor of God. Thus he usurps the place of God, makes a god of self, falls into self-adoration and pays self the homage which belongs to God alone. This is the extreme iniquity of sin. This is what we have done every time and as often as we have sinned. Hence we should despise ourselves as a bottomless pit of sin.

SECOND POINT

THE SINNER MAKES HIMSELF GOD OF ALL CREATURES

Not only does the sinner make a god of self, but he also makes himself the god of all creatures made by God. Man wants other creatures to offer him what belongs only to God; he desires them to prefer his inclinations, interests, pleasure and honor to those of God. Instead of attributing and referring every good to God alone as to its only source, man desires creatures to esteem him as if he possessed good in himself, and to praise and applaud his actions as if he could do good, independently.

He desires created beings to imitate him instead of God. He desires them to have no other rule than his inclinations, to be directed by his spirit, to love him to the prejudice of God and to do everything for him instead of doing everything for God. We have frequently been guilty of this and so we have usurped the place which God alone should hold towards creatures. What an abomination! How true it is that I am an abyss of every sin! O my God, impress these truths upon my mind; grant that I may regard, treat and hate myself as much, and that I may be glad to be so treated by others.

THIRD POINT

The Sinner Makes Himself the God of God

There is another and a last extremity of sin, the deepest abyss of iniquity, which consists in making oneself the god of God. The sinner would wish God to prefer his interests, will, pleasure and honor to the interest, will, pleasure and honor of His divine majesty. He would wish that his human will might rule the Providence of God and that God should be guided by the sinner's whims and fancies. He would seek to be the end of God and to have God adore him and make him His idol. O abomination of abominations! Behold the bottomless pit of sin! See what we have done every time we have sinned! Here we have an infinite source of infinite humiliation.

O my God, let me see these truths in the light of faith! O my God, enrich their fruitfulness within me! Let me know myself, let me know that I am nothing and that Thou art all! Let me no longer consider myself, let me do nothing for self, but all for Thee. Let no creature think of me, speak to me, nor of me, do anything for me nor give me anything, but all for Thee; and do Thou Thyself give me nothing, do nothing for me, nor consider me any more, but everything for Thyself! For Thou alone shouldst be Thy object! Let nothingness be obliterated with regard to itself, with regard to all Thy creatures and with regard to Thy supreme majesty! Let All be all, in all things and everywhere.

Ejaculatory prayer:

"O Lord rebuke me not in thy indignation, nor chastise me in thy wrath."

Domine, ne in furore tuo arguas me, neque in ira tua corripias me (Ps. 6, 2).

ELEVENTH MEDITATION

On the Same Words: "We Were Born Children of Wrath."

WE DESERVE to be the object of the wrath of God and all God's creatures and of our own condemnation, for three reasons.

FIRST POINT

THE EVIL WHICH THE SINNER WORKS UPON HIMSELF

Since by sin the sinner kills his body, so far as he may, and kills his soul, he deserves that God should take away the life and being imparted to him, in punishment for his abuse of existence, in using it to fight against his Creator. Moreover, the sinner robs himself of the grace and friendship of God, and of eternal happiness, meriting the torments of hell. Thus he injures himself far more than the demons in hell and the creatures in the world could harm him even if they all united for his ruin.

Therefore I, a sinner, should despise, humble and hate myself more than all the abominable and contemptible things in the world. If God were to surrender me to the demons, they would exercise upon me the hatred I have merited by my sins and so would perform an act of justice. And I, instead of humbling and hating myself, exalt, love, praise and revere myself.

O my God, what a contradiction! Let it exist no more! Let me hate and fear myself more than death, more than the devil, more than hell. Permit me to hate nothing but myself, who am nothing but sin, and let me vent all my wrath, hatred and vengeance upon myself, out of zeal for Thy divine justice towards sin and the sinner!

SECOND POINT

THE SINNER DESTROYS ALL THE WORKS OF GOD
INSOFAR AS IS POSSIBLE

We have merited God's wrath because the sinner, so far as possible, destroys all the works of God in nature, grace and glory. In nature, since he commits sin, for which God might justly annihilate the whole world. The damnation of a single soul is a greater evil than the destruction of the entire world of nature. Now God may justly damn a soul for a single mortal sin. Therefore He might justly annihilate the world of nature in punishment for a mortal sin. I say, furthermore, that, according to all theologians, the extinction of every natural being is not so great an evil as a venial sin. So he who commits a venial sin works an evil greater than the destruction of the whole world; consequently God might justly destroy the whole world in punishment for a venial sin.

He who sins mortally annihilates also the world of grace and glory. For, if all God's graces were in his soul, by committing mortal sin, he would destroy them all and consequently all the glory destined for him in heaven. Hence, the sinner merits the anger of every creature of nature, grace and glory and they will vent their just wrath upon him in the day of judgment. Even now they would do so if the mercy of God and the Blood of Jesus Christ did not restrain them: "The mercies of the Lord that we are not consumed" (Lam. 3, 22).

O my God, let me behold this devastating truth in Thy divine light, so that I may know that no creature, rational or irrational, owes me anything; no one should consider, nor love, nor give me anything, nor render me any service or assistance, nor even think of me. Rather do I deserve that every creature should employ all his strength in destroying and annihilating me.

THIRD POINT

THE SINNER EVEN ATTEMPTS TO DESTROY GOD

We have merited God's wrath because the sinner annihilates not only all the works of the Creator, but also all the works of the Redeemer. The sinner renders void and useless to himself all the meritorious labors, sufferings, the Precious Blood, the life and death of the Divine Son of God, together with all the Sacraments and means of salvation established in Holy Church.

Moreover, the sinner even "annihilates God as far as lies in his power," says St. Bernard. In the first place, the sinful man obliterates the will of God replacing it with his own; secondly, he destroys within himself the Spirit of God Who is God; thirdly, he destroys the life of God in his soul by grace; fourthly, he crucifies Jesus Christ in himself after having already crucified Him with the Jews: "Crucifying again to themselves the Son of God" (Heb. 6, 6). Therefore, we may say that the sinner annihilates all things, since he annihilates, as far as he may, God the author of all things. The sinner deserves to be an object of wrath and malediction to created and uncreated things, and all creatures should unite to crush him. So he may say with the prophet: "Correct me, O Lord, but yet with judgment: and not in thy fury, lest thou bring me to nothing" (Jer. 10, 24).

If I carefully consider these truths, O my God, how is it possible that I can still be proud? O Lord, crush this serpent of pride in my soul at any cost.

Ejaculatory prayer:

"Correct me, O Lord, but yet with judgment and not in Thy fury, lest thou bring me to nothing."
  Corripe me, Domine, verumtamen non in furore tuo, ne forte ad nihilum redigas me (Jer. 10, 24).

TWELFTH MEDITATION

On the Same Words: "We Were Born Children of Wrath."

WE ARE unworthy of every good, and deserving of every evil; therefore we should humble and hate ourselves.

WE ARE INFINITELY UNWORTHY OF EVERY GOOD

Our existence as children of wrath, death and iniquity makes us unworthy of every good, corporal, spiritual, temporal and eternal, of nature, grace, or glory either emanating from the Creator or derived from creatures, unworthy to receive any assistance, gifts or favors from our Creator or from creatures, nay, infinitely unworthy even that they should think of us or speak of us or on our behalf. I say *infinitely unworthy*, because no human mind is capable of realizing our unworthiness except the mind of God alone. The following are the reasons:

First, by our sins we have robbed ourselves of blessings, that come from infinity, namely, the grace and friendship of God, the title of children and heirs of God and the enjoyment of God and all the treasures He possesses in Himself.

Secondly, we have deprived God of a good, that in a way is infinite in depriving Him of the service, honor, love and obedience we owe Him, a good that is eternal in its duration, for anything we do for God renders Him an honor that will last for all eternity. We deprive God of a good, infinite in a way because it is due to God on account of His infinite perfections and our obligations towards Him; infinite because God purchased it at an infinite price, the Precious Blood of His Divine Son.

Thirdly, by sin we have willed to deprive God of Jesus Christ, the God-Man, by crucifying Him anew, and consequently we have also willed to deprive Him of the mystical body of Jesus Christ and of all the honor, praise, glory and adoration that Jesus Christ will render to His Father for all eternity, either in Himself or by His mystical body, the Church.

Fourthly, we have willed, as a result of this, to deprive all creatures of their Redeemer.

For these reasons, we have rendered ourselves so to speak infinitely unworthy of every good. Therefore, let us not complain when we are forgotten or when we do not receive the recognition we expect, but let us humble ourselves.

SECOND POINT

WE ARE DESERVING OF ALL EVIL

We are infinitely deserving of every evil, of contempt, punishment and suffering. I say infinitely because we are so despicable that only God Himself can understand the measure of our guilt. I say that we infinitely deserve every evil, corporal and spiritual, temporal and eternal, from God and from creatures, because by sin we have done an injury to the infinite God, to ourselves and to all creatures, and sin is an evil which may be said to be infinite in its nature, its object, its end and its effects.

The sinner inflicts an injury which we call infinite on God Himself, for as St. Bernard says, "he annihilates God so far as it lies in his power."

Man does an injury to himself for he kills his body, and murders his soul, as completely as possible.

He perpetrates an injury against all creatures in the order of nature, grace and glory since he destroys them to the extent of his ability. Should we not call it an infinite injury?

This being so, let us not be surprised when other creatures injure us by word or act, nor when God chastises us. Let us only be surprised that our Divine Creator and all His faithful creatures suffer us to exist anywhere but in hell and in nothingness.

WE SHALL NEVER HUMBLE OURSELVES SUFFICIENTLY

From these two truths follow other realities:

1. We shall never completely fathom the abyss of our unworthiness and misery. Even after we are well advanced in this knowledge, we must believe that there is infinitely more left to be known in the un-fathomed depths of our nothingness.

2. We can never humble ourselves sufficiently, and even if we were to accomplish our very utmost in this respect, we would still be re-moved from the humiliation due to our baseness, and from the final degree of humility. Our Lord alone attained this final degree for He alone humbled Himself infinitely.

3. If all the creatures of heaven, earth and hell were to employ all their strength in vilifying us, it would be but a trifle of the shame we deserve.

4. God alone can humble us suitably.

Let us beg Him to engrave these truths upon our mind and make them fruitful in us. O great God, if we believe these truths, how can we still be proud? How can we seek to avoid suffering, or find it so hard to humble ourselves? How can we love honor and dread con-tempt so much? Lord Jesus, have mercy on us.

Ejaculatory prayer:

"To us sinners therefore be confusion and shame and to Thee be honor
    and glory forever and ever. Amen."
*Nobis peccatoribus confusio et ignominia, tibi autem honor et gloria
    in saecula saeculorum. Amen.*

THIRTEENTH MEDITATION

On the Same Words: "We Were Born Children of Wrath."

WE HAVE merited the wrath of God and of all His creatures, and deserve eternal torments.

WE HAVE MERITED THE WRATH OF GOD

The greatest torment of the damned is the wrath of God: "They shall be called . . . the people with whom the Lord is angry for ever" (Mal. 1, 4). "They would prefer being burned in a fire ten times more intense," says St. Chrysostom, "than see the face of God enkindled with wrath against them." Therefore, they will cry out on the day of judgment, "Fall upon us and hide us from the face of him that sitteth upon the throne and from the wrath of the Lamb. For the great day of their wrath is come, and who shall be able to stand?" (Apoc. 6, 16-17) and St. Paul tells us: "Who shall suffer eternal punishment in destruction, from the face of the Lord" (2 Thess. 1, 9).

We have merited like condemnation and would infallibly and eternally have become the object of the wrath of God, of the wrath of the Father, of the Son and of the Holy Ghost, if Our Lord Jesus Christ had not delivered us by bearing the wrath of His Almighty Father for our sake according to His own words: "Thy wrath hath come upon me" (Ps. 87, 17). Let us love and bless our merciful Saviour and humble ourselves at the thought that, since we have incurred the wrath of God, we have, in consequence, merited to be deprived of all His graces and all the effects of His bounty; and much more have we merited all the sufferings of this life and even the torments of hell; yet even these are much less than the wrath of God.

SECOND POINT

We Have Merited the Wrath of All Creatures

Not only are the damned the object of God's wrath, but also of the wrath of all creatures rational and irrational, animate and inanimate, in heaven, on earth and in hell. For the justice of God arms all His creatures against them: "He will arm the creature for the revenge of His enemies. He will put on justice as a breastplate, and will take true judgment instead of a helmet. He will take equity for an invincible shield. And He will sharpen His severe wrath for a spear: and the whole world shall fight with him against the unwise" (Wisd. 5, 18-21).

1. The Blessed Virgin, all the angels and saints in heaven are all animated by God's wrath against the damned. God communicates all His sentiments to His loved ones and the more closely they are united to God, the more they share in His dispositions. They love what God loves and hate what He hates. Whence it follows that the Blessed Virgin is more wrathful against the sins of the damned than all the angels and saints together; and so it is with all the other saints in proportion.

2. All creatures upon earth, even the inanimate things of nature, are enkindled with wrath against the damned. Even every single atom is full of wrath against the damned and aids God's justice in avenging the injuries these sinners perpetrated against their Creator.

3. Even the damned and the demons cooperate with God's justice and are wrathful against one another, so that they are mutual executioners, tearing, cursing and tormenting one another perpetually.

4. Every reprobate is his own executioner raging against himself, hating himself and finding himself more intolerable than all the other demons and damned, because of the just judgment of God and the operation of the wrath of God which animates the lost soul against himself.

We have merited that this punishment should be ours, and we should look upon ourselves as wretches who have merited the eternal wrath of God and of all His creatures forever. We should infallibly have been reduced to such a state if our Lord had not delivered us, by taking our place and willing to be hated and persecuted by the world and all creatures. Let us love and bless our Saviour and make Him the only object of our love. Let us be humbled, venting our hatred, anger and contempt upon ourselves. Let us reflect that, having merited the wrath of God and all His creatures, we do not deserve to be well treated by anyone and, if all creatures were to do their utmost to humiliate and persecute us, it would be justly deserved.

THIRD POINT

WE HAVE DESERVED ETERNAL TORMENTS

In addition to the wrath of God and creatures, the damned will also suffer many other eternal torments: the gnawing worm: "their worm dieth not" (Mark 9, 45), the unbearable stench, the shouts, the blasphemies, hunger, thirst, fire, suffering in every part of body and soul, rage, despair, confusion, infamy and the endless eternity of all these torments.

We have merited all these punishments and much more have we merited all the confusion and ignominy of this world. Let us die of shame if we are still proud and vain, and cling to a high esteem of ourselves, after studying these realities, or if we still think anyone owes us anything. Let us beg God to engrave deeply on our mind the knowledge of our three portions, namely, nothingness, sin and the wrath of God, of creatures and eternal torments. This is expressed in our protestation of humility: "We are nothing; we are worth nothing; we are worthless servants; we have nothing but sin; we are born children of wrath." Let us not let a day pass without remembering and reflecting on our just deserts, so that when we have occasion to humble ourselves as we do hourly, we may ever have them in mind and they may serve to keep us constantly humble as the Holy Spirit teaches: "Humble thyself in all things" (Ecclus. 3, 20).

Ejaculatory prayer:

"To us sinners be confusion and shame, and to Thee be honor and
    glory forever and ever. Amen."
*Nobis peccatoribus confusio et ignominia, tibi autem honor et gloria
in saecula saeculorum. Amen.*

FOURTEENTH MEDITATION

On the Words: Novissimi Virorum—"The Last of Men."

FIRST POINT

OUR LORD ADVISES US TO TAKE THE LOWEST PLACE

BY THESE words we profess our desire to regard ourselves as the least of men and to rejoice that others should treat us similarly. To enter into this disposition and to realize the truth of these words, let us first consider and adore our Lord pronouncing the words: "Sit down in the lowest place" (Luke 14, 10). Let us adore His admirable designs for each one of us in giving this counsel of humility. Let us humble ourselves and ask His forgiveness for having opposed His holy will and beg the grace not to do so again. Let us give ourselves to the spirit in which He pronounced those words so that they may be faithful in us. And on our part, let us cultivate the desire to practise His counsel in constant lowliness.

SECOND POINT

OUR LORD CHOSE THE LAST PLACE IN ALL HIS WORDS

Let us consider that our Lord taught nothing that He did not first practise, and He always chose the last place in His words, thoughts, interior dispositions and actions.

By His words, He said of Himself, "I am a worm and no man" (Ps. 21, 7). Let us adore Him uttering these words and consider that the worm is the most abject of creatures. It lives in the ground and everyone tramples it underfoot. In the same way the Son of God abased Himself beneath the feet of every man.

Very frequently, too, He called Himself "the Son of man" (Luke 12, 8), to confound our pride, for we prefer to be called by what is most excellent in us, whereas Jesus Christ, God and man, Son of God and Son of man, takes His name from what is lowest in Him, calling Himself the Son of man, that is, the Son of the sinner who, of himself, is only nothingness, sin and damnation. Thus our Lord calls Himself a sinner, which is the greatest of all humiliations.

Moreover, after saying of St. John the Baptist: "Amen I say to you, there hath not risen among them that are born of women a greater than John the Baptist," our Saviour says of Himself: "Yet he that is the lesser in the kingdom of heaven (that is, in the Church) is greater than he" (Matt. 11, 11). But how can we reconcile those ideas: "He that is lesser is greater?" If He is greater than St. John the Baptist, how is He lesser in the Church? And if He is the least in the kingdom of heaven, how is He greater than St. John? He is truly and indeed greater, but He calls Himself lesser because He treated Himself and willed to be treated as the last of men.

Lastly, He wished to be called "the most abject of men" in Sacred Scripture (Isa. 53, 3). This was one of His titles of honor. He gloried in it and wished it to be mentioned among His titles in Scripture. Let us adore Him humbling His greatness in this manner and taking the last place by His words.

Let us humble ourselves for having so often in our words exalted ourselves, resolving to refrain carefully from everything contrary to humility, asking God's grace to enable us to do so.

THIRD POINT

OUR LORD TOOK THE LAST PLACE IN HIS THOUGHTS AND INTERIOR DISPOSITIONS

The Son of God took the last place in His thoughts and interior dispositions. These thoughts certainly correspond with His words and His Heart was not in opposition to His lips. Therefore, He considered Himself the last of men and always remained in this attitude before God. Interiorly, He always took the lowest place for He regarded Himself as the bearer of the sins of all men, taking the place of all criminals, and obliged to endure the humiliation of their crimes, and consequently, to humble Himself below all creatures. Let us adore Him in these dispositions; let us give ourselves to Him, asking Him to let us share the depths of His sublime Humility.

Ejaculatory prayer:

> "Lord Jesus, I will sit down in the lowest place."
> *Domine Jesu, recumbam in novissimo loco.*

FIFTEENTH MEDITATION

On the Same Words: "The Last of Men."

OUR LORD TOOK THE LOWEST PLACE IN HIS INCARNATION AND CHILDHOOD

OUR Lord took the last place in His actions throughout the whole course of His life, as well as in His words, thoughts and interior dispositions.

In becoming man, He might have assumed the most perfect state of human life at the very moment of His Incarnation, by forming Himself as perfect a body as that of Adam at his creation. Instead He chose the lowest state of human life, that of infancy.

In choosing a mother, He might have chosen one of high rank, a queen, a princess or a titled lady. Instead He chose a woman from the lowest rank, from among the poor who earn their livelihood by manual labor. He chose a virgin who esteemed herself as the least of all His creatures.

He also chose a foster-father of lowly condition, who likewise esteemed himself the least of all men. For, after the Blessed Virgin, no one was so humble as St. Joseph.

Since it was ordained for Him to become incarnate in Judea, Jesus might have chosen Jerusalem or some other famous city; but he chose Nazareth, a despicable place, as these words of Nathaniel show: "Can any thing of good come from Nazareth?" (John 1, 46).

For His birth, He might have chosen a palace or honorable edifice; but He willed to be born in a most abject place, in a stable, in a cave which was a shelter for beasts. And He wished to be laid on the straw in the manger, between an ox and an ass.

Eight days after His birth, He willed to be marked with the seal of sin by circumcision, which was to rank himself amongst the lowest, for there is nothing lower than sin and the quality of sinner whose likeness He assumed.

Then, too, He chose the most trying season and month of the year for His birth; and He willed to be born not as Lord and Master, but enrolled as a subject and vassal of Emperor Augustus.

When He was presented in the Temple, He would not have His parents offer a lamb, the offering of the rich and the first of the nation, but two pigeons or turtle-doves which was the offering of the poor and the last of the people.

When Herod sought His life, He chose flight, the last and most ignominious of all means of escape; He chose the country most unworthy of His presence, Egypt, where idolatry was rife and where Satan held sway.

In the Temple with the doctors, He was not the doctor but the disciple, not learned but ignorant, questioning the doctors as if to learn of them.

Let us adore our Lord in all these mysteries and in all these humiliations. Let us strive to exalt Him the more, the more He has humbled Himself. Let us bless Him for the glory He rendered the Eternal Father by His abasement. Let us ask our Blessed Saviour to give us a share in His spirit of humility.

SECOND POINT

Our Lord Took the Last Place During His Entire Life

In the house of His Blessed Mother and St. Joseph, the first place was rightfully His but He took the last. Although He is infinitely higher than either of His parents, He coveted no other rank with them than that of subject: "And (He) was subject to them" (Luke 2, 51).

Among all the conditions of human life, He takes not that of a prince nor of the wealthy, but the last of all, that of a poor man who earns his bread by the sweat of his brow: "Is not this the carpenter's son?" (Matt. 13, 55).

In His baptism in the Jordan He again takes the lowest place, willing to be baptized as if He were a sinner. "For so it becometh us to fulfil all justice" (Matt. 3, 15), that is, all humility.

When He retired into the desert, He spent forty days among wild beasts. He permitted the vilest of creatures, the demon, to approach Him, to tempt Him and consequently to treat Him as if He were a sinner and capable of sin, and even to touch Him and carry Him from one place to another; hence He took the last place, in Satan's hands.

With the apostles and disciples He takes the last place, for He says: "I am in the midst of you, as he that serveth" (Luke 22, 27).

At the Last Supper, He knelt and performed the humblest action possible, which was to wash their feet, even those of Judas, thus placing Himself at the traitor's feet, at the feet of a devil, as He Himself said: "One of you is a devil" (John 6, 71). This was the lowest place in the world, for Judas was the most wicked creature the world has ever known.

In His Passion our Lord subjected Himself to the power of darkness: "This is your hour, and the power of darkness" (Luke 22, 53). He was treated as a fool and a madman by Herod and his army and in the streets of Jerusalem, and He died on a Cross. If there is question of poverty, our Lord was born, lived and died in the greatest poverty ever experienced. If there is question of suffering, He suffered extreme torments in body and soul. If there is question of privation, no one has ever endured or will ever endure any lot comparable to His. If there is question of humiliation, there never was and never will be abasement and lowliness like His. He died "with the wicked" (Isa. 53, 12). "He shall be filled with reproaches," says the Prophet Jeremias (Lam. 3, 30).

He also takes the last place in Holy Church where in the Blessed Sacrament, He is the Victim bearing the sins of the world, where He dwells in the greatest humiliation and annihilation imaginable, according to both the manner and duration of this humiliation.

Lastly, even in the midst of His glory in heaven, He wills to bear for all eternity the marks of the greatest ignominy ever known, His Sacred Wounds—the marks of His Crucifixion and His dreadful death of shame.

Let us adore, bless and exalt the Son who thus first practises what He

teaches in the words: "Sit down in the lowest place." Let us give ourselves to Him to enter wholly into His dispositions.

REASONS FOR THE DIVINE CHOICE OF THE
LAST PLACE

Let us consider the reasons which inspired the Son of God to take
the last place. The four chief motives are: (1) To render adequate
homage by this extreme abasement to the supreme majesty of His
Eternal Father; (2) to repair the dishonor given to His Heavenly
Father by the pride of men who always desire the first place everywhere; (3) to confound our pride and to oblige us by His example
to humble ourselves; (4) to merit and acquire the grace for us to overcome our pride and imitate Him in His humility.

Let us thank Him for all these lessons. Let us die of shame at finding
ourselves so proud. Let us cultivate a great desire to imitate Him and
obey His blessed words. In order to do this let us surrender ourselves
to His spirit of humility.

Ejaculatory prayer:

"Lord Jesus Christ, I will sit down in the lowest place."
Domine Jesu Christe, recumbam in novissimo loco.

SIXTEENTH MEDITATION

On the Same Words: "The Last of Men."

FIRST POINT

OUR LORD WILLED TO BE TREATED AS THE LAST OF MEN BY HIS CREATURES

NOT only did the Son of God treat Himself as the last of men, but He also willed to receive similar treatment from others.

1. He was so treated by men and by sinners, members of Satan, for never was man treated by men with such ignominy and cruelty as was inflicted on the Son of God.

2. Not only was He reviled by men, but also by the demon in the desert when the evil spirit tempted Him as if He were capable of all types of sin. The devil even carried Him from one place to another, which so far as we know, Satan was never permitted to do to anyone else. Our Lord was also assailed by the demons during His Passion, according to His own words: "This is your hour, and the power of darkness" (Luke 22, 53), which show that He subjected Himself to the powers of darkness.

SECOND POINT

OUR LORD WILLED TO BE TREATED AS THE LAST OF MEN BY THE HOLY GHOST

Our Lord was also treated as the last of men by the Holy Spirit. The Gospel says that after our Lord was baptized in the River Jordan, that is, after He had taken our sins upon Him, "The Spirit drove him out into the desert" (Mark 1, 12). These words signify ignominy, and that the Holy Spirit treated our Lord as one burdened with all the sins of the world and obliged Him to endure confusion and penance for them.

138

This was prefigured by the emissary goat led yearly to the Temple, over which the high priest confessed all the sins of the people, then committed it to a herdsman who drove it out into the desert (Lev. 16, 5-10). Thus the Eternal Father charged His divine Son with all our sins: "The Lord hath laid on him the iniquity of us all" (Isa. 53, 6). And the Holy Ghost drove Him into the desert like a man burdened with all the crimes of men and obliged to endure their humiliation.

THIRD POINT

OUR LORD WILLED TO BE TREATED AS THE LAST OF MEN BY HIS FATHER

Our Lord was also treated as the last of men by His Eternal Father. God looked upon His Son as taking the place of sinners and treated Him as such; nay, He treated Him almost as if He were sin itself: "He hath made sin for us" (2 Cor. 5, 21). Wherefore He says: "For the wickedness of my people have I struck him" (Isa. 53, 8). "He that spared not even his own Son, but delivered him up for us all" (Rom. 8, 32), to the Cross, to death, to the powers of darkness and to the greatest opprobrium that ever was and ever will be. Nay, it would seem that divine justice treated Him with more severity than the reprobate in hell, the vilest of creatures. For it is not unwarranted that those wretches, who are rebels, should be treated as they are, for they assuredly deserve it; but it is a very strange thing to witness the only Son of God treated by His Eternal Father for the crimes of others.

Thus did our Lord take the lowest place and treat Himself as the last of men in His words, thoughts, actions and interior dispositions throughout His whole life. Thus did He will to be treated as the last of men by sinners, members of Satan, by the demons, by the Holy Ghost and by His Eternal Father. He did so in order to glorify His Father absolutely by humbling Himself to the very utmost to repair the dishonor given to His Father by our pride. He stooped to confound our arrogance, to make us hate vanity and love humility.

How pride dishonors God and how horribly displeasing it must be to Him since it was necessary that God-made-man should thus humble Himself in order to repair such dishonor! What a dreadful vice is vanity when the Son of God had to lower Himself to such depths of abasement in order to destroy it! How precious is humility in the sight of God, and how pleasing to His divine majesty since the Son of God wished to be treated in this way in order to make us love humility, to attract us to it by His example and obtain for us the grace to practise it! How guilty we are if we still yield to pride, if we will not humble ourselves! How great will be the shame of the ambitious on the day of judgment!

Let us adore our Lord in all these humiliations. Let us desire Him to be exalted in proportion to His abasement. Let us enter into His dispositions. Let us take the lowest place everywhere in mind and heart, and be glad to be treated both by God and creatures as the last of men. Let us beg the Son of God to destroy our pride and imprint in our hearts His dispositions of humility.

Ejaculatory prayer:

> "Lord Jesus, I will sit down in the lowest place."
> *Domine Jesu, recumbam in novissimo loco.*

SEVENTEENTH MEDITATION

On the Words: Primi Peccatorum—"The First of Sinners."

FIRST POINT

OUR LORD WILLED TO BE TREATED AS THE CHIEF OF SINNERS

LET us consider that the Son of God treated Himself and willed to be treated not only as the last of men, but also as the first of sinners: "(He) was reputed with the wicked" (Isa. 53, 12). He willed to die between two criminals as if He had been their leader. He was treated with as much opprobrium as if He had been sin itself: "Being made a curse for us" (Gal. 3, 13), says St. Paul. Our Divine Redeemer regarded Himself as laden with all the crimes of all sinners and He considered all the sins of men as His own. "He willed that our sins should be His own," says St. Augustine.

Let us adore and exalt Him in His profound annihilation. Let us beseech Him to destroy our pride and share His humility, showing us how we should treat ourselves and be glad to be treated, since the Son of God so humbled Himself.

SECOND POINT

MANY GREAT SAINTS TREATED THEMSELVES AS THE FOREMOST OF SINNERS

Let us consider that only the greatest saints shared the dispositions of our Lord and treated themselves as the foremost sinners. Such was St. Paul's opinion of himself: "A faithful saying, and worthy of all acceptation, that Christ Jesus came into this world to save sinners, of whom I am the chief" (1 Tim. 1, 15). St. Francis, St. Bernard, St. Dominic and many other great saints practised the same self-abasement. The

Holy Ghost inspired them with these thoughts and sentiments; consequently they were founded upon truth. For He is the Spirit of truth and not of lies. We must not ask how we can reconcile the idea that St. Paul is the first of sinners, if St. Francis is the greatest sinner. And how St. Francis is, if St. Bernard is? Although the spirit of human reason does not understand, it nevertheless holds true before God and according to the Spirit of God.

We must not follow our own light, which is nothing but darkness, but we must draw this conclusion and fruit from the verdict of the saints. If I had the light of those saints, I would see clearly that they were right in believing themselves the first of sinners. And, if those great saints lived in such dispositions and esteemed themselves so vile, what should be my opinion of myself, and how much more reason have I to believe that I am "the first of sinners," and to treat myself as such and rejoice to be so inspired by others?

Let us honor those sentiments in the saints. Let us bless God for their presence and thank Him for their meritorious application. Let us ask our Lord through the intercession of the saints to let us share their abnegation. Let us ask St. Paul, St. Francis and the other saints to engrave similar sentiments of profound humility in our own hearts.

THIRD POINT

REASONS WHY WE SHOULD CONSIDER OURSELVES THE GREATEST OF SINNERS

Although human reason cannot penetrate the things of God, and the truths and maxims of the Gospel, the following reasons may serve to prove that we are: "The first of sinners."

In the first place, we may easily compare ourselves with Lucifer, Judas and Antichrist for, as children of Adam, we have within us the source of every sin of earth and hell. But, in order to put ourselves below Judas, Lucifer and Antichrist, we should believe with St. Francis, that if God gave to the greatest of all sinners the graces He has bestowed upon us, that sinner would become better than we, and if God were to withdraw His graces and leave us to ourselves, as He will withdraw them from Antichrist, we would be worse than His arch-enemy.

We should, moreover, compare our sins not with the sins of other men but with the graces we have received from God. Now, we have received more graces from His divine bounty than all pagans, Jews and heretics together. If we are priests, we have received more graces than all other Christians for the grace of the priesthood surpasses every other. Consequently, the sins of a priest are greater than the sins of all other men; therefore, a single sin of ours makes us as guilty and more so than the sins of all other men put together.

As priests, we are obliged in imitation of our Sovereign Priest, to take the sins of others upon ourselves and to expiate them by humiliation and penance as if they were our own sins. Wherefore, every priest should humbly treat and consider himself as laden with the sins of the whole world and rejoice in being treated as such even as if he were the chief and greatest of sinners.

Let us beg our Lord to imprint these truths upon our minds and engrave these dispositions in our hearts. Let us desire them ardently. Let us give ourselves to the Spirit of God to treat ourselves henceforth, and to wish to be treated by others with lowest esteem.

Eiaculatory prayer:

"O God, be merciful to me a sinner."
Deus propitius esto mihi peccatori (Luke 18, 13).

IV

MEDITATIONS
ON
OUR BIRTH AND BAPTISM

IV

MEDITATIONS
ON OUR BIRTH AND BAPTISM[1]

[1] "Meditations on Our Birth and Baptism" are taken from "Part Seven" of *The Kingdom of Jesus*, pp. 295-312. They may be used very profitably during the Christmas Season as an exercise in honor of the Child Jesus.

Saint John Eudes prefaces the first meditation with the following remarks: "I can never tell you enough, nor should you grow tired of hearing and considering (so important is it) that Jesus Christ, Who is your Head and Whose members you are, passed through all the stages of human life, through which you are passing. He did almost all the things that you do, and performed not only His outward acts but also all His interior actions for Himself and for you. Therefore, Christian sanctity and perfection consist in ceaselessly uniting yourself to Him as His members, and in continuing to do what He did, as He did it, to the best of your ability, uniting yourself with His dispositions and intentions. It likewise consists in consenting and adhering to what He did for you in the presence of His Father and in ratifying it. So, too, it consists in performing all your inward actions not only for yourself, but also for the whole world, in imitation of the Son of God, and especially for those with whom you have some special connection with respect of God. This Christian devotion inspires similar acts of union and imitation proportionately, towards the Blessed Virgin, never separating the Mother from the Son."

FIRST MEDITATION

Duties to Be Rendered to God on the Anniversary of Our Birth

FIRST POINT

LET US ADORE JESUS IN HIS ETERNAL AND TEMPORAL BIRTH

O JESUS, I adore Thee in Thy eternal birth and Thy divine dwelling for all eternity in the bosom of Thy Father. I also adore Thee in Thy temporal conception, and in Thy presence in the sacred womb of Thy most pure Mother, for the space of nine months, and in Thy birth into this world at the end of that time. I adore and revere the great and admirable occurrence of all these mysteries. I adore and honor the holy dispositions of Thy Divine Person and Thy holy soul in these mysteries. With my whole heart I adore, love and bless all the acts of adoration, love, oblation Thou didst render to the Eternal Father, and all the other divine acts and practices offered Him in these mysteries.

SECOND POINT

LET US UNITE OURSELVES TO THE HOMAGE THAT JESUS RENDERED TO HIS HEAVENLY FATHER FOR US

Again I adore and glorify Thee, O Good Jesus, as performing all these things for Thyself, for me and for everyone in the world. On this anniversary of my birth I give myself to Thee, O my Dear Jesus, that I may now repeat the acts Thou didst perfect while dwelling from all eternity in the bosom of the Father, and for nine months in the bosom of Thy Mother. I unite myself to Thee to perform this duty as Thou didst perform it, in union with love, humility, purity and other

148

holy dispositions of Thy adorable soul. Since Thou didst perform this act for Thyself and for me and for all men in the world, I also desire to exercise this present devotion, not only for myself, but for all the men in the world.

I now desire, O my Saviour, to render unto Thee as far as I can, with the help of Thy grace, all the rightful homage I should have paid Thee if I had been gifted with the use of reason, from the first moment of my life. So, too, I desire to pay Thee all the due meed of adoration, praise and love, which should have been given to Thee at that same time by all my friends, and by all people who ever were, are, or shall be in the world; and even that which should have been rendered to Thee by the evil angels at the moment of their creation. I give myself again to Thee, my Lord Jesus. Enter into me, and unite me to Thyself in order that in and by Thee I may fulfil these desires for Thy pure glory and satisfaction.

THIRD POINT

LET US ADORE, LOVE AND THANK JESUS FOR OUR BIRTH AND BAPTISM

In union, therefore, with the devotion, love, humility, purity and sanctity, and all the other sublime dispositions with which Thou didst honor, bless, love and glorify the Eternal Father in Thy eternal and temporal birth, and in Thy dwelling from all eternity in the bosom of Thy Father, and during nine months in the bosom of Thy Mother: I acclaim Thee; I adore, love, bless and glorify Thee together with the Father and the Holy Spirit as my God, my Creator and Sovereign Lord. I adore, love and glorify Thee also on behalf of all creatures— angels, men, animals, plants and inanimate things. I wish I could possess in myself the totality of their being, all their strength and all their actual or potential capacity to glorify and love Thee, that I might now use it all in paying Thee this homage for myself and for them, especially those for whom, before Thee, I have both the obligation and desire to pray with special zeal.

I give Thee infinite thanks, O my God, on behalf of myself, all creatures, and especially my particular friends, for the gift of life, and the capacity to know and love Thee. I thank Thee for having preserved our existence and allowed us to be born alive to receive Holy Baptism. If we had died before being delivered from original sin by the grace of Holy Baptism, which has been the misfortune of many souls, we should never have seen Thy divine face, and we should have been deprived forever of Thy holy love. May all the angels and saints bless Thee forever for this most special favor Thou hast accorded us.

Ejaculatory prayer:

> "He made us, and not we ourselves."
> *Ipse fecit nos, et non ipsi nos* (Ps. 99, 3).

SECOND MEDITATION

Our Obligation of Loving and Serving God

FIRST POINT

LET US CONSECRATE OUR BEING AND OUR LIFE TO JESUS

OMNIPOTENT Creator, Thou didst give me being and life solely that I might employ them in Thy love and service. Therefore, I offer my life to Thee. I consecrate and sacrifice it altogether to Thee, together with the being and life of all the angels, all men and all creatures, in testimony that I desire no longer to live save to serve Thee with all the perfection Thou dost ask of me.

O my God, what a source of humiliation and pain it is for me to think that, during the first months of my life, I was Thine enemy and under the power of Satan, in a continual state of sin that infinitely displeased and dishonored Thee! For this I most humbly beg Thy forgiveness, O my Lord, and in satisfaction for the dishonor I gave Thee while I remained in the state of original sin, I offer Thee, O Father of Jesus, all the glory given Thee by the immaculate Mother during the time she dwelt in the blessed womb of St. Anne, her mother.

O my Jesus, in honor of and in union with the love with which Thou didst accept and bear all the crosses and sufferings that were permitted by the Heavenly Father to attend Thy temporal birth, I offer Thee all the trials and afflictions I have suffered since my birth, and those remaining for me to suffer until the end of my life, accepting and loving them for love of Thee, and begging Thee to consecrate them to the homage of Thine own sufferings.

O Most Kind Jesus, I offer Thee all the circumstances of my birth, and I implore Thee by Thy very great mercy to wipe out all that displeases Thee in the first part of my life. Deign to make up for my faults, giving to Thy Father and to Thyself all the honor I ought to have given Thee at that time, if I had been capable of honoring Thee; and mayest Thou grant that the earliest phase of my life may render an undying homage and glory to the divine state of Thy dwelling in the bosom of Thy Father and in the womb of Thy Mother, and to Thy eternal and temporal birth.

SECOND POINT

LET US RATIFY THE ACTS DONE IN OUR BEHALF BY JESUS ON THE DAY OF HIS BIRTH

Such, O my Lord, is the rightful homage I ought to have rendered to Thee, had I been able, at the moment of my birth, and indeed from the first moment of my life, that I now endeavor to render to Thee, although very tardily and imperfectly. But what gives me infinite consolation, O my Dear Jesus, is that I know Thou didst atone for my deficiencies by Thy temporal birth. Then Thou didst render all this just homage to God the Father, performing in a most holy and divine manner all these acts and devotions for Thyself and for me. Thou didst refer and consecrate to His glory all Thy being and Thy entire life, present and to come, and together with it all my being and every state of my life, and of all creatures that ever were, are, or shall be, all the past, present and future state of created things being just as vividly present to Thee then as now. Thou didst look upon every life as Thine own, as something given to Thee by the Father, according to Thy blessed words: "All things are delivered to me by my Father" (Matt. 11, 27). Thou wast consequently obliged, by Thy profound love for Him and Thy zeal for His honor, to refer and give and sacrifice everything to Him. And this Thou didst do most excellently.

Thou didst also offer to Thy Father the holy and divine state of Thy dwelling in the sacred womb of the Virgin, all filled with glory and love for Him, in satisfaction for the dishonor that was to be rendered to Him by myself in the state of original sin. And at the same moment when Thou didst accept and offer to Thy Father all the crosses and sufferings of Thy whole life, Thou didst offer Him also all the past, present and future trials and afflictions of all Thy members: for it is the function of the head to act for himself and on behalf of all his members, because the head and the members are but one, and also because all that pertains to the members belongs to the head, and conversely all the attributes of the head belong to the members.

And so, O divine Head, Thou hast turned my whole being and the whole condition of my life to meritorious purpose. In Thy temporal birth, Thou didst render for me to Thy Father all the rightful homage I should have rendered Him at my own birth, and Thou didst then practise all the acts and exercises of devotion that I should have practised. Be Thou blessed for ever! How willingly I consent and adhere to all that Thou didst do at that time for me! Indeed I ratify it with my whole will, and would gladly sign that ratification with the last drop of my blood. I also endorse all Thou didst do for me in all the other phases or actions of Thy life, to compensate for the faults Thou didst know I was going to commit.

In imitation of Thee, O my Jesus, in honor of and in union with the same love which led Thee thus to accomplish all things for Thyself and for all Thy brothers, members and children, and for all creatures, I henceforth desire in all my functions and activities to render to Thee all the honor and glory I can, for myself and for all Christians, who are my brothers, and members of the same Head and Body. I desire to honor Thee on behalf of all men and all other creatures that are unworthy or incapable of loving Thee, as if all of them put together had entrusted me with their duties and obligations towards Thee, and had charged me to love and honor Thee on their behalf.

THIRD POINT

PRAYER TO THE BLESSED VIRGIN

O Mother of Jesus, I honor thee, as far as I am able, in the moment of thy holy conception, and in the instant of thy birth into the world. I honor all the love, all the adoration, praise, oblations and blessings thou didst offer to God at that time. In union with thy love, purity and humility as thou didst adore, love and glorify Him, and didst refer thy being and thy life to Him, I adore, bless and love my God with thee, my Mother, with my whole heart. I consecrate and sacrifice to Him forever my life, my being and my whole self.

So also, acclaiming thee, O Blessed Virgin, as Mother of God and consequently as my Sovereign Lady, I refer to thee, after God, the whole state of my being and my life. I implore thee most humbly to offer to God, for me, all the love, the glory and rightful homage thou didst render to Him at thy birth, by way of satisfaction for my faults, and to cause, by thy prayers and merits, all the phases, actions, and sufferings of my life to pay undying homage to all the phases, actions and sufferings of thy Son's life and thine own.

Ejaculatory prayer:

"I am thine."
Tuus sum ego (Ps. 118, 94).

THIRD MEDITATION [2]

Institution of the Sacrament of Baptism [3]

Let Us Adore Jesus as the Institutor of the Sacrament of Baptism

O Jesus, I adore Thee as divine Author of the holy Sacrament of Baptism, which Thou didst institute for my salvation. Thou didst also acquire and merit the grace contained in that Sacrament, by Thy Incarnation, Thy Baptism in the River Jordan and by Thy holy death.

I adore the exceeding great love with which Thou didst merit and institute this same Sacrament.

I adore all the designs which Thou didst cherish in its institution, for the whole Church and for myself in particular.

I thank Thee countless times for all the glory Thou hast given to Thyself and for all the graces Thou hast transmitted to Thy Church, and to me in particular, by this Sacrament.

I offer Thee all that glory and all the graces Thou hast produced in Thy Holy Church by this means.

[2] Before these Meditations on Baptism, St. John Eudes says:
"Holy Baptism is the beginning of your true life, that is, your life in Jesus Christ, and it is the origin of all happiness. Therefore, it is certain that you would have been obliged to render a very special tribute to your Heavenly Father on the occasion of your baptism. But you were incapable of fulfilling your obligation then because you did not have the use of reason. It is logical that you should each year set apart a little interval near the anniversary of your baptism, or else some other time, to devote yourself to prayer and thanksgiving for this priceless sacrament." Cf. *The Kingdom of Jesus*, p. 302.

[3] Saint John Eudes begins this meditation with the following reflections:
"The author of the holy Sacrament of Baptism is Jesus Christ our Lord. He is the source of all its graces, acquired and merited by His Incarnation, by His Baptism in the River Jordan, by His Passion and Death. He applied these infinite merits to you by virtue of His Resurrection, out of His exceeding great love." *Ibid.*, loc. cit.

SECOND POINT

ACT OF REPARATION FOR HAVING SO LITTLE PROFITED
BY THE GRACE OF BAPTISM

I beg Thee to forgive me for neglecting to take advantage of the grace Thou didst give me in holy Baptism, and for having made it valueless by my cowardice and infidelities in Thy service, and for having even destroyed it entirely in my soul, by my sins.

I give myself to Thee, O Good Jesus; renew in me the treasure of baptismal grace, and accomplish in me, by Thy very great mercy, all the plans of Thy Providence on my behalf in the divine Sacrament of Baptism.

THIRD POINT

LET US ADORE JESUS RECEIVING BAPTISM
IN THE RIVER JORDAN

O Jesus, I adore Thee in the mystery of Thy Incarnation, Passion and Death, as meriting the grace of the Sacrament of Baptism; but especially do I adore Thee in the mystery of Thy holy Baptism in the River Jordan. I adore all the dispositions of Thy divine soul in this mystery, and all the designs Thou didst then deign to have in my regard. How different was Thy Baptism, Lord, from ours! In Thy Baptism Thou didst take upon Thyself our sins, to make satisfaction and do penance for them before the Father of heaven, in the desert and on the Cross, while in our baptism Thou didst lift from us the burden of our sins, washing and effacing them in Thy Precious Blood. Baptize me with the Baptism of the Holy Ghost and of fire, even as Thy blessed precursor, St. John the Baptist, assures us Thou dost baptize, that is, consume all my sins in the fire of Thy holy love, and by the power of Thy divine spirit.

Ejaculatory prayer:

> "We are baptized in Christ Jesus."
> *In Christo Jesu baptizati sumus* (Rom. 6, 3).

FOURTH MEDITATION
The Mysteries of Which Baptism Makes Us Participants[4]

FIRST POINT

LET US ADORE JESUS AS THE EXEMPLAR OF OUR BAPTISM IN THE
MYSTERY OF HIS TEMPORAL AND ETERNAL BIRTH

O JESUS, Son of God and at the same time Son of man, I adore Thee
in Thy temporal and eternal birth. I give Thee infinite thanks for
all the glory Thou didst thus render to Thy heavenly Father. I adore
the thoughts and designs Thou didst then deign to have for me, thinking of me from the very first, O Good Jesus; Thou didst love me and
didst plan to make in me a living image of Thyself, of Thy birth and

[4] The following reflections should be read before the meditation:
"All things outside of God have their idea, their exemplar, and their prototype in
God; so also Sacramental Baptism has for prototype and exemplar four great mysteries,
namely:

(a) The mystery of our Lord's eternal birth, because His Father, by eternal generation, imparted to Him being, life and all the divine perfections, by reason of which He
is the Son of God and the perfect image of His Father. Likewise, by Baptism He
imparted to you the celestial and divine life He received from His Father; He implanted in you a living image of Himself, and He made you children of His Own
Heavenly Father.

(b) The mystery of our Lord's temporal birth, because at the moment of His Incarnation and birth in the Blessed Virgin, He united our nature with His and His essence
with our nature, and filled it with Himself and clad Himself in it as in a garment; similarly in the holy Sacrament of Baptism He united Himself with you and incorporated you
with Him; He formed Himself and, as it were, took flesh in you. He clothed and
filled you with Himself, according to these words of St. Paul: "As many of you as have
been baptized in Christ have put on Christ" (Gal. 3, 27).

(c) The mystery of His death and burial, for St. Paul also tells us that "All we,
who have been baptized in Christ Jesus, are baptized in His death" (Rom. 6, 3), and
that "we are buried together with Him by baptism into death" (Rom. 6, 4). This means

Thy life. Just as God the Father communicates to Thee His divine and immortal life, and just as Thou art consequently His Son and His most perfect image, so also Thou didst plan to transmit to me by Baptism Thy holy and celestial life, and to make me a living image of Thyself, and to transform me by grace into what Thou art by nature, that is, a child of God, and by participation and resemblance, God and another Jesus Christ.

Who could ever thank Thee for such great favors! How culpable I am for having, by my sins, so often impeded the perfect fulfilment of Thy divine plan! Forgive me, my Saviour, with all my heart I beg Thee to forgive me, and I give myself to Thee so that Thou mayest make amends for my faults and renew in me that image of Thyself, of Thy birth and of Thy life. Separate me from myself and from all that is not Thee, in order to unite and incorporate me with Thee. Empty me of myself and of all things, destroy me utterly, in order to fill me with Thyself and to form and establish Thyself in me. Cause me henceforth to be a perfect image of Thyself, just as Thou art a most perfect image of Thy Father.

Grant that I may share in Thy filial love for Him, since He is my Father as He is Thine; enable me to live by Thy life, that is, a holy and perfect life, truly worthy of God, since Thou hast made me God by participation; and, finally, invest me so fully with Thy qualities, perfections, virtues and dispositions, and so transform me into Thee that men may see only Jesus in me, only His life, His humility, His meekness, His charity, His love, His spirit, and His other virtues and qualities, since Thou dost will me to be Thy other self on earth.

precisely the same as the thought expressed by the same Apostle in other words: "You are dead: and your life is hid with Christ in God" (Col. 3, 3), that is: You have entered by baptism into a state which obliges you to die to yourself and to the world, and to live no longer except with Jesus Christ, by a totally holy and divine life, hidden and absorbed in God, resembling the life of Jesus Christ.

(d) The mystery of the Resurrection, because by His Resurrection the Son of God entered into a new life, totally heavenly and spiritual, entirely separated from the earth. And so St. Paul instructs the faithful: "We are buried together with him by baptism into death; that, as Christ is risen from the dead by the glory of the Father, so we also may walk in newness of life" (Rom. 6, 4).

For these reasons, then, we owe our Saviour a great tribute of homage and should lift up our minds and hearts to Him." *The Kingdom of Jesus*, p. 303-304.

LET US ADORE JESUS AS THE EXEMPLAR OF OUR BAPTISM IN THE MYSTERIES OF HIS DEATH, BURIAL AND RESURRECTION

O Jesus, I adore Thee in the mystery of Thy holy death, Thy burial and Resurrection. I give Thee thanks for the glory Thou didst render to the Eternal Father in these mysteries, and for the thoughts and plans Thou didst have in them for me. For Thou didst constantly think of me in all these mysteries, and at every moment of Thy life, and Thou didst always have a special plan for me. Thy special Providence was to imprint on my soul, by holy Baptism, an image of Thy death, burial and Resurrection, causing me to die to myself and to the world, hiding me in Thyself, and with Thee in the bosom of the eternal Father, and raising me up again and causing me to live like Thee a new life, altogether celestial and divine. For this, be Thou blessed forever!

Alas, by my sins I have destroyed in myself the great effects produced by Thy goodness, and for this I beg Thee, with all humility and contrition, to forgive me. I give myself to Thee, O Good Jesus, I surrender myself to the spirit and the power of the mystery of Thy death, burial and Resurrection, that Thou mayest cause me to die again to all things; that Thou mayest hide me in Thyself and with Thyself in the bosom of the Heavenly Father; that Thou mayest dissolve my mind in Thy mind, my heart in Thy Heart, my soul in Thy soul, my life in Thy life; and that Thou mayest establish in me the new life into which Thou didst enter by Thy Resurrection, so that I may no longer live, save in Thee, for Thee, and by Thee.

Ejaculatory prayer:

"We are buried together with him by baptism into death."
Consepulti sumus cum illo per baptismum in mortem (Rom. 6, 4).

FIFTH MEDITATION
Administration and Ceremonies of Baptism[5]

FIRST POINT

LET US ADORE JESUS AS THE ONE WHO BAPTIZED US
IN THE PERSON OF THE PRIEST

O MY Most Beloved Jesus, I adore and recognize Thee as the One who baptized me, in the person of the priest, whom Thou didst use as a living instrument to confer this grace upon me. Alas, Lord, I knew Thee not at that time! I did not think of Thee, I did not love Thee, nor did I appreciate the very great favor conferred upon me. Yet this did not deter Thee from loving me, and receiving me among the number of Thy children, and even of Thy members, by the sanctifying grace of Baptism. O my adorable Saviour, I desire with all my heart to bring back that holy time, that happy moment in which Thou didst baptize me, in order that I may adore, bless, love and glorify Thee infinitely, imploring Thy Eternal Father, Thy Holy Spirit, Thy Blessed Mother, all the angels and saints and all creatures to love, bless and thank Thee for me forever.

[5] All the Fathers of the Church teach us that our Lord Jesus Christ Himself, by the power of His Holy Spirit, confers all the Sacraments in the person of the priest, who represents Him and acts in His name and by His authority. It is He who consecrates in Holy Mass and gives us absolution in the Sacrament of Penance; also He baptizes us, with various symbolic ceremonies, inspired by His Spirit in Holy Mother Church and filled with mysteries that signify great graces that are conferred upon us in Holy Baptism. We should, therefore, pay Him homage in this connection. *The Kingdom of Jesus*, p. 306.

Let Us Adore Jesus Inspiring the Ceremonies of Baptism to the Church

O Jesus, I adore Thee as the One who, by Thy Holy Spirit, didst institute and inspire in Thy Church all the ceremonies which accompany the solemn administration of Sacramental Baptism. I adore all Thy admirable designs in their institution. I give myself to Thee that Thou mayest effect them in my person, and that by Thy great mercy Thou mayest produce in me the great and holy effects signified by these symbolic ceremonies.

O Jesus, cast out the evil spirit from me forever and fill me with Thy Divine Spirit. Give me a lively and perfect faith. Fortify my bodily senses and my spiritual faculties against every kind of temptation by the virtue of Thy holy Cross and consecrate them to Thy glory. Fill my soul with Thy divine wisdom, that is, with Thyself; excite in me the most avid hunger, thirst and desire of Thee, the principal and only food of my soul, so that I may no longer find any savor or relish in anything save Thee alone. Keep me safe in Thy Church, as in the bosom of a mother, apart from whom there is no life or salvation, and give me the grace to honor her in all her observances, as in customs taught and inspired by Thee. Give me the grace to obey all her laws and commandments, as those of a mother most worthy of honor who commands nothing save in Thy Holy Name. In all things and everywhere teach me to follow the maxims and guidance of the Spirit of the Church which is entirely Thine own.

Let Us Beg Jesus to Make Us Participants in the Graces Symbolized by the Last Ceremonies of Baptism

O Good Jesus, open my ears to Thy word and Thy voice, as Thou didst open the ears of the man possessed by the deaf and dumb spirit, by the application of Thy sacred spittle, and close them altogether to the voice of the world and of Satan. Anoint me with the oil of Thy grace so that I may spread abroad, as it were, the divine odor of Thee in every place. Give me a firm and lasting peace with Thee and with every kind of creature. Clothe me in the white robe of Thy holy innocence and divine purity, both bodily and spiritually. Dispel the shadows of my darkness, filling me with Thy heavenly radiance.

Set me on fire with Thy sacred love and cause me to be a shining and a burning light, to illumine and enkindle all my associates with the light of Thy knowledge and the fire of Thy love. Finally, if I became a source of joy to all the citizens of heaven, to the Blessed Virgin, the Eternal Father, Thyself, and the Holy Spirit, when by Baptism I was delivered from the power of Satan and admitted into the divine company of angels and saints, and even of the Three Divine and Eternal Persons, and if in token of this joy the church bells were rung after I was baptized, cause me now to live henceforth in such a way as to continue to be a source of joy and satisfaction to the court of heaven, the Queen of Angels and the Most Blessed Trinity. Grant also that I may find all my satisfaction and joy in serving and loving Thee.

Ejaculatory prayer:

> "You are the light of the world."
> *Vos estis lux mundi* (Matt. 5, 14).

SIXTH MEDITATION

Profession of Baptism

RENEWAL OF OUR BAPTISMAL PROMISES

O JESUS, my Lord and my God, I adore Thee as the mystical Head whom I must follow and imitate in all things, according to my solemn and public profession made at Baptism. I promise, through my sponsors, before heaven and earth, to renounce Satan utterly with all his works and his pomps, that is, sin and the world, and to adhere to Thee as my Head, and to give and consecrate myself altogether to Thee, to dwell in Thee forever.

Great indeed are this promise and profession, which oblige me, as a Christian, to practise great perfection and sanctity. To profess to · dwell in Thee and to adhere to Thee as my Head is to profess to be one with Thee, as the members are one with their head; it is to promise to have but one life, one mind, one heart, one soul, one will and one thought, one devotion and disposition with Thee. It means to profess not merely poverty, chastity and obedience, but to profess Thy very self, that is, Thy life, spirit, humility, charity, purity, poverty, obedience and all other virtues. In a word, it is to make the very profession Thou didst make before the Eternal Father at the moment of the Incarnation, a profession perfectly fulfilled throughout Thy life. It means to make profession never to follow my own will, but to seek all happiness in doing everything willed by God, to remain in a state of perpetual subjection to God, and submissive to men for the love of God. It means existing always as a host and victim continually sacrificed to the pure glory of God.

Such is the vow I made at Baptism, O Jesus my Lord. How holy and divine is that profession! How far is my life from this sanctity

163

and perfection! How often have I failed in every respect to live up to so sacred a promise! Forgive me, most merciful Lord, forgive me. O Divine Redeemer, I implore Thee to repair all my failings, and in satisfaction for them, to offer to Thy Father the inestimable honor Thou didst accord Him all Thy life long, by carrying out perfectly the profession made to Him at the Incarnation.

O my Jesus, in honor of and in union with the very great love and holy dispositions of Thy profession, I now desire to enact in my own person what I promised through others at my baptism, that is, I will to renew the profession then made by my godparents. Therefore, in the virtue and might of Thy Spirit and Thy love, I forever renounce Satan, sin, the world and myself. I give myself to Thee, O Jesus, to adhere to Thee, to remain in Thee, to be but one with Thee in heart, mind, spirit and life. I offer myself to Thee, never to do my own will, but to seek all my happiness in doing everything commanded by Thy holy will. I sacrifice myself to Thee as a host and victim to be immolated to Thy pure glory in any way that may be pleasing to Thee.

O most compassionate Jesus, I implore Thee by Thy great mercy, grant me the grace to carry out this holy profession perfectly. Do Thou fulfil it Thyself in me and for me, or rather for Thyself and for Thine own good pleasure, in all the perfection Thou dost desire; for I offer myself to Thee to do and suffer whatever pleases Thee for this intention.

SECOND POINT

Prayer to the Most Holy Trinity[6]

O Holy and Adorable Trinity, I adore Thy divine essence and Thy Three Eternal Persons; I adore Thee for having been present at my baptism; I adore all the designs of Thy Providence for me. I beg Thee

---

[6] St. John Eudes makes the following reflections before this prayer to the Blessed Trinity:

"As has been said, it is our Lord Jesus Christ who baptizes the faithful; but each soul is baptized in the Name and by the power of the Most Holy Trinity. The Three Divine Persons are present at Holy Baptism in a particular manner. The Father is present generating His Son in the soul and imparting to it a new being and new life in His Son. The Son is present, being born and receiving life in the soul, transmitting

to forgive me for impeding their fulfilment and in satisfaction I offer Thee the life, actions and sufferings of my Lord Jesus Christ and of His most holy Mother. I give myself to Thee, O Divine Trinity, for the accomplishment of those same designs.

O Eternal Father, O Thou the only Son of God, O Holy Spirit of the Father and the Son, enter into me; enter into my heart and my soul; separate me from all that is not Thyself, draw me to Thyself, live and reign in me, destroy in me all that displeases Thee, and cause my being and my life to be completely consecrated to Thy pure glory.

Ejaculatory prayer:

"I renounce thee, Satan; I adhere to Thee, O Christ."
Abrenuntio, Satana; adhaeres tibi, Christe.

His divine sonship, by which the neophyte becomes a child of God, just as He is Son of God. The Holy Spirit is present, forming Jesus in each even as He was formed in the bosom of the Virgin. The Father, Son and Holy Ghost are present, separating the new-born Christian from all things, taking possession of him and consecrating him specially to Themselves, imprinting Their divine character and image on his soul and establishing in his being (as in Their living temple, Their sacred tabernacle, or Their holy throne and heaven) the dwelling-place of the Blessed Trinity, Their glory, kingdom and life. And consequently, if only sin did not stand in the way, the Three Eternal Persons would dwell always in each Christian heart in a particular and ineffable manner; They would most wonderfully glorify one another by living in the soul a most holy and divine life So, too, it follows that we belong to God as creatures entirely consecrated to Him and we must consequently pursue no other purpose in life save His glory and service. In this connection it would be well to pay the following tribute of praise to the Holy Trinity" *The Kingdom of Jesus,* p. 310.

V

MEDITATIONS
ON
THE PREPARATION FOR DEATH

V

MEDITATIONS
ON
THE PREPARATION FOR DEATH [1]

DEATH is usually preceded by such violent throes of intense weakness that the dying person is unable to direct his thoughts to God and cannot render the homage owed to His divine majesty at that crucial time. Therefore, it is extremely advisable to anticipate this disability by setting aside a few days each year to carry out now what one ought rightfully to render to God at the hour of death. St. Gertrude tells us that when she had once performed this exercise, our Lord revealed that it was most pleasing to Him, and He promised to set aside her preparation and keep it for the day of her death. We should be confident that in His goodness He will give this grace to us also, if we make use of the same exercise. To this end, we may make, during ten consecutive days, the following meditations, or else choose one each month in our retreat.

[1] These meditations are found in "Part Seven" of *The Kingdom of Jesus*, pp. 312-344. They are both inspiring and practical. Religious communities will find them most useful for the monthly retreat and for the preparation for death.

FIRST MEDITATION
Submission to the Will of God

FIRST POINT

LET US ACCEPT DEATH AS A PUNISHMENT FOR OUR SINS AND
AS A HOMAGE TO THE SOVEREIGNTY OF GOD

O MY Lord Jesus, behold me prostrate at Thy feet, adoring my Judge and Sovereign, as Thou dost pronounce on me the sentence of death, pronounced to Adam and in his person to all sinners, by Thy words: "Dust thou art, and into dust thou shalt return" (Gen. 3, 19). In honor of Thy exceeding great love and most profound humility with which Thou didst hear and accept the sentence of death, spoken by Pilate, the Roman Governor, but willed by Thy Eternal Father, in honor of and in homage to His divine justice, I submit with my whole heart to the sentence of death Thou didst pass upon me even at the beginning of the world, recognizing that I have deserved it not only by original sin, but each time I have committed sin.

O my God, I recognize that even if I were guilty of no sin, whether original or actual, nevertheless, by Thy absolute sovereignty and power over me Thou couldst in all holiness take away my life, annihilate me and do with me as Thou wilt.

And so in honor of the very great love and in union with the deep submission with which the Blessed Virgin, Thy Mother, accepted death even though she was not obliged to die, by reason of any sin, original or actual, I, too, accept death in homage to Thy sovereignty, abandoning myself entirely into Thy hands, that Thou mayest dispose of me in time and in eternity, according to Thy holy will, for Thy greater glory.

Let Us Accept Death to Honor the Death and the Sovereignty of Our Lord

O Jesus, Thou art eternal and immortal; Thou art the source of all life, yet Thou dost will to die on the Cross the most cruel and igno-minious of all deaths in homage to the justice and sovereignty, the divine and eternal life of Thy Father, and to give me a token of Thy love. And so, my Saviour, even if I were not obliged to die on account of my sins, and even if (to suppose the impossible) I depended in no way upon Thy sovereignty, and even indeed if Thou hadst not died for me in particular, I ought not only to accept death, but even to desire to die, in order to honor Thy holy death, which is so exalted and worthy of honor that all living creatures ought to subject them-selves to death voluntarily even if they were not already obliged to die, in homage to the death of their Creator made Man.

Even if Thou hadst not died, O my God, all living things ought most willingly to sacrifice their very existence to pay homage to Thy supreme and eternal being, and to bear witness by this sacrifice that Thou alone art worthy to live, and that no other being or life has any right to show itself, but should be annihilated in Thy presence as the stars of heaven are extinguished in the light of the sun.

Thy death is so worthy of honor and homage, Thy life is most worthy to be adored. With excessive love Thou didst will to die, not only to satisfy the justice of God the Father and to honor His sover-eignty, but also to sacrifice Thy human and temporal life for the glory of the divine and eternal life with Thy Father and Holy Spirit. By this sacrifice Thou didst bear witness before heaven and earth, that there is none but the divine life alone that is worthy of existence, and all other created life, however noble and excellent, should be extin-guished in the sight and in the presence of this supreme and un-created life. Therefore, in honor of Thy death, in homage to Thy Life, in union with the infinite love with which Thou didst thus will to die, for such great and divine intentions, and also in honor of the burning love with which Thy Blessed Mother and all Thy saints, especially Thy holy martyrs, embraced death with a very ready will for the same intentions, I accept and embrace death with my whole heart, in whatever form it may please Thee to send it to me, that is, in the place, time, manner and under all the circumstances it shall please Thee to decree.

And so if Thou dost order me to die a painful or even a shameful death, or that I be left desolate and abandoned by all human help, or if I am to be deprived of the use of my senses and reason, provided Thou art always with me, Thy holy will be done. I desire to accept and embrace all this in honor of Thy most sorrowful and ignominious death, in honor of the unspeakable desolation Thou didst suffer on the Cross, abandoned by all when even the face of Thy All-loving Father seemed veiled. I accept it in homage to the surrender of Thy senses Thou didst make in earliest childhood. I honor Thee in the humiliation Thou didst suffer, being treated as a madman by Thine own people, at the beginning of the preaching of the Holy Gospel, and by Herod and his court during Thy Passion.

Finally, my Dear Jesus, I place myself entirely in Thy hands. I abandon myself so completely to Thy good pleasure that I no longer desire to have any other will or desire, save to let Thee will, desire and choose for me, in this and in everything else. Thou dost possess infinite wisdom and power and Thou hast a far greater knowledge and power and will to further Thy glory than I ever could have. One thing alone I beg of Thee, and it is that, since Thou didst die in love, by love and for love, if I am not worthy to die for Thy love or by that love, at least Thou mayest permit me to die in Thy dear love.

O my Jesus, I implore that, just as Thou didst perform all actions and functions for Thyself and for all men, especially for Thy children and friends, I may be permitted, in honor of and in union with Thy love, to perform all these actions and render unto Thee all due homage not only for myself but for all men, especially for all those for whom Thou knowest that I am both bound and anxious to pray with particular fervor.

THIRD POINT

Let Us Accept Death to Honor the Death of the Blessed Virgin Mary

O Mother of Jesus, surely it would seem that thou shouldst not have died, since thou art the Mother of the Eternal and Immortal Son of God, who is life itself! Yet thou didst willingly submit to death, in homage to the most adorable death of thy Son. Thus, thy death is so exalted and worthy of honor that all creatures ought to subject themselves to death by their own free will, in order to honor the death of their Sovereign Lady, the Mother of their Creator. Therefore, O holy Virgin, even if I were not obliged to die, I should, nevertheless, wish to accept death freely, and offer it to thee together with the death of each one who is dear to me, and of all mankind, in homage to thy most holy death. I most humbly implore thee, O Mother of Life, to unite my death to thine in honor of the death of thy Son and to obtain from Him the grace to die in His favor and in His love.

Eiaculatory prayer:

"Dust thou art, and into dust thou shalt return."
Pulvis es, et in pulverem reverteris (Gen. 3, 19).

SECOND MEDITATION

Thanksgiving for Graces Received

LET US THANK OUR LORD FOR ALL THE GRACES THAT WE HAVE RECEIVED FROM HIM ·

AFTER we have made the solemn act of acceptance, we should prepare for a holy death, first by thanking Our Lord for all the favors we have received from Him in our whole lifetime. And it is very wise to devote a day to this exercise as follows:

O Jesus, I contemplate and adore Thee as the principle and source of all good things and all temporal and eternal graces past, present and future, in heaven and on earth, especially those I have received from Thee. I refer all these graces to Thee, for Thou art their source and Thy glory is their destiny. O good Jesus, who could ever describe all the favors that Thou hast done me? They are numberless and I am utterly incapable of thanking Thee for them as Thou dost deserve. O dearest Lord, may all that ever was, is, or shall be in me, may all earthly and heavenly creatures, all the angels and saints, Thy Holy Mother, Thy Holy Spirit, Thy Eternal Father, all the powers of Thy divinity and humanity, and all the graces and mercies which emanated from Thee, may all these be employed in praising Thee forever. May they be entirely transformed into everlasting praise of Thee, of all that Thou art together with Thy Father, Thyself and Thy Holy Spirit, and of all the graces Thou didst ever impart to Thy sacred humanity, Thy Blessed Mother, the angels and saints, and all creatures, and especially the graces Thou hast given me, or would have given me if I had not stood in Thy way.

O Father of Jesus, Holy Spirit of Jesus, Mother of Jesus, angels of Jesus, saints of Jesus, and all creatures of Jesus, bless and give thanks to Him for me forever. O Divine Jesus, do Thou glorify Thyself for me and return to Thyself a hundredfold all the thanks I ought to render to Thee.

SECOND POINT

LET US THANK OUR LADY, AND ALL THE ANGELS AND SAINTS
FOR THE MANY FAVORS RECEIVED THROUGH THEM

O Good Jesus, Thou knowest how many favors and benefits I have received from Thy Blessed Mother, the angels and saints in heaven, and from many persons on earth. Thou knowest also how incapable I am of acknowledging them and giving thanks for them as I ought. And so I have recourse to Thee, imploring Thee most humbly to make up for my deficiencies and to give, on my behalf, to all those Souls, both in heaven and on earth, all that I ought to render to them for the benefits I have received through their intercession.

O Mother of Grace, Mother of my God, it is through thy mediation that I have received all the graces ever bestowed on me from heaven. May heaven and earth bless thee for them all, on behalf of myself and of all the thoughtless persons who have received favors from thee and give thee no thanks whatever.

Ejaculatory prayer:

"Let us return thanks to the Lord our God."
Gratias agamus Domino Deo nostro.

THIRD MEDITATION
Confession, Satisfaction for Our Sins

FIRST POINT

In Reparation for Our Sins Let Us Offer Jesus All the Glory
that He Received from His Father, His Holy Spirit,
the Blessed Virgin, the Angels and the Saints

HAVING set aside one day to thank God for all the graces He has given us in our lifetime, it is most necessary that we devote another day to ask forgiveness for our sins and to make satisfaction to Him. To that end, we ought on this day to make a good confession, either an extraordinary confession or one marked by unusual contrition and self-abasement, with as much care as if it were to be our last confession. As a preparation for this confession we should set aside a little time during the day to meditate on this matter, in the presence of God, in the following way:

O Most Lovable Jesus, infinitely worthy of all service and love, to Whom I owe debts without number, Thou didst create me only to love and serve Thee. Yet I have done scarcely anything but offend Thee by thought, word and deed, by all my bodily senses and spiritual faculties, by my misuse of Thy creatures, against all Thy commandments, in countless different ways. O what sins! What ingratitude! What betrayals! Lord Jesus, I cast all my offenses upon Thy divine love, into the abyss of Thy mercies. Grant that I may be utterly transformed into sorrow and contrition, with tears of blood to detest and wipe out the sins I have committed against that immense Goodness, so deserving of love and honor! My God, what is there that I could ever do to make reparation for my sins? But even if I were to suffer all the torments and martyrdom in the world, I still could not of myself alone repair the insult given Thee by even the least of my faults.

LET US OFFER TO GOD IN REPARATION FOR OUR SINS
THE HONOR WHICH JESUS RENDERED TO HIM

O Good Jesus, I offer Thee instead all the glory, love and service given Thee by all the saints and Thy most Blessed Mother, by their holy thought, words and actions, by holy use of their bodily senses and their spiritual powers, by their eminent virtues and sufferings, in satisfaction for the failures of my lifetime. I offer Thee likewise all the honor given Thee forever by all the angels, by the Holy Spirit, by Thyself, and by the Eternal Father, in reparation for the dishonor I have given Thee all my life.

O Heavenly Father, O Holy Spirit, O ye angels and saints, offer up for me, to my Saviour, all the love and glory you ever gave Him, in satisfaction for the wrong I have done Him by my offenses.

Miserable sinner that I am, by offending my God I have offended all things. I have offended the Father, the Son, the Holy Ghost, the Mother of God, all the angels and saints, and all creation, for all are concerned and offended in offense to their Creator. How, O my God, how can I make reparation for so many offenses, make satisfaction to so many persons and pay off so many debts? I know what I will do: I have my Jesus who is in Himself an infinite wealth of virtues, merits and good works. He has been given me to be my riches, my virtue, my sanctification, my redemption and reparation. I shall offer Him to the Eternal Father, to the Holy Ghost, to the Blessed Virgin, to all the angels and all the saints in reparation and satisfaction for all the faults I have committed. O Holy Father, O Divine Spirit, I offer all the love and honor that my Jesus gave you by all His divine thoughts, words and actions, by His divine employment of all the members of His body and of His soul, by all His glorious virtues and heroic sufferings, in satisfaction for all the offenses I have committed against you all my life long.

O holy Virgin, O holy angels, O blessed saints, I offer you my treasure and my all, my Saviour Jesus Christ; I conjure you to draw from His infinite storehouse of merit whatever you require in payment and satisfaction for all the debts I owe you, by reason of my sins and negligence.

O my Jesus, my divine Redeemer, do Thou make reparation for all my faults, and by Thy very great mercy atone for all my sins committed against the Eternal Father, Thyself the Son, the Holy Spirit, Thy most Blessed Mother, the angels and saints and all persons I have offended. I give myself to Thee to do and suffer in atonement whatsoever may be pleasing to Thy holy will, accepting now all the sufferings of body or spirit that I may have to bear, whether in this world or in the next, in satisfaction for my sins.

O most holy Virgin, I have so many obligations to serve and venerate thee; yet I have so little honored and so greatly offended thee by offending thy Son! I beg thy forgiveness, O Mother of Mercy, and I offer thee in satisfaction all the honor ever accorded thee in heaven and on earth. I implore all the angels and saints, the Holy Ghost, thy Son, and the Eternal Father to supply for my deficiencies, and fill up the measure of glory I ought to have rendered to thee all my life long.

Ejaculatory prayer:

> "My sin is always before me."
> *Peccatum meum contra me est semper* (Ps. 50, 5).

FOURTH MEDITATION
Holy Communion

FIRST POINT

INTENTIONS FOR OUR LAST HOLY COMMUNION

HOLY COMMUNION is the most precious and effective means given us by God to render to Him all the honor and service we owe to Him. To prepare for a holy death, we should make a point of taking one day of this exercise to dispose ourselves for an exceptionally well-prepared Communion, marked by extraordinary devotion and approached with as much care and recollection as if it were to be our last.

We should offer this special Communion to our Lord:

1. In honor of all that He is in Himself and towards us.
2. In thanksgiving for all the effects of His love for His Father and for all creatures, but especially for us.
3. In satisfaction for all the dishonor and pain given Him by all the sins of the world, especially by our own.
4. For the fulfilment of the plans of His Divine Providence for all men, especially for us.

SECOND POINT

DISPOSITIONS FOR OUR LAST HOLY COMMUNION

Let us offer ourselves to the Eternal Father, begging Him to unite us with the surpassing love of His paternal heart when He received His Son Jesus Christ into His bosom on the day of the Ascension. Let us give ourselves to Jesus and beg Him to unite us with the most ardent love and profound humility with which He instituted the Holy Sacrament of the Altar, on the eve of His death. Let us offer ourselves to the

Blessed Virgin, to St. John the Evangelist, to St. Mary Magdalen and St. Mary of Egypt, and all the other saints, praying that they may cause us to participate in the love and fervor, the humility, purity and sanctity with which they received Holy Viaticum.

THIRD POINT

LET US ASK OUR DEAR LORD TO ACCOMPLISH AND COMPLETE ALL HIS HOLY DESIGNS IN US

After we have received Communion and made the usual thanksgiving to our Lord with unusual fervor, let us adore His divine plans from all eternity for us. Let us beg Him to remove all the obstructions we have ever placed in the way of their operation. Let us beg Him fervently not to let us die until He has completed the plans of His goodness and the work of His grace in our souls. Let us give ourselves to Him with a great desire and mighty resolution to work manfully to consummate His work in us, and to destroy in ourselves everything that might stand in His way, so that we may be able to repeat to Him, on the last day of our life, His words to the heavenly Father on Good Friday: *Opus consummavi quod dedisti mihi ut faciam,* "I have finished the work which Thou gavest me to do" (John 17, 4).

Ejaculatory prayer:

"He that eateth this bread shall live for ever."
Qui manducat hunc panem vivet in aeternum (John 6, 59).

FIFTH MEDITATION

Extreme Unction

LET US ADORE JESUS AS AUTHOR OF EXTREME UNCTION

O JESUS, I adore Thee as the author of the Holy Sacrament of Extreme Unction, and as the source of its priceless graces, which Thou hast acquired and merited for us by the shedding of Thy Precious Blood. I refer to Thee all the graces Thou didst ever produce in souls through Extreme Unction. I bless Thee a thousand times for all the glory Thou hast given to Thyself by this last Sacrament. I adore the infinite design of Thy Providence in the institution of Extreme Unction and I surrender myself to the accomplishment of Thy divine Plan for me according to Thy holy will. I implore Thee most humbly to grant me the grace of receiving this Sacrament at the end of my life. And if I should not be able to receive it, I implore Thee to produce in my soul, by Thy great mercy, the same graces I would acquire by its reception.

O Jesus, I adore Thee in the holy anointing of Thy sacred body in the last days of Thy life by St. Mary Magdalen, and at Thy burial by St. Nicodemus and St. Joseph of Arimathea. I offer Thee all the holy unctions ever performed, in this last Sacrament, upon the bodies of all Christians who have received it or ever shall do so, in honor of and homage to the divine anointing of Thy deified body.

SECOND POINT

LET US ASK JESUS TO PREPARE OUR SOULS TO RECEIVE EXTREME UNCTION AND ALL ITS ATTENDANT GRACES

O Good Jesus, I adore Thee as High Priest to Whom, before all others, belongs the right of conferring all the Sacraments. I give myself to Thee as High Priest and implore Thee to inspire in my soul all the dispositions required for the fruitful reception of Extreme Unction and to produce in me all the graces represented by its consoling ceremonies.

In order to dispose myself for its reception, O my Saviour, behold I cast myself down at Thy feet, accusing myself most humbly before Thee and Thy heavenly court of all my sins, most humbly begging Thy forgiveness with all the humility and contrition I can muster, with my whole heart imploring Thee, together with Thy Blessed Mother and all the angels and saints, to ask forgiveness from Thy Eternal Father, and to offer to Him in satisfaction for my sins the full measure of Thy infinite merits and sufferings.

O Good Jesus, come into my soul and into my heart. Come to bring me Thy holy peace and to destroy in me all that might disturb the peace and repose of my spirit. Come unto me, and with Thy Precious Blood purify me of the foulness of my sins. Come to grant me full and total absolution, indulgence and remission of all my sins.

O Most Kind Jesus, I offer Thee all the senses and members of my body and all the powers of my soul. Anoint me, I beg Thee, with the sacred oil that ever flows from Thy divine Heart, that is, with the oil of Thy grace and mercy and, by this heavenly anointing, cleanse me of the evil effects of my sins. O Dearest Jesus, I offer Thee the holy employment of bodily senses and spiritual powers ever made by Thy Divine Self, by Thy Blessed Mother and all the saints, in satisfaction for my abuse or misuse of the members and senses of my body and the faculties of my soul. May it please Thee to grant me the grace to employ them in future only for Thy pure glory.

Finally, O Most Amiable Jesus, may it please Thee to give me Thy holy blessing. Ask the Beneficent Father and the Holy Spirit to bless me with Thee, so that this divine and mighty benediction may destroy in me all that displeases Thee, and transform me utterly into eternal benediction and praise of the Father, the Son, and the Holy Spirit.

Ejaculatory prayer:

"Come, Lord Jesus."
Veni, Domine Jesu (Apoc. 22, 20).

SIXTH MEDITATION

The Last Will and Testament of Jesus and the One Which - We Should Make in Its Honor

FIRST POINT

THE FIRST THREE BEQUESTS OF CHRIST'S LAST WILL

O JESUS, I adore Thee in the last days of Thy life. I adore every aspect and event of these last days, but especially Thy divine Testament pronounced in the Canacle, on Mount Olivet and from the Cross. I adore, bless and glorify the supreme love for Thy Father, the most burning charity towards us and all the other holy dispositions of Thy last Testament to mankind.

The last will of Our Saviour comprises five bequests:

The *first* bequest is to His enemies, for, O wonder of wonders, O immensity of goodness, His first word and first prayer on the Cross is for His enemies, begging the Father to pardon them, in the very hour when they were blaspheming and crucifying Him.

The *second* bequest is to the Heavenly Father, the final gift of His holy soul with these words: "Father, into thy hands I commend my spirit" (Luke 23, 46). These words were uttered not only with reference to His deified soul, but to my soul and the souls of all who belong to Him, which were present at that moment before His sight, and He looked upon them as His veritable possession, forming all together but one soul by virtue of their most intimate union with Himself. When our dying Saviour said to the Father: *Pater, in manus tuas commendo spiritum meum,* He spoke for Himself and for me; He didst commend my soul together with His into the hands of the Eternal Father, addressing this prayer to Him who is at once Thy Father and mine, in Thy Name and my own, against the hour when my soul shall leave my body. And He made the offering of my soul with the same love with which He said *Pater* or *Father* in general, not *My Father* in particular, to show that He regarded Him not only as His special Father, but as the common and universal Father of all His brethren and members. He prayed to Him not only for Himself in particular, but also in general for all who belong to Him, with filial confidence and love, as much for Himself as for them, for which may He be loved and blessed forever.

The *third* bequest in His will concerns the Blessed Mother, to whom He didst give the friend who was most dear to Him after herself, the beloved disciple, St. John the Evangelist. At the same time there were represented in the person of St. John all the other disciples and children until the end of Time. When He said to Mary the words, "Woman, behold thy son" (John 19, 26), He gave her not only St. John, but all other Christians to be her children. Reciprocally, in saying to St. John the words: "Behold thy Mother" (John 19, 27), He gave to him and also to all Christians, represented in his person, His most precious possession in the order of created beings, namely, His most Blessed Mother, He gave her to them to be their Mother just as she was His Mother, imparting to them His precious relationship and character with her. That was the reason He called her no longer His Mother, but *Mulier,* "woman" to show the transfer to us of His relationship to her as Son, and the gift to us, as Mother, of her who was to cease to be His Mother for a time by reason of her Son's death. And so, Jesus bequeathed me in His will to His Blessed Mother, not only as a servant and subject, but actually as a son: *Mulier, ecce filius tuus.* He gave her to me not only as my Queen and Lady, but in the most honorable and lovable character there is—that of a Mother. O love! O excess of goodness! May the whole world be transformed into love for so great a goodness!

THE LAST TWO BEQUESTS OF CHRIST'S WILL

The *fourth* bequest in His will is particularly ours and concerns us so diversely that it seems to have been made for us alone.

1. During His last days on earth, He expressed a surpassing and extraordinary love, assuring us that the Father loves us as He loves Him (John 17, 23), and that He dost love us as the Father loves Him (John 17, 9). And He consequently urges us to love one another as He has loved us (John 13, 34).

2. He likewise commended us with most particular affection to the most exalted and powerful persons most dear to Him, by Whom He is most loved in heaven and on earth—that is, His Eternal Father and His divine Mother. Just before setting out on the road to Calvary, He addressed a beautiful prayer to the Father: "Holy Father, keep them in thy name whom thou hast given me. . . . Not for them only do I pray, but for them also who through their word shall believe in me" (John 17, 11-20). While hanging on the Cross, He placed our souls in His hands together with His own, as has been said. He also commended us to His divine Mother.

3. We share in His will because in His last, solemn and public prayer, He obtained from the Heavenly Father the greatest favors that we could ask for, or could obtain from God. Here are the prayers He addressed to Him for us: "Father, I will that where I am, they also whom thou hast given me may be with me" (John 17, 24), that is, that they should have their dwelling and take their rest with Him forever in the bosom and Heart of His Father. "Just Father, ... that the love wherewith Thou hast loved me, may be in them" (John 17, 25-26), that is, to say: Love them as Thou lovest Him, love them with the greatest, the most burning and most divine love that could ever possibly exist. Look upon them as Thou dost regard Him; love them with the very heart with which Thou lovest Him; treat them as Thou dost treat Him; give them all that Thou givest Him. "That they may be one, as thou, Father, in me and I in thee; that they also may be one in us . . . I in them, and thou in me; that they may be made perfect

in one" (John 17, 21-23). What love! What more could He ask the Father for us?

4. We share in Thy will because He gave us the most rare and precious gift, His Eternal Father to be our Father, praying Him to love us as He loves Thee, as His children with sublime paternal love. He gave us His Blessed Mother to be our Mother. He gave us His most Holy Body in the Eucharist, His holy soul on the Cross in death with the words: "I lay down my life for my sheep" (John 10, 15). He gave His Precious Blood to the very last drop, His life, merits, sufferings, humanity and divinity, as expressed in these words: "The glory which thou hast given me, I have given to them" (John 17, 22). He gave us all without reserve. How admirable is His goodness, poured forth for us in the very hour when we were causing Him to suffer so many evils! How can we love Him so little and think so seldom of Him? How can so great a love be held so cheap and be so despised by those whom He so loves?

The *fifth* and last bequest in His will was made on Mount Olivet when, departing from the apostles and ascending into heaven, He gave His holy blessing. We share in this bequest also, for in imparting His blessing to the holy apostles and disciples He blessed all of us, each one in particular, for we were all just as much present in His sight then as we are now. May heaven and earth bless the Author of all gifts, and may all things in heaven and earth be transformed into eternal blessings of Him!

Such are the five clauses of His admirable will, in honor of which I desire to draw up my own testament.

THIRD POINT

OUR SPIRITUAL WILL SHOULD BE MADE IN HONOR AND IMITATION OF THE WILL OF JESUS

1. O Most Kind Jesus, in honor of and in union with the love with which Thou didst shed Thy Precious Blood and die for Thine enemies and pray to the Eternal Father to pardon those who crucified Thee, with my whole heart I fully forgive all those who have ever offended or

injured me, and I implore Thee to grant them full pardon. I offer myself to Thee to do and suffer whatever may please Thee for their sake,
even to shed my blood and die for them, if necessary. So, too, in all the
humility I can muster, I beg all whom I have ever offended or displeased in my whole life to forgive me, and I give myself to Thee to
make whatever satisfaction to them Thou mayest desire.

2. In honor of and in union with the exceeding great love, the most
perfect confidence and all the other dispositions with which Thou didst
commend Thy soul and all the souls that belong to Thee into the hands
of the Father, I surrender my soul, with the souls of all those for whom
I am bound to have special concern, into the gentle hands and the
most loving heart of the Divine Father, who is my God, my Creator
and my Most Lovable Father, that He may dispose of them according
to His good pleasure. I trust that His infinite goodness will place them
with Thy soul, Good Jesus, in His fatherly bosom, there to love and
bless Him eternally with Thee, according to the desire of Thy soul,
expressed in the words: "Father, I will that where I am, they also
whom thou hast given me may be with me" (John 17, 24).

3. In honor of and in union with Thy great charity in giving all
Thy friends and children to Thy most Blessed Mother, I resign into
her hands all those entrusted to my care, imploring Thee, good Jesus,
to commend them Thyself to Thy Virgin Mother. I implore her with
my whole heart, by Thy very great love for her and hers for Thee, and
by the same love with which Thou didst give her Thy friends and children, to look upon them henceforth as her children in a more special
way, and to be their Mother.

4. In honor of and in union with the exceedingly powerful love
whereby Thou didst commend me to Thy Father on Thy last day, and
didst beg Him, on my behalf, for such great favors, giving me all that
was most dear to Thee, with such extraordinary tokens of that love,
urging me also to love my neighbor as Thou didst love me: I commend
to Thee all those whom Thou knowest I should commend particularly
to Thee, and I beg Thee on their behalf for all that Thou didst ask
for me on Good Friday from Thy Eternal Father. I abandon myself
to Thee to love Thee as Thou lovest the Father and as the Father loves

Thee. I give myself also to Thee to love my neighbor as Thou didst love me, and to shed my blood and give my life for him, if it is Thy holy will.

5. O Jesus, God of all blessings, I adore Thee in the last moment of Thy sojourn on earth, upon Mount Olivet, as Thou didst leave the earth to ascend into heaven. I adore Thee giving Thy most holy blessing to Thy Blessed Mother, Thy apostles and disciples; I adore the exceeding great love and all the other dispositions which filled Thy divine soul when Thou didst impart this supreme blessing as is related in the Holy Gospel (Luke 24, 50).

O Good Jesus, behold me prostrate at Thy feet, in union with the humility and the other holy dispositions of the Blessed Mother and the holy apostles and disciples as they received Thy blessing. I most humbly implore Thee, by all Thy love for them, and theirs for Thee, to give now to me and to all I have commended to Thee, Thy most holy blessing, so that by the power of that divine blessing all that displeases Thee in me may be destroyed and I may be altogether transformed into everlasting praise, love and benediction of Thee.

Ejaculatory prayer:

"Father into thy hands I commend my spirit."
In manus tuas commendo spiritum meum (Luke 23, 46).

SEVENTH MEDITATION

Our Last Agony and the Moment of Death

FIRST POINT

WE SHOULD LOOK UPON THIS DAY AS THE LAST OF OUR LIFE AND UNITE OURSELVES TO JESUS AND HIS HOLY MOTHER

WE SHALL consider this day as if it were to be our last. We must strive to spend it with as much care and devotion as if we had only this one day in which to love God. For this purpose, we should apply ourselves to the contemplation and adoration of Our Lord in the last day of His life on earth, and to do everything in union with the holy and divine dispositions of His last actions. With the last day of our life in view, we should implore Jesus to unite us to His Dispositions and foster them in our hearts, that we may be of the number of those of whom it is said: "Blessed are the dead who die in the Lord" (Apoc. 14, 13), that is, who die in the dispositions of the death of our Lord Jesus Christ.

Similarly we should consider and honor the Blessed Virgin on the last day of her life, uniting ourselves to her dispositions, offering her the last day of our life. The prayers addressed to Jesus Christ and His Blessed Mother for the end of the year should also serve our purpose here.

SECOND POINT

WE SHOULD ADORE JESUS IN HIS AGONY AND OFFER HIM OUR AGONY AND DEATH IN HONOR OF HIS

I may also add at this point that it is a good thing on this day to adore Jesus and honor His most holy Mother in their agony and death,

189

offering our agony and death in union with theirs, imploring them to
bless and sanctify our death by their own. It is also most beneficial to
adore the infinite power of the divine love that caused the death of
Jesus and of His most holy Mother, for they both died of love and by
love. We should implore that divine love to cause us to die with Jesus
and His divine Mother, and to consume and sacrifice our life in its
sacred flames.

We should also honor the holy martyrs and all saints in their agony
and death. Let us offer them our agony and death, in union with their
own, begging them to unite us with their holy dispositions as they
prepared for death. Let us implore them specially to associate us with
all the love and glory they gave to Our Lord on the last day of their
life and at the moment they died for Him.

We should pray specially to St. John the Evangelist, St. Mary Magdalen and the good thief who died with Jesus, and all the other saints
who were present at the death of the Son of God, that through the
merits of their privilege in being near Him in death, they may give
us special assistance at the hour of our own death.

On this same day it would be most advisable to read the Passion of
Our Lord, the seventeenth chapter of St. John, containing His last
words and prayers before setting forth to be crucified, as well as the
prayers of Holy Mother Church for the agonizing soul, which are to
be found at the end of the Breviary. We do not know whether we will
be in a fit state on the last day of our life to complete these prep-
arations for a holy death. Hence, it is a good thing to anticipate that
day, and to read the Passion of Our Lord and the above-mentioned
prayers with all the devotion we would wish to put into them at the
hour of death, and all the devotion with which they have ever been
read by the whole Church.

But above all, when we read the seventeenth chapter of St. John,
which contains the last words and prayers of Jesus, let us give ourselves to Him in a sincere effort to pronounce these words and prayers
in union with His love, dispositions and intentions when He spoke
them, imploring Him to foster in our hearts these sublime dispositions
in preparation for the last day of our life and to produce the effects
of these holy words.

Finally, let us cast ourselves down at the feet of Jesus and His most holy Mother, to implore them to give us their blessing. "O Jesus, O Mother of Jesus, give me your blessing for the last moment of my life. By your great goodness, grant that the last moment of my life may be consecrated to the glory of the last moment of yours, and that my last breath may be an act of most pure love of you."

Ejaculatory prayer:

"Blessed are the dead who die in the Lord."
Beati mortui qui in Domino moriuntur (Apoc. 14, 13).

EIGHTH MEDITATION

The Particular Judgment

FIRST POINT

LET US ADORE JESUS IN THE JUDGMENT PRONOUNCED AGAINST HIM BY HIS HEAVENLY FATHER

O JESUS, Thou art the Saint of Saints and Sanctity Itself, infinitely above all sin and imperfection. Yet, I behold Thee prostrate with Thy face to the earth at the feet of the All-just Father in the Garden of Olives, and the following day at the feet of Pilate, where the Eternal Father contemplates Thee as the Victim who has taken upon Himself all the sins of the world, giving Himself without reserve for the ransom of mankind. Thou hast taken the place of all sinners and borne the heavy judgment of our sins by dying on the Cross for our salvation. Thou dost accept that judgment with most perfect submission, most profound humility and most ardent love for Thy Father and for us. O Jesus, I adore and glorify Thee in this judgment and in all holy dispositions of humiliation, contrition, submission and love with which Thou didst suffer to be judged and condemned to save us.

SECOND POINT

LET US SUBMIT OURSELVES IN ADVANCE TO THE SENTENCE PRONOUNCED AGAINST US AT THE HOUR OF OUR DEATH

In honor of and in union with these dispositions, behold me prostrate at Thy feet, great Jesus, adoring Thee as my sovereign judge. I most willingly submit myself to Thy supreme power. I infinitely rejoice that Thou hast sovereign power over me and over all men and angels. A thousand times I bless the Eternal Father for having given Thee this power. I affirm sincerely that if, to imagine the impossible,

Thou didst not have this power, and I did have it, I would want to
strip myself of it to give it to Thee; if I were not subject to Thy power
to judge me, I should wish to subject myself voluntarily to that power,
out of homage to Thy divine justice and to the condemnation Thou
didst undergo from Thy Father during Thy holy Passion.

O Jesus, I adore Thee in Thy coming at the hour of my death and
at the moment of Thy judgment of my soul. I adore now every aspect
and detail of my particular judgment. May it please Thee to grant
me now some measure of the divine light by which Thou wilt clearly
show me every event of my whole life, compelling me to give an account of everything. Grant me a share in the zeal for justice with
which Thou wilt be avenged for my offenses, so that I may from now
on see my sins clearly and make reparation by perfect contrition, horror
and detestation for these same sins.

O my God, how many sins I have committed against Thee all my life
long, by thought, word and deed, in every way! They can not be num-
bered, I confess; and I accuse myself before Thee, before Thy Blessed
Mother, before all the angels and saints, and, if it be Thy holy will,
before the whole world. I accuse myself of my sins, just as they are in
Thy sight, as Thou knowest them. If only I could see my offenses as
Thou seest them! If only I knew myself as Thou knowest me, and as
I shall see and know myself in Thy light at the moment of judgment!
How I shall be confounded and humiliated then by the realization of
what I am! What horror my crimes will awaken in me! What regret,
what anguish at having so little loved and so greatly offended so tran-
scendent a goodness as Thine! How quickly will I then accuse and condemn my own self! Indeed there will be no need of any other judge,
for I shall be the first to pass sentence upon my own misdeeds and ignominy.

But why wait until that final hour? Lord, at this very moment I
surrender myself to the zeal of Thy divine justice and to the spirit of
Thy just hatred and righteous horror for sin. In honor of and in union
with Thy extreme hatred of sin, I hate and detest all my sins; I hold
them in abhorrence; I renounce them forever; I offer myself to Thee
to suffer for them all the penance Thou shalt order. Casting myself
down before Thy face, in the ultimate depths of abjection, to which,

O great God, I have deserved to be reduced by my sins, I pronounce against myself, in the presence of heaven and earth, that final sentence. Since I, who am nothing but a worm of the earth, a handful of ashes and mere nothingness, have in so many ways offended so exalted and great a majesty, there are no tortures, either on earth, in purgatory or in hell, capable of worthily expiating my sin, without the intervention of Thy mercy and the power of Thy Precious Blood. For all these torments are finite, while the offense of my sins is infinite, since they offend an infinite majesty, and consequently deserve an infinite punishment.

So, my sovereign Judge, falling down once more at Thy feet, and in the lowest depths of the bottomless pit of my sins, I adore and bless and love Thee with my whole heart, as pronouncing the sentence that Thou shalt pronounce at the hour of my death, and I voluntarily, with all the love possible to me, submit to this sentence, whatever it may be, telling Thee with the Royal Prophet, with all the power of my will: "Thou art just, O Lord, and thy judgment is right" (Ps. 118, 137). And I most obediently accept anything it may please Thee to ordain in my regard, in time and eternity, giving myself to Thee to bear not only all the sufferings of Purgatory, in homage to Thy divine justice, but any other penalty Thou mayest impose upon me. I take no thought of what is to become of me nor what is to be done to me in time and eternity, provided only that the wrong and dishonor I have done Thee may be made good, no matter what the cost.

THIRD POINT

Let Us Beg Jesus to Be Merciful

And yet, O God of mercy, do not permit that I should be numbered among those who will never love Thee. O most merciful Lord, what am I that Thou deignest to open Thy blessed eyes to look upon me, to summon me into Thy presence in judgment and to exercise Thy justice upon me? It is all too true that I deserve Thy mercy far less than Thy justice. But, O Thou Saviour of my soul, remember that Thou didst will to be judged for me, and that Thou art most worthy that my sins should be forgiven in Thee, since Thou didst ask the All-merciful

Father to pardon them for me. And yet, Lord, enter not into judgment with Thy miserable and unworthy servant, but offer for me to Thy Father the judgment Thou didst sustain for my sins, and pray that His divine forgiveness be granted, not to me but to Thee.

O Father of mercy, I confess that I have deserved to bear the stern weight of Thy judgments, and that I am not worthy that Thou shouldst give me the least grace, nor that Thou shouldst pardon the very smallest of my sins. I offer Thee the terrible judgment Thy Son sustained for my faults, and I implore Thee to pardon them, not to me, but to Thy Beloved Son, Who begs Thy forgiveness on my behalf, and to give Him, also, all the graces I need for Thy service. All possible punishments in the world, visited upon me, are incapable of giving Thee fitting satisfaction for the very least of my crimes. Thy Son alone can make perfect reparation for the dishonor I have given Thee. And so I offer to Thee, and I implore Him to offer with me, all that He did and suffered in His whole life, and all the honor He ever rendered to Thee, whether by Himself or through His Blessed Mother, His angels and all His saints.

O Mother of Mercy, Mother of Jesus, O angels and saints of Jesus, offer to God all your merits and works on my behalf and all the glory you ever gave Him, in satisfaction for my offenses and implore Him to treat me not according to the rigor of His justice, but the multitude of His mercies, in order that I may love and bless Him with you forever.

Ejaculatory prayer:

"According to the multitude of thy tender mercies blot out my iniquity."
Secundum multitudinem misericordiarum tuarum dele iniquitatem meam (Ps. 50, 3).

NINTH MEDITATION
Death and Burial

FIRST POINT

LET US OFFER OUR DEATH TO JESUS IN HONOR OF HIS

O JESUS, Thou art eternal life and the source of all life, yet I behold Thee cold in the darkness and shadow of death. I see Thee bid fare-well, for a little while, to Thy most lovable Mother, to Thy dearly be-loved apostles and disciples, and to all Thy friends left bathed in tears, in the greatest mourning and lamentation of all time. I contemplate Thy holy soul separated from Thy divine body, with which it had so holy, so close and so sublime a union. I see this same body, more holy and sacred than all the heavenly bodies,—I mean than all heaven itself, —lying in a sepulchre, among the rocks in the dust.

O my Jesus, I adore, praise and glorify Thee thus. I offer Thee all the honor rendered to Thee in this state by Thy holy Mother, by St. Mary Magdalen, by the holy apostles and disciples, by the angels, by the holy souls Thou didst free from Limbo and by the whole Church, with all the glory Thy Father gave Thee, and which Thou now en-joyest in heaven, in recompense for that humiliation Thou didst bear on earth. I offer Thee the state of death which will one day be mine, in honor of that state of death in which Thou didst remain before the Resurrection.

I offer Thee the separation from the company of my friends and relatives that I shall one day have to bear, in honor of the most bitter separation which Thou didst suffer, torn from the most sweet company of Thy dearest Mother, of Thy dearly beloved apostles and disciples. I offer Thee all the sorrow and the tears of my relatives and friends in honor of the sorrow and tears of Thy harrowed Mother and sorrowing apostles. I offer Thee the separation of my soul from Thy sacred body.

I offer Thee all the states of my soul, until its reunion with its body, whatever they may be, in homage to the state in which Thy holy soul existed during the time it was separated from Thy body. I offer Thee the burial of my body and all the actions that shall be done in performing this burial, in honor of the burial of Thy holy Body.

In honor of and in union with the same love with which Thou, O good Jesus, didst will that Thy sacred body should lie upon the dust within a hollow rock, and by which Thou hast so often given me this same body in Holy Communion, although I am nothing but a worm of the earth, I most willingly surrender my body to the ground, and to the worms. I consent to be reduced to ashes and dust, but only on condition, O crucified Saviour, that all the grains of dust into which my flesh and bones shall crumble, may be so many voices praising and glorifying without interruption the adorable mystery of Thy burial, and that I may thus sing with the holy psalmist: "All my bones shall say: Lord, who is like to thee?" (Ps. 34, 10).

- SECOND POINT

LET US ADORE JESUS BURIED IN THE SEPULCHRE

O Divine Jesus, even though Thy body and soul were separated, nevertheless they are continually united to Thy divinity. Thus, they never ceased to be worthy of infinite honor and adoration. Therefore, I adore Thy holy soul in its descent into Limbo. I adore all that happened in Thy soul and all the effects produced in the souls of the Holy Patriarchs in Limbo. I also adore Thy body in the tomb, in all its members, for there is no part of it that is not infinitely adorable. I adore you, O most holy eyes of my Saviour's body. I adore you, O sacred ears of my God. I adore and praise you, O most blessed mouth and tongue of Him who is the Word and eternal utterance of the Father. I adore and bless you, O most divine hands and feet of my Lord. I adore and love you, O most amiable Heart of Jesus.

Alas, my Beloved! Thy perfect body is lifeless because of my sins! Those sacred eyes, that by their sweet aspect gave joy to all who came in contact with Thee, are now darkened by the shadow of death. Those holy ears, always open to hear the cries and prayers of all unhappy creatures, are now closed and hear no more. Those divine lips, which pronounced the words of life, have become mute and speak no words. Those blessed hands that wrought so many miracles are lifeless and still. Those holy feet, so often wearied for the salvation of the world, are no longer able to walk. But above all, the most loving Heart of my Jesus, the most exalted and noble throne of divine love, is without life or feeling. Ah! My dear Jesus, who has brought Thee to this pitiable state? My sins and Thy love! Cursed and detestable sin, how I abhor you! O love of my Saviour, may I love you, may I bless you without ceasing!

THIRD POINT

LET US GIVE OURSELVES TO JESUS, BEGGING HIM TO MAKE US DIE TO OURSELVES IN ORDER TO LEAD A HIDDEN LIFE WITH GOD

O Good Jesus, I surrender myself completely to the power of Thy holy love, I implore Thee by that love, to reduce me now into a state of death that may imitate and honor Thy state of death. Utterly extinguish in me the life of sin and of the old Adam. Cause me to die to the world, to myself and to all that is not Thee. Mortify my eyes, ears, tongue, hands, feet, heart and all the other powers of my body and soul, so that I may no longer be able to see, nor hear, speak, taste, act, walk, love, think, will, nor make any other use of all the parts of my body or the faculties of my soul, save in accordance with Thy good pleasure, led by the guidance of Thy divine spirit.

O my Well-beloved Jesus, I give myself to Thee to derive the benefits of these words of Thine apostle: "You are dead: and your life is hid with Christ in God" (Col. 3, 3). Hide me utterly with Thee in God. Bury my mind, my heart, my will and my being, so that I may no longer have any thoughts, desires, or affections, any sentiments and dispositions other than Thine own. And just as the earth changes and transforms into itself the bodies buried within it, do Thou change and transform me completely into Thyself. Bury my pride in Thy humility, my coldness and tepidity in the fervor of Thy divine love, and all my other vices and imperfections in Thy virtues so that, just as the earth consumes all the corruption of the body buried in it, so all the corruption of my soul may be consumed and annihilated in Thy divine perfections.

O Mother of Jesus, I honor and revere thee in the state of thy death and burial. I offer thee all the honor then given thee by the angels and holy apostles. I thank thee for all the glory thou didst give to the death and burial of Thy Son by thine own. I offer thee my own death and burial, imploring thee to obtain for me, by thy holy prayers, the grace that every aspect of my earthly end may pay everlasting homage to the death and burial of thy spotless self and of thy beloved Son, our Saviour.

Ejaculatory prayer:

"For you are dead: and your life is hid with Christ in God."
Mortui estis, et vita vestra est abscondita cum Christo in Deo (Col. 3, 3).

TENTH MEDITATION

The Entrance of the Soul into Heaven

FIRST POINT

LET US OFFER JESUS CHRIST OUR ENTRANCE INTO HEAVEN IN HONOR OF
HIS ASCENSION AND OF THE ASSUMPTION OF HIS HOLY MOTHER

O JESUS, I adore, praise and glorify Thee countless times at the moment
of Thy triumphant entrance into heaven. I offer Thee all the glory,
love and praises that were given to Thee in welcome by the Father, the
Holy Spirit, Thy Blessed Mother and all the angels. I also honor Thy
Blessed Mother in the moment of her assumption into Paradise. I offer
her all the glory and praises that were bestowed upon her by the Omnipotent Father, by her Beloved Son, Thyself, Thy Holy Spirit, all the
angels and all the saints. I offer to Thee and to Thy glorious Mother,
my own entrance into Paradise, which, I hope, by Thy great mercy, to
make one day, in honor of the glorious and triumphant entry of Thy
ascension and her assumption. O my Most Adorable Jesus, I desire to
consecrate everything that ever was, is, and shall be in me, in time and
in eternity, to the honor and homage of Thee and Thy most holy
Mother.

SECOND POINT

LET US OFFER PRAISE AND LOVE TO THE THREE DIVINE
PERSONS, TO JESUS, MARY, THE ANGELS
AND THE SAINTS

O Most Admirable and Most Adorable Trinity, I adore, bless
and magnify Thee infinitely for all that Thou art in Thy manifold
works of mercy and justice toward me and to all Thy creatures, in

heaven, on earth and in hell. I offer Thee all the adoration, love, glory, praise and benediction accorded Thee forever. O my God, how I rejoice to behold Thee so full of greatness, of marvels, of glory and joy! It is enough. I desire no other glory, felicity or happiness in eternity save to behold the incomprehensible glory, felicity and happiness of Him whom I love more than myself. O my glory and my love, may all heaven and earth be transformed into glory and love for Thee! Finally, I sacrifice myself all to Thee to be sacredly annihilated and consumed forever in the most pure fire of Thy divine love.

O Jesus, Thou only object of my love, with what love, with what praises can I ever repay Thee for all that Thou art in Thyself, and for all the innumerable effects of Thy goodness towards all Thy creatures, myself in particular? Lord, may all Thy creatures, all Thy angels and saints, Thy Blessed Mother, and all the powers of Thy divinity and humanity be employed in blessing and loving Thee forever.

O Mother of God, O holy angels, O blessed saints, I hail, honor and thank you all in general, and each one in particular, especially those to whom I owe some special obligation and with whom I am to be most closely associated in eternity. In thanksgiving for all the favors I have received from you, and much more for all the glory and services you have rendered to my God, I offer to each one of you the most amiable Heart of my Jesus, source of all joy, all glory and all praise. I give you my mind and my heart; unite them with your minds and hearts and associate me in your constant chorus of praise to Him who created me, that I may praise and love Him eternally with you. Pray ardently that I may bless and love Him through you, while awaiting the day when it may please Him to unite me with you to love and glorify Him to perfection.

O blessed day, when I shall begin to love most purely and perfectly my Lord and Saviour who is infinitely amiable! O thousand times happy day in which I shall begin to be all love for Him who is all love for me! O Jesus, my sweet love, how consoled I am when I think that I shall love and bless Thee eternally! My eyes dissolve in tears and my heart melts with joy at the sweetness of the thought that some day I shall be completely transformed into praise and love for Thee. But, alas, when will it come, this day, so longed for and a thousand times desired? Will it yet delay for long? "Woe is me, that my sojourning is prolonged" (Ps. 119, 5). "How long, O Lord, wilt thou forget me unto the end? How long dost thou turn away thy face from me" (Ps. 12, 1)?

No more the hunted stag desires,
Fleeing in woe and weariness,
Waters to quench his burning thirst,
Than my poor heart with sadness pressed
Sighs after Thee, O Lord, my rest.

My heart is driven nigh to death
By cruel desires, merciless,
And longs for Thee, Lord, Mighty God,
And in its longing, cries apace:
When shall my eyes behold Thy face?
When, ah, when will come that day
To take my earthly woes away
And bring me home at last to Thee?

THIRD POINT
Let Us Resolve to Lead a Heavenly Life Here Below

While waiting for that day, I desire, O my Saviour, to realize in myself St. Paul's words: "Our conversation is in heaven" (Phil. 3, 20), as well as Thy words of reassurance and guidance: "The kingdom of heaven is within you" (Luke 17, 21). I desire to live on earth as though I were not here, but living by my heart and spirit in heaven. I desire to concentrate all my powers on the establishment of the kingdom of Thy glory and holy love within myself. But Thou knowest, Lord, that of myself I can do nothing; therefore, I give myself to Thee, that Thou mayest destroy every obstacle and perfectly establish the kingdom of Thy pure love in my body, in my soul, and in all my thoughts, words and actions.

Ejaculatory prayer:

"Our conversation is in heaven."
Conversatio nostra in caelo est (Phil. 3, 20).

VI

MEDITATIONS
ON
THE ADMIRABLE CHILDHOOD
OF
THE MOST BLESSED VIRGIN
MARY

MARY IN THE CRIB

Fac-simile of the "Bambino Romano" which adorned the Novitiate of Our
Lady of Charity of Caen until the destruction of the Monastery in 1944.

VI

MEDITATIONS ON THE ADMIRABLE CHILDHOOD OF THE MOST BLESSED VIRGIN MARY [1]

FIRST MEDITATION
The Feast of the Most Holy Name of Mary

FIRST POINT

ORIGIN AND MEANING OF THE HOLY NAME OF MARY

THE most holy name of Mary was sent from heaven from the adorable Heart of the Most Holy Trinity, where it was cherished from all eternity. It was carried to earth by the Archangel Gabriel, who announced it to St. Joachim and St. Anne. This blessed name is a marvelous treasure containing within itself all riches.

It embraces the divine maternity, since Mary, according to St. Ambrose, signifies "God born of my race."

Mary signifies also "enlightened" and enlightening," which is most fitting. For the infant Mary was so replenished with the light of grace from the first moment of her life, that she knew the Creator and all creatures, and all things necessary to Almighty God. If she was so enlightened at the commencement of her life, judge what progress she

---

[1] At the end of his work, *The Admirable Childhood of The Most Holy Mother of God*, St. John Eudes added this series of meditations on the holy childhood of Mary. He recommended them for the days following September 8, the Feast of the Nativity of Our Lady, and for the eighth day of each month, which he dedicated to the childhood of the Blessed Virgin Mary.

must have made during the years of her childhood, inasmuch as her light and grace continually grew and multiplied from moment to moment.

Return thanks to the Father of Light and supplicate Him to make you feel the effects of that precious name, Mary, which not only signifies "enlightened" but also "enlightener" and "enlightening." Pray Our Lady of Light to give you a share in that radiance that you may know the infinite goodness of God, in order to love Him; the frightful horror of sin, in order to hate it; the vanity of the things of this world, in order to despise them, and the abyss of your own nothingness, that you may humble yourself.

ANOTHER MEANING OF THE NAME OF MARY

The name, Mary, also signifies "Imitator of God." The most holy Virgin imitated God perfectly throughout her holy childhood, in the love God bears Himself, in His charity towards men, in His goodness, His liberality, His mercy, purity, sanctity and other perfections, appearing as a more perfect image of the Divinity than all the saints together.

St. Thomas calls Our Lady "a perfect image of the divine Goodness."

Rejoice then with her; thank with her the most Holy Trinity, offering all the honor this holy maiden rendered the Blessed Trinity by her marvelous imitation. Weigh well the words of the Holy Ghost, speaking by the mouth of St. Paul: "Be ye therefore followers of God, as most dear children" (Eph. 5, 1). Humble yourself for having until now so inadequately practised His counsel. Resolve to do better, especially in imitating the Blessed Virgin in the virtues most necessary for you, and supplicate her constantly to assist you by her powerful prayers.

THIRD POINT

THIRD MEANING OF THE NAME OF MARY

Mary signifies Lady. From her infancy this holy maiden was Sovereign Lady of heaven and earth, of men, of angels and of all creatures.

Her power is absolute in heaven, earth and hell, over the demons and in all things, spiritual and corporal. Her power is threefold: first by her title of eldest daughter, and, consequently, of heiress to all the estates of the Eternal Father; second, by title of Mother of God, having been chosen by the Son of God, from the first moment of her life, to be His Mother; third, by title of Spouse of the Holy Ghost, as endowed with all the rights of spouse of the omnipotent Sanctifier.

Mankind, Christians included, tends generally to rob this glorious lady in so far as possible, of the authority and power God has given her over them, and bestow their authority and power upon Satan, her enemy. This is what you have done every time and as often as you have been guilty of mortal sin.

Beg pardon of the Son and the Mother, and endeavor to establish their reign in your heart, removing every obstacle and imploring the Blessed Virgin Mary to employ in your behalf the power God has given her.

Ejaculatory prayer:

> "O clement, O loving, O sweet Virgin Mary."
> *O clemens, O pia, O dulcis Virgo Maria.*

SECOND MEDITATION

Our Obligations to Honor and Imitate the Blessed Virgin Mary in Her Admirable Childhood

EXCELLENCE OF THE HOLY CHILDHOOD OF MARY

WE ARE obliged to honor the sacred Virgin in her childhood. First, because the twelve years of this sacred period contain in themselves almost an infinitude of greatness and holiness, which merits the highest honor, and will be for eternity the object of the praises of the denizens of heaven. Count the mysteries, the virtues, the thoughts, affections, words, actions and mortifications of this maiden. Reflect upon her holy use of the powers of her soul, and of her interior and exterior senses. You will find herein sufficient reasons for entertaining a singular devotion to her. For all that passed in the interior or exterior of this blessed child was filled with perfection and sanctity, worthy of most particular veneration.

Secondly, we should revere this admirable maiden because her infancy was a continual exercise of adoration, praise and love towards God. She was full of grace, therefore she gave more glory to God by the smallest action than the chief among the saints by the practice of most heroic virtue.

Thirdly, we should render all possible honor to her pure sanctity because all the virtues of her infancy were employed in preparing her to give us a Saviour and to cooperate with Him in our salvation. May all these reasons inspire in us a singular devotion and particular love for this inviolate and amiable maiden.

SECOND POINT

ADVANTAGES DERIVED FROM THE HOLY CHILDHOOD OF MARY

Among other considerations, we must remark that we are indebted to the holy childhood of Mary for three great favors. The Son of God when about to be born into the world could have created a virgin of perfect age and become incarnate in her. But His infinite goodness towards us obliged Him to choose for His Mother a daughter of Adam, thus to honor all the human race with three signal favors.

First, by this birth of the Infant Mary, divine Bounty gave us two treasures of sanctity, St. Joachim and St. Anne.

The second favor is that, by the birth of the holy Infant Mary, God bestowed upon the race of Adam another inestimable gift, an immense treasure of good, the holy and precious Mother of God, born of Adam's race, our sister and our Mother.

The third favor consists in the treasure our Lady herself has given us, the God-man, our Brother.

Weigh well these three great favors God has given us in the birth of the most holy Infant Mary and let these considerations excite in us a great desire to honor our Blessed Lady in every possible way.

THIRD POINT

THE HOLY CHILDHOOD OF MARY IS A MODEL FOR ALL CHRISTIANS

The Son of God wished His admirable Mother to pass through the state of infancy that she might give an example and rule of life for all Christians to follow. For all men are obliged by the laws of the Gospel to be children in innocence, in simplicity, in humility, in obedience and in all virtues. "Amen, I say to you, unless you be converted, and become as little children, you shall not enter into the kingdom of heaven" (Matt. 18, 3).

Render thanks to the Son of God for having given us an example so noble and so charming, and a rule so holy and so sweet. Venerate this divine example, love this amiable rule. See if you have followed it in the past. Humble yourself and ask pardon for the shortcomings of which you have been guilty. Begin carefully to imitate the virtues of the precious infancy of your most holy Mother. Beg her to assist you to eradicate in yourself any obstacle to your loving imitation of her virtue.

Ejaculatory prayer:

"Unless you . . . become as little children, you shall not enter into the kingdom of heaven."
Nisi efficiamini sicut parvuli, non intrabitis in regnum caelorum (Matt. 18, 3).

THIRD MEDITATION

The Innocence and Simplicity of the Blessed Virgin in Her Admirable Childhood

INNOCENCE OF MARY DURING HER CHILDHOOD

AN INNOCENT person is an individual who does not know what it is to injure another, or, in different words, to commit sin, because sin alone dishonors God and injures men.

Consider that, among all pure creatures, the Immaculate Virgin alone was conceived, born and lived until her last breath in perfect innocence. She was not only preserved from all sin, but was in reality impeccable. The goodness of God endowed her will with this happy impossibility. First, by a singular favor of His divine Providence, God preserved her from all perils, and occasions of danger, as much by His immediate protection as by the ministry of millions of angels who accompanied her everywhere and guarded her most carefully. This privilege was most appropriate to the dignity of the Mother of the Saint of saints and Sovereign Monarch of the universe.

Secondly, the great and marvelous light within her soul revealed, with unerring clearness, the tiniest atom of imperfection, and the superabundance of the grace which filled her vanquished the very shadow of sin. St. Augustine says: *"Ad vincendum omni ex parte peccatum."*

Thirdly, the sacred fire of divine love so inflamed her heart that she lived in the continual exercise of most pure love, without fatigue or interruption. This held her will under a moral inability to choose any fault, even the slightest.

Thank God for the marvelous innocence with which He clothed this most holy Virgin from the first moment of her life. Ask the grace to imitate this shining innocence, carefully avoiding any offense against

God, against your neighbor, against your own soul. Endeavor to apply yourself as ardently as possible to the exercise of divine love, for the greater your love for God, the farther removed you are from sin. Offer your heart to this Mother of Fair Love, and beseech her to kindle therein one spark of the ardent fire of love with which her own heart is consumed.

SECOND POINT

SIMPLICITY OF MARY DURING HER CHILDHOOD

The virtue of Christian simplicity is most pleasing to God. The divine Word assures us that He takes His pleasure and delight in those who walk in simplicity before His Countenance: "His will is in them that walk sincerely" (Prov. 11, 20). This virtue shuns multiplicity in thoughts, desires, affections, words and actions, and employs all the exertions of the soul, mind and heart in pleasing God. It causes moderation in speech, it eliminates useless actions which serve to dissipate the mind and distract the heart from Him who should be the only object of its thoughts and affections.

Simplicity detests that curiosity which is eager to see, to hear and to know things that are not at all necessary to render it more pleasing to God. It is the sworn enemy of duplicity, artifice and disguise, of lying and deceit. It causes the soul to pursue the straight road of candor, frankness and dove-like sincerity, turning neither to the right nor the left. It chooses by preference simple and plain taste in eating, speaking, walking and dressing, and has a horror of the novel fashions of the world, which are vain and frivolous.

To what an eminent degree this holy simplicity adorned our amiable Mary! The Holy Spirit says of her: "Thy eyes are as those of doves" (Cant. 1, 14).

Give thanks to God for the glory rendered Him by this most Holy maiden in her practice of the virtue of shining simplicity.

THIRD POINT

OUR OBLIGATION TO IMITATE THE INNOCENCE AND SIMPLICITY OF MARY

Adore the designs of the Son of God towards you when He pronounced these words: "Be ye therefore as wise as serpents and simple as doves" (Matt. 10, 16). For you were present before His eyes, He bore you in His mind and in His heart, which was filled with ardent desire to behold you adorned with simplicity for the glory of His Father and the salvation of your soul.

Endeavor to acquire this virtue. Examine your failure to observe simplicity in your intentions, desires and affections; by excess in words; by curiosity of the eyes, ears and mind; by artifice, lying and deceit; by aversion to simple food, clothing, lodging or furniture; by your inclination to follow worldly vanities. All these vanities are opposed to the spirit of the Blessed Virgin.

Ask pardon for all your faults and promise to eliminate all that is contrary to Christian simplicity. Imitate the simplicity of your heavenly Queen, that you may be of the number of those whom St. Paul calls the simple children of God, who are without reproach (Phil. 2, 15), in whom He delights. You may repeat: "For our glory is this, the testimony of our conscience, that in simplicity of heart and sincerity of God, and not in carnal wisdom, but in the grace of God, we have conversed in this world" (2 Cor. 1, 12).

Ejaculatory prayer:

> "(Be) blameless, and sincere children of God."
> *Simplices filii Dei* (Phil. 2, 15).

FOURTH MEDITATION

The Humility of the Blessed Virgin in Her Admirable Childhood

WHY GOD LOVES HUMILITY

THERE are three reasons why God loves humility and hates presumption, pride and ambition.

God, who is the essential Truth, loves truth. He hates lying because it is the enemy of truth. As truth and humility are one, so pride and falsehood are one.

Humility is simply a lowly opinion of ourselves and true consciousness of our own misery and nothingness. It is only the truth to assert that we are nothing but sin and misery. What is pride but a high esteem of ourselves in the belief that we are something, which belief is only falsehood and deceit? "For if any man think himself to be some thing, whereas he is nothing, he deceiveth himself," says St. Paul (Gal. 6, 3).

God who is infinite Justice, hates injustice as the enemy of justice and, consequently, His own enemy. Humility is that justice which renders to God the honor and glory which are His due, and pride is that injustice which robs God of His glory to attribute it to self.

Idolatry is an abomination in the sight of God for it renders to creature the sovereign honor due to God alone; the virtue of religion is loved by God because it renders Him His due. Now, pride causes the sinner to make an idol of self, and put himself in God's place, since he prefers himself to God when his own interests, his satisfactions, his own will and desires are at stake. But, God loves humility, inasmuch as it is animated by the spirit of religion, which refers to God the honor and glory of all things.

Adore in the heart of the great God His infinite love for humility and His hatred of pride. Beg Him to enkindle in your heart some portion of His love for humility and His detestation of pride.

HUMILITY OF MARY DURING HER CHILDHOOD

God inspired in the heart of the pure Virgin Mary His own intense love for humility, and abhorrence of pride. She possessed, even from her infancy, a far greater horror of pride and ambition, and a far deeper love for humility than did all the saints together. It was the first virtue that she practised. She abased and humbled herself before all. She esteemed herself, and would have been happy to be treated by others, as the last of all creatures.

By the marvelous radiance of her Immaculate Conception, she beheld herself susceptible to the guilt of the children of Adam, except that God miraculously preserved her, and she considered that she might have been capable of all the sins in the world, whose source is original sin.

It was this humility which attracted to her the countless graces which rendered her worthy to be the Mother of God, Queen of heaven and earth. Give thanks to Almighty God who resists the proud and gives grace to the humble, and offer Him all the glory that this maiden accorded to His majesty by her practice of richest humility during her childhood and throughout the rest of her life.

OUR NEED OF HUMILITY

The practice of humility is not only a counsel of perfection but also a precept of obligation, since our Saviour Himself has declared that unless we become little and humble as children, we shall not enter into the kingdom of heaven (Matt. 18, 3).

Consider the frightful castigation the just anger of God has hurled upon the apostate angels, upon Core, Dathan and Abiron and many other proud persons. This realization should help us to hate pride, which is so detestable before God. On the other hand, consider the prodigious humility of our Saviour, of His Blessed Mother and of all the Saints.

Excite in yourself a true desire to practise this virtue and to shun its opposite. Examine well your thoughts, desires, affections, your words and actions, to see if they reveal anything contrary to humility. See what esteem you hold for yourself, what motives actuate you, how you bear humiliations and corrections, how you react to honor and praise. See if you love to speak about yourself and to your own advantage, if you obey without murmuring, if you prefer yourself to others or indulge in envy of them, if you perform your actions to gain applause and esteem, if you are vain and worldly in your choice of clothing and lodging.

Humble yourself profoundly before God at sight of all the faults of which you have been guilty. Beg Our Lord and His Holy Mother to repair them. Offer to the Eternal Father the glorious honor of their profound humility. Take a strong resolution for the future to guard yourself against pride and to practise this counsel of the Holy Ghost: "Humble thyself in all things: and thou shalt find grace before God: for . . . he is honored by the humble" (Ecclus. 3, 20-21).

Ejaculatory prayer:

"Humble thyself in all things: and thou shalt find grace before God."
Humilia te in omnibus, et coram Deo invenies gratiam (Ecclus. 3, 20).

FIFTH MEDITATION

The Obedience of the Blessed Virgin Mary in Her Admirable Childhood

FIRST POINT

SUBMISSION OF THE BLESSED VIRGIN TO GOD'S WILL

WE HAVE been placed in the world for one purpose only, to do God's will. This is our first beginning and our last end, and consequently our sovereign good. In His holy will as in our centre, we ought to find repose of mind, peace of heart, our perfect felicity and true paradise. As our own will is opposed to the will of God, we should regard and hate it as His sworn enemy and our own foe. We should treat self-will as a beast of prey, a ravening wolf, a ferocious lioness, the source of hell, for without it there would be no hell. It is the mother of all the abominations of the earth. Self-will is a venomous serpent, a detestable homicide that kills body and soul at the same time, an execrable deicide that kills God insofar as it is able.

Our blessed Lady, by the light of her incomparable grace, saw clearly this monster of self-will and renounced it utterly, although she was not corrupted nor depraved by sin as we are. She united herself inseparably to the divine will, seeking all her glory and contentment and joy in following it everywhere and in all things, with entire submission and perfect obedience.

Let us praise Almighty God for having given her this grace, and offer to His Divine Majesty all the glory she rendered Him by the practice of obedience, in reparation for our rebellion against God and our disobedience to the divine will.

OBEDIENCE OF THE BLESSED VIRGIN TO HER PARENTS AND SUPERIORS

Let us consider that the Blessed Virgin was obedient, not only directly to God, but to His will as manifested by His commandments, by the law of Moses, by her parents and superiors, in whom she perceived and honored God, whose voice she obeyed as the voice of God. She followed literally the injunction of St. Peter: "Be ye subject therefore to every human creature for God's sake" (1 Peter 2, 13). Never was there obedience so simple because never was there humility so profound. Her obedience was unquestioning, prompt and joyous for this thrice holy maiden had no other delight than to follow the most adorable will of God, pointed out to her by those who held His place.

Give thanks to the divine majesty, and offer God the honor rendered Him by the obedience constantly practised by His little Handmaid in reparation for your faults against this virtue.

NEED TO RENOUNCE OUR OWN WILL TO DO THE WILL OF GOD

Let us consider that all our happiness consists in following the divine will of God, manifested to us by His commandments and those of His Church, by the obligations of our state of life and by those who represent God to us. Obedience is the mother of happiness.

To follow God's will we must renounce our own, for they are diametrically opposed, since man's will is perverted, corrupted and poisoned by sin.

Let us regard our own will as the sworn enemy of our salvation, and even of our happiness in this life. There is nothing on earth nor in hell we should fear more than self-will for it is the source of all the miseries and evils of earth and hell. It is a dragon which will strangle us if we do not crush it. Fear it more than all the demons for they are chained dogs that can bite only those who come within their reach, but self-will is a serpent which we bear in our very selves.

Let us work, then, to crush this reptile. Examine the faults we have committed through self-will, in thought, word, deed and omission. Let us ask God's pardon, pray to Him and to His most holy Mother for the grace of amendment.

Finally, let us engrave upon our heart these words: "The blessing of God follows the obedient everywhere, and His malediction is inseparable from disobedience." Follow the example of Jesus and Mary in their submission to the divine will, that you may become like Jesus Christ: "The man of my own will" (Isa. 46, 11).

Ejaculatory prayer:

> "An obedient man shall speak of victory."
> *Vir obediens loquetur victorias* (Prov. 21, 28).

SIXTH MEDITATION

The Charity and Meekness of the Blessed Virgin Mary in Her Admirable Childhood

FIRST POINT

LOVE OF THE BLESSED VIRGIN FOR ALL MANKIND

CONSIDER that God chose the Blessed Virgin from the first moment of her life to establish her in the place of Eve, as Queen and Mother of all the living. He bestowed upon her at the same time a universal love for all mankind. Grace and charity are one and the same thing, therefore it follows that the charity of the infant Mary at the commencement of her life was far greater than that of all the saints. And as her grace multiplied from moment to moment, so did her charity, until it reached so high a degree that it was comprehensible only to that of God Himself.

Consider also that when the Eternal Father chose this glorious Mary, to communicate to her His divine Paternity, He made her at the same time a participant in His paternal love for His Well-beloved Son and for all His other children. Therefore, her heart burned with a love proportionate to her dignity of Mother of God, and of the children of God.

It was this charity which drew her, when yet an infant, to solicit with tears and prayers the advent of the Saviour, and by her ardor to advance the moment of the Incarnation. It was this charity, joined to her humility and virginal purity, that disposed her to become the Mother of the Redeemer.

Let us thank the God of charity, and offer Him the glory which accrued to Him from the love of the Immaculate maiden for Him and her charity towards mankind. Let us ask her to repair our deficits in the love of God and of our fellowmen.

Meekness of the Blessed Virgin

The holy Virgin, among all pure creatures, is the most powerful in heaven and on earth. She shares in the infinite omnipotence of God. She participates in the immense wisdom of the Son of God, and in the sweetness, benignity and gentleness of the Holy Ghost, the infusion of Whose potent and benign gifts has filled her virginal heart with incomprehensible sweetness. Except the Son of God, never has there been beheld upon earth, nor will there ever be again one so gentle, so gracious, so delectable, so merciful as this lovely maiden. Her benign charity extended itself even to her cruelest enemies, the enemies of the Saviour of the world, for she knew by divine revelation, and by reading the Prophets, that the Messiah was to be persecuted and crucified by the perfidious Jews, who would vent upon the Saviour all their hatred and cruelty. Instead of praying heaven to punish these murderers, the spirit of charity and benignity animated His most sweet handmaid to pray for these miserable wretches in the words which the all-merciful Redeemer would one day utter from His Cross: "Father, forgive them, for they know not what they do" (Luke 23, 34).

O all amiable maiden, I am not astonished that the divine Spouse exclaims: "Thy lips, my spouse, are as a dropping honey-comb, honey and milk are under thy tongue" (Cant. 4, 11). And He continues, "Thy spirit is sweet above honey" (Ecclus. 24, 27). Holy Mother Church cries out in the same strain: "O clement, O loving, O sweet Virgin Mary." Immortal thanks be given to the Holy Spirit for having filled thee with the nectar of heavenly sweetness and transformed thee into His own divine gentleness. May the Eternal Father receive in satisfaction for my sins against meekness, the honor thou hast given Him by its perfect practice.

WE SHOULD STRIVE TO IMITATE THE CHARITY AND MEEKNESS OF THE BLESSED VIRGIN

If we desire to be among the true children of the benign Jesus and the gentle Mary, let us strive to imitate them in these virtues. Let us weigh often these words of the Holy Ghost: "But before all things have a constant mutual charity among yourselves" (1 Peter 4, 8). "God is charity: and he that abideth in charity, abideth in God, and God in him" (1 John 4, 16). "Shewing all mildness towards all men" (Tit. 3, 2). "Charity is patient, is kind: charity envieth not, dealeth not perversely; is not puffed up; is not ambitious, seeketh not her own, is not provoked to anger, thinketh no evil; rejoiceth not in iniquity, but rejoiceth with the truth; beareth all things, believeth all things, hopeth all things, endureth all things" (1 Cor. 13, 4-7).

Above all, let us listen to the Saviour, who says: "This is my commandment, that you love one another, as I have loved you" (John 15, 12). "Learn of me, because I am meek, and humble of heart" (Matt. 11, 29).

Let us make profitable use of these holy precepts. Examine the faults we have committed against them in any way. Pray the Son of God and His holy Mother to repair our defects, and to impart to us a share in their admirable charity and incomparable sweetness.

Ejaculatory prayer:

"For my spirit is sweet above honey."
Spiritus enim meus super mel dulcis (Ecclus. 24, 27).

SEVENTH MEDITATION

The Silence of the Blessed Virgin Mary
in Her Admirable Childhood

SILENCE OF OUR LORD DURING HIS LIFE

THE virtue of silence is most agreeable to God. The Son of God, the Eternal Word of the Father, came into the world to converse with men. He had many great and important things to say to them, yet He was silent throughout the greater part of His life. His Infancy passed in silence, He was silent in His hidden life up to the age of thirty years, in the solitude of the desert and in the anguish of His bitter Passion, without ever dispensing Himself, although He had weighty reasons for so doing.

When the holy kings came from afar to adore Him, when cruel Herod sought to kill Him, He maintained His wonderful silence. And not content with observing it in His mortal and passible life, He yet continues it in His glorious life, in the holy Sacrament of the Altar, where He has resided in the continual silence of two thousand years.

Among the reasons for our Saviour's observation of silence there are three principal ones.

By silence He wishes to teach us that He came upon earth principally and primarily to honor His Eternal Father. He knew perfectly well the means by which He could best accomplish this, and His choice of silence is an infallible proof that it is a most excellent means of honoring God and pleasing Him.

Again, He lived a silent life to repair the dishonor done to God by sins of the tongue.

Finally, by the practice of silence He merited and acquired for us the grace to make beneficial and worthy use of the gift of speech.

Let us thank the Son of God for the example He has given us of this virtue, and beg of Him the grace to profit thereby.

SECOND POINT

SILENCE OF THE BLESSED VIRGIN

The Blessed Virgin was animated by the same spirit as her Son in the practice of silence, as of every other virtue. She was eminently fitted to repeat those words of St. Paul: "Let this mind be in you, which was also in Christ Jesus" (Phil. 2, 5). This caused her to love silence, and to hate a multitude of words. We do not read anywhere that she ever broke the sacred silence of her holy childhood. And, we find in the Holy Gospel seven instances of her having spoken at any time of her life, and even then her words are few.

O most holy Virgin, I consecrate to thee my powers of speech. Grant that I may henceforth use them to speak only the language of my Most Adorable Father and my most amiable Mother.

THIRD POINT

IMPORTANCE OF SILENCE IN THE CHRISTIAN LIFE

Consider these words of St. James: "The tongue is a fire, a world of iniquity" (James 3, 6). It is the source of blasphemy, impiety, maledic-, tion, calumny, detraction, false testimony, perjury and lying; of deceit, murmuring, raillery, injurious and lascivious words. Silence preserves the soul from all these sins, and a multitude of others that follow in their train. Therefore: "If any man think himself to be religious, not bridling his tongue but deceiving his own heart, that man's religion is vain" (James 1, 26). And on the contrary: "If any man offend not in word, the same is a perfect man" (James 3, 2).

God loves silence. For, it is a sacrifice we make of our constant inclination to talk. So eminently agreeable to Him is this silence, that He is pleased when we abstain sometimes even from good words. "I was dumb and was humbled and kept silence from good things," says the Prophet David. Thus, in their silence Our Saviour and His holy Mother abstained from speaking good and holy things for they could speak naught else. St. John the Baptist retired into the desert to avoid staining the purity of life by a single useless word.

Thousands of saints have spent their lives in silence and solitude for the same reason. This is why all the founders of religious Orders have recommended silence and mortification of the tongue in their established rules, for even the praises of our tongue to God are no better than hypocrisy when the tongue alone recites them and the heart is not united thereto (Matt. 15, 7-8). "The voice of the tongue is not heard by God if that of the heart is not present," says St. Augustine. This being so, we should cultivate a deep esteem and affection for the virtue of silence. What a desire to imitate our most holy Mary! What care to guard our tongue against the least injurious word! For we must remember that our Lord has declared that on Judgment Day He will demand a severe account of every idle word.

Let us crave pardon for the sins we have committed by our tongue. Let us implore the Blessed Virgin to obtain for us the grace to imitate her and her Divine Son in the devout use of speech and in their singular love for holy silence.

Ejaculatory prayer:

"In silence and quiet the devout soul maketh progress."
  In silentio et quiete proficit anima devota (Imitation of Christ, Ch. 20, 6).

EIGHTH MEDITATION

The Modesty of the Blessed Virgin Mary in Her Admirable Childhood

EXCELLENCE OF MODESTY

MODESTY is a virtue which regulates the exterior of the individual in a manner edifying to the beholder. It is one of the fruits of the Holy Ghost, and, where modesty is, there is the Holy Spirit.

Modesty, according to St. Paul, is a visible mark of predestination. It is one of the recognizable characteristics of the elect, the saints, and the well-beloved of God: "Put ye on therefore, as the elect of God, holy and beloved, the bowels of mercy, benignity, humility, modesty, patience" (Col. 3, 12).

In the early days of the Church when the Christians were very few, they were recognized by their great modesty, which converted many of the pagans.

Let these considerations fill your mind and heart with a high esteem and great love for this virtue, and with an ardent desire to acquire it.

SECOND POINT

ADMIRABLE MODESTY OF OUR LORD DURING HIS LIFE ON EARTH

Endeavor to picture the Son of God upon earth, conversing with men. Behold the marvelous modesty which appeared in His visage, His eyes, His speech, His gait, His gestures and His entire person. The Blessed Virgin declared to St. Bridget that her Divine Son was endowed with such beauty, sweetness and modesty that His aspect gave comfort and joy not only to the good, but even to the wicked and His enemies, and that the Jews, when they were in distress and affliction, would say to one another: "Let us go and gaze upon Mary's Son: the sight of Him will console us."

Let us adore the admirable modesty of the Saviour. Let us give thanks for the honor He rendered the Eternal Father by the practice of this virtue. Let us entreat Him to grant us grace to eradicate from ourself whatever is contrary to holy modesty.

THIRD POINT

ANGELIC MODESTY OF THE BLESSED VIRGIN

Picture the angelic modesty of Mary, the little Handmaid of God. Never was there anything comparable in any creature. Her carriage, her speech and gestures, her whole exterior, whether standing or seated, whether reposing or at work, whether conversing with her neighbor or praying to God in the Temple, her angelic visage, and simple dress and manner suggested a visible angel in whom modesty had become incarnate.

The modesty of this most holy maiden proceeded from three causes.

First, from the virginal chastity which enveloped her whole exterior. Second, from her constant dwelling in the presence of God and conversing with Him in her mind and heart. Third, from her complete possession of this gift of the Holy Ghost, who was the rule of all her actions, and imprinted in her being a living and perfect image of the adorable modesty befitting the Mother of God.

Let us give thanks to God for having clothed Mary with such incomparable modesty. Let us offer this peerless modesty in reparation for our faults against this virtue. Let us resolve to practice earnestly these words of the Apostle: "Let your modesty be known to all men; the Lord is nigh."

Let us examine our own behaviour in all the exterior acts of our life, and ask the grace to correct our faults against modesty. Let us beg the Blessed Virgin to obtain this grace for us for the sole glory of her Son.

Ejaculatory prayer:

"Let your modesty be known to all men."
Modestia vestra nota sit omnibus hominibus (Phil. 4, 5).

VII

MEDITATIONS
ON
THE HOLY HEART OF MARY

VII

MEDITATIONS
ON
THE HOLY HEART OF MARY[1]

*Meditations for the Feast and Octave
of the Holy Heart of Mary*

FIRST MEDITATION

The Vigil of the Feast

Preparation for the Feast

FIRST POINT

THE FIRST DISPOSITION FOR THE FEAST OF THE
HOLY HEART OF MARY IS HUMILITY

LET us bear in mind that all the feasts celebrated in the Church are
fountains of grace, especially those of Our Lord and His Blessed
Mother. But among the feasts of our Lady that of her admirable Heart
is the essence and queen of all, for the heart is the seat of love and
charity, the queen of all virtues and the source of every grace. This
solemnity is a veritable ocean of graces and blessings which are most
valued by Our Saviour, having been acquired at the cost of His Pre-

---

[1] The two series of meditations on the Holy Heart of Mary are found in the eleventh
book of St. John Eudes's work, *The Admirable Heart of Mary*. The first series is made
up of nine meditations for the Feast of the Holy Heart of Mary and for the Octave of
the Feast. The second series dealing with the perfections of the Heart of Mary may be
used on any occasion for private devotion or community meditation. These beautiful
meditations contain an excellent summary of St. John Eudes's doctrine of the devotion
to the Holy Heart of Mary.

cious **Blood** and countless torments. For this reason Our Lord desires that we, too, should have a great esteem and singular veneration for these graces, and, consequently, that we should prepare, with much care and diligence, to receive the gifts He wishes to bestow on this great solemnity, to enable us to celebrate it worthily.

For this end there are three things to be done. First, we must humble ourselves profoundly, recognizing that we are most unworthy to participate in such a wonderful solemnity, which being the feast of a heart totally on fire with divine love, belongs rather to the Seraphim than to sinful souls such as we are, and in our position as sinners we cannot humble ourselves too deeply.

Then, again, we are deeply unworthy to share in the graces and blessings of this feast on account of our inadequate and faulty use of the graces God has already showered upon us, and by the obstacles we have put in the way of those He would have given us, had we not prevented Him. Let us humble ourselves most profoundly before God at the sight of these defects, which are only too true.

SECOND POINT

THE SECOND DISPOSITION IS PURITY OF CONSCIENCE

The second thing to be done in preparation for the Feast of the Holy Heart of Mary is to excite a lively desire to celebrate it with appropriate devotion, divesting ourselves of all that is displeasing to Our Lord and His Blessed Mother. For this end, let us carefully and seriously examine our failings, in thought, word, deed and affection, also the misuse we have made of the powers of our soul, and our interior and exterior senses, in order to humble ourselves, beg God's pardon for our offenses, confess them faithfully and correct them in our lives.

THIRD POINT

THE THIRD DISPOSITION IS UNION WITH THE ANGELS, SAINTS AND THE THREE DIVINE PERSONS OF THE BLESSED TRINITY

In order to celebrate worthily the feast of the Heart of the Mother of Fair Love, it is little, or rather, it is nothing, if we employ only the affections of our own hearts; so, as far as possible, we must make use of the complete treasures of love in heaven and on earth. The Holy Spirit, speaking by the lips of St. Paul, assures us that all things are ours (1 Cor. 3, 22), our Heavenly Father having given us all in giving us His Son. "How hath he not also, with him, given us all things?" (Rom. 8, 32). We have the right to employ all hearts as our own in celebrating the praises of our heavenly Mother.

Very particularly should we ask our good angels and all the other choirs of heavenly spirits—especially the Seraphim—also the holy patriarchs, prophets, apostles, martyrs, confessors, virgins, all holy priests and levites, and those saints who belong in a special way to the Heart of the Queen of Heaven, to unite our love with theirs, to make us sharers in their devotion to their glorious Queen, and do their utmost to help us to celebrate this rich solemnity worthily, as far as poor, weak human nature is capable of doing so.

Above all, let us offer our hearts, our bodies, our souls, our whole existence, to the infinite love of the Father, Son and Holy Ghost for the spotless Mother of our Saviour, begging Them to associate us in their divine love, and to prepare us to celebrate this feast in the way most pleasing to the Most Holy Trinity.

Ejaculatory prayer:

"My heart is ready, O God, my heart is ready."
Paratum cor meum, Deus, paratum cor meum (Ps. 107, 2).

SECOND MEDITATION

The Feast of the Holy Heart of Mary

The Holy Heart of Mary

EXCELLENCE OF THE HOLY HEART OF MARY

LET us concentrate on the subject of this feast. It is the Immaculate Heart of the Queen of Heaven and earth, the sovereign empress of the universe; it is the Heart of the only and beloved daughter of the Eternal Father, the Heart of the Mother of God, the Heart of the Spouse of the Holy Ghost; it is the Heart of the most dear Mother of all the faithful; a Heart the most worthy, noble, august, and generous, the most magnificent and charitable, the most lovable, most loved and most loving heart of all pure creatures; a heart on fire with love of God, inflamed with ardent charity towards us, deserving as many feasts as it has made acts of love and charity. Unite to it, also, the Divine Heart of Jesus, whose heart was one with His dearest Mother, through unity of spirit, affection and will. Add to these the love of all the saints and angels, who are so closely united in thought and affection with Jesus and Mary.

Such is the subject of this great and admirable feast, which is worthy of boundless veneration and praise. Be eager to celebrate it with all possible devotion.

•

SECOND POINT

THE ETERNAL FATHER GAVE US THE HOLY HEART OF MARY

We should regard this feast as a day of extraordinary joy for ourselves, the Heart of our heavenly Mother being ours on four accounts,

being given to us by the Eternal Father, by the Son of God, by the
Holy Ghost, and by our Lady herself, therefore, the love of the Heart
of Jesus and that of the saints and angels are ours also, being all united
and one in the fire of charity.

What a treasure, and what happiness for us to possess such riches!
How great should be our joy and delight! O, Dear Jesus, what return
shall I make for the innumerable and tremendous favors I am constantly receiving from Thy holy Mother? I offer Thee my heart, which
belongs to Thee, but what is it to offer Thee the love of one so worthless? I offer Thee the hearts of all Thy angels and saints, but this again
is inadequate in comparison with the immense treasure Thou hast
given me in the Heart of Thy Blessed Mother.

I offer Thee her pure Heart, which is more pleasing to Thee than
all the hearts in the universe; but even that offering is not enough to
fulfill my obligations entirely. I offer Thee Thine own Adorable Heart,
which is all on fire with infinite and boundless love for Thyself and
Thy Eternal Father. O Mary, Queen of my heart, I offer thee likewise,
the Sacred Heart of thy Divine Son, so lovable and overflowing with
love, in thanksgiving for the inestimable treasures thou hast given me
in thine own maternal Heart.

THIRD POINT

GRATITUDE TO JESUS AND MARY FOR THIS
PRECIOUS GIFT

How would we feel if a great monarch opened his vaults, all filled
with money and precious stones, giving us permission to take as much
as we wanted?

This favor would be nothing in comparison with the indescribably
rich gift the King of kings has bestowed in giving us the most lovable
Heart of His glorious Mother.

If our Holy Father the Pope allowed us to have the choice of the
most precious relics in the city of Rome, it would undoubtedly be a
very great favor, but, again, it would be slight compared with the unspeakable favor of our Lord in granting to men the treasure of the
Heart of the Queen of all Saints.

If Our Lord were to take from each one of us our own heart of flesh and blood and miraculously substitute the love of a seraph, it would be wonderful indeed, but the gift He has made of the Heart of His Blessed Mother is, in comparison, more magnificently noble and more precious.

O my Jesus, would that the hearts of all Thy creatures were employed to praise and love Thee for this incomprehensible favor! Mother of my God, Mother of Fair Love, may all the creatures in the universe be changed into so many tongues and hearts blessing thee with constant love throughout eternity. Since thou hast given me thy most admirable Heart, do thou take complete possession of my poor heart, to sacrifice it without reserve to the undiluted love and pure glory of Thy Divine Son.

Ejaculatory prayer:

"Infinite thanks to Jesus and Mary for their unspeakable gift."
Gratias infinitas Jesu et Mariae, pro inenarrabili dono ipsorum.

THIRD MEDITATION

Second Day of the Octave

The Holy Heart of Mary Reflects the Adorable Love of the Eternal Father

FIRST POINT

THE HOLY HEART OF MARY IS WITH THE HEART OF THE ETERNAL FATHER THE PRINCIPLE OF THE MYSTERY OF THE INCARNATION

WE SHOULD look upon and honor the most pure Heart of the Blessed Virgin as a living portrait and perfect image of the infinite love of the Eternal Father. The divine love of the Father of Jesus was the first cause of the Incarnation and of His Son's birth on earth, and the most pure Heart of the Mother of Jesus is its second principle. For it was the love of the Father of Mercies that moved Him to send His Son into this world to become incarnate for the salvation of men, and it was the most pure and burning love of the virginal Heart of the Mother of Grace, inflamed with charity towards God and our souls, that drew down the Eternal Son from the bosom of His Father to be born of her and thus accomplish our salvation.

SECOND POINT

OTHER REASONS WHICH MAKE THE HOLY HEART OF MARY THE IMAGE OF THE HEART OF THE ETERNAL FATHER

The holy Heart of the Blessed Virgin is the living image of the adorable love of the Eternal Father, because as the Son of God has ever dwelt and will never cease to dwell in His Father's love, so, too, He has always lived and will ever live and dwell in the Heart of His Mother. His Father's divine felicity is a paradise of delight, love and glory for Him, and His Mother's Heart as a heaven, a heaven of heavens, in which He is, in a way, far more loved and glorified than in the empyrean sphere.

Furthermore, the Father of Mercies and the God of all consolation, in His exceedingly great and Fatherly love, gave us His Well-beloved Son at the time of His Incarnation, and gives Him to us daily in the most Blessed Sacrament. So, too, the most Blessed Mother of Mercy and Consolation, in the boundless charity of her maternal Heart, gave us her dear Jesus at His birth, and does so continually in the Holy Eucharist, because being one with Him in spirit, in love and in will, she wills all that He wills and does all that He does.

Finally, the Eternal Father Himself accomplished in the holy Heart of His beloved daughter, the glorious Virgin Mary, that which He commands all faithful souls to do when He says: "Put me as a seal upon thy heart" (Cant. 8, 6). With His own hand He has impressed on her Heart a perfect semblance of the divine qualities of His love, which consequently is a perfect image of the sanctity, wisdom, goodness, mercy, benignity, charity and all the other perfections of the infinite love of our Heavenly Father.

O wondrous goodness of our eternal King, may all men and angels bless, love and praise Thee to all eternity, for having imprinted Thy likeness on the Heart of the Queen of my heart! O lovable Heart of my heavenly Mother, how I rejoice to see thee so noble, so royal, so holy, so perfect and so like unto the Creator and Sovereign Ruler of all hearts!

O holy Mother of God, art thou not my true Mother, and am not I thy poor child, although unutterably unworthy? And should not the heart of the child resemble that of the Mother? Thou seest, nevertheless, how unlike mine is to thine! O Mother of Mercy, take pity on my misery. I offer and give thee my wretched heart, whole and entire. I beseech thee by all the goodness of thy motherly Heart completely to destroy in thy unworthy child all that is displeasing to thee, and to imprint a perfect image of the holiness reigning in the Heart of its revered Mother.

Ejaculatory prayer:

> "Jesus, Fruit of the Heart of Mary, have mercy on us."
> *Jesu, fructus cordis Mariae, miserere nobis.*

FOURTH MEDITATION

Third Day of the Octave

The Holy Heart of Mary Is One with the Eternal Father and Is the Mirror of the Sacred Heart of Jesus

FIRST POINT

THE HOLY HEART OF MARY IS BUT ONE HEART WITH
THE HEART OF THE ETERNAL FATHER

THE Holy Heart of the glorious Virgin Mary is not only a vivid likeness of the infinite love of the Eternal Father, the Father of Virgins, but is one with it, one, not in unity of nature or essence, but in unity of spirit, with love and affection. For the Mother of Jesus never had any other spirit, will, or affections but those of the Father of Jesus, and attained that union, or rather that unity, by three means:

1. By entire separation from all sin.

2. By perfect detachment from the world, from self-love and from all created things.

3. By a most ardent love for the Divine Will, and by a prompt and cordial submission and abandonment to all its designs and orders.

O dearest Mother, I rejoice unspeakably to see thy blessed Heart thus united and conformed to the adorable will of our Heavenly Father, and render Him infinite thanks for this exalted union. To thee, my great and powerful Queen, I offer my heart. Cause it to share thy boundless hatred of sin; sever the bonds and break the chains that bind this poor slave; detach me entirely from the world, from self-will and from all that is displeasing to God. Consecrate me to His divine will, praying that it may be established in my heart, and reign there absolutely for ever more, so that in imitation of thee I may be one in mind, will and heart with my loving Heavenly Father.

The Holy Heart of Mary Is the Mirror
of the Heart of Jesus

The Heart of the Mother of our Divine Saviour is a beautiful mirror in which her Beloved Son has depicted, reflected and represented most excellently, all the virtues that reign in His Sacred Heart. They who see the Heart of the Queen of Angels, as the angels do, find therein a vivid and perfect reproduction of the love, charity, humility, obedience, patience, purity, contempt of the world, hatred of sin and all the other virtues of the most adorable Heart of Jesus. From the very depths of our own heart, then, let us return Him fitting thanks, and offer it to our Blessed Lady, earnestly begging her to obtain for us the grace that, as her Heart is a living portrait of the Sacred Heart of her Son Jesus, ours may be in like manner an image of hers.

Let us, on our part, cultivate a great desire to behold that virginal heart, on which, as on a beautiful mirror, we should often fix our eyes that we may see the stains on our soul, in order to efface them and engrave on our heart by earnest imitation all the virtues which shine forth in the peerless Heart of our heavenly Mother, especially humility, obedience and charity; for all the happiness, perfection and glory of our hearts consist in so living that we may be vivid reproductions of the Sacred Hearts of Jesus and Mary.

The Holy Heart of Mary Is but One Heart with
the Heart of Jesus

Although the Heart of Jesus is distinct from that of Mary, and infinitely surpasses it in excellence and holiness, nevertheless, God has so closely united these two Hearts that we may say with truth that they are but one, because they have always been animated with the same spirit and filled with the same sentiments and affections. If St. Bernard could say he had but one heart with Jesus: *"Bene mihi est, cor unum cum Jesu habeo,"* and if it was said of the first Christians that they had but one heart and one soul, so great was the union amongst them, how much more can we say that Jesus and Mary had but one heart and one soul, considering how closely they were bound together by the perfect conformity of mind, will and sentiment that existed between the Divine Son of God and His Immaculate Mother.

Add to this that Jesus so lives and reigns in Mary that He is the Soul of her soul, the Spirit of her spirit, the Heart of her heart; so much so that we might well say that Jesus is enshrined in the Heart of Mary so completely that in honoring and glorifying her Heart, we honor and glorify Jesus Christ Himself.

O Jesus, living in the Heart of Mary! be the life of my heart. Mary, Mother of Jesus, obtain by thy intercession, I beseech thee, that I may have but one heart with thy Beloved Son and thyself.

Ejaculatory prayer:

"Who will grant me that my heart may be one for ever with the Heart of Jesus and Mary?"
Quis dabit mihi ut cor meum, cum Corde Jesu et Mariae cor unum fiat in aeternum?

FIFTH MEDITATION

Fourth Day of the Octave

Reasons Inspiring Us to Honor the Holy Heart of Mary

FIRST POINT

THE HOLY HEART OF MARY IS, AFTER THE HEART OF JESUS,
THE MOST EXALTED THRONE OF DIVINE LOVE

LET us recollect that God has given us the feast of the most pure Heart of the Blessed Virgin so that we may render on that day all the respect, honor and praise that we possibly can. To enkindle this spirit within us let us consider our motivating obligations.

The first is that we ought to love and honor whatever God loves and honors, and that by which He is loved and glorified. Now, after the adorable Heart of Jesus there has never been either in heaven or on earth, nor ever will be, a heart which has been so loved and honored by God, or which has given Him so much glory as that of Mary, the Mother of Jesus. Never has there been, nor will there ever be a more exalted throne of divine love. In that Heart divine love possesses its fullest empire, for it ever reigns without hindrance or interruption, and with it reign likewise all the laws of God, all the Gospel maxims and every Christian virtue.

This incomparable Heart of the Mother of our Redeemer is a glorious heaven, a Paradise of delights for the Most Holy Trinity. According to St. Paul, the hearts of the faithful are the dwelling-place of our Lord Jesus Christ, and Jesus Christ Himself assures us that the Father, the Son and the Holy Ghost take up Their abode in the hearts of those who love God. Who, therefore, can doubt that the Most Holy Trinity has always made His home and established the reign of His glory in an admirable and ineffable manner in the virginal Heart of her who is the Daughter of the Father, the Mother of the Son, the Spouse of the Holy Ghost, who herself loves God more than all other creatures together?

How much then are we not obliged to love this exalted and most lovable Heart?

The Holy Heart of Mary Is the Principle of all the Greatness of the Blessed Virgin

There is another very special obligation embodied in these words of the Holy Ghost: "All the glory of the king's daughter is within" (Ps. 44, 14). All the glory, all the grace, all the sanctity, and all that is great and worthy of honor in the Queen of Heaven takes its origin from within, from her Heart, because it was by the profound humility, the peerless purity and burning love of her virginal Heart, that she, the Virgin of virgins, won the Well-beloved of the Eternal Father, that is His Only Son, whom she drew down to her heart and caused to dwell within her. In consequence she has been raised to the sublime dignity of eldest Daughter of the Father, the Mother of the Son, Spouse of the Holy Ghost, the Sanctuary of the Blessed Trinity, the Queen of the Universe, and has, moreover, been given to us as our Mother and our Sovereign. For this reason we ought not only to honor the most holy Virgin Mary in some of her mysteries or qualities, or in certain of her actions, nor even in her exalted person alone, but we ought first and chiefly to honor in her the source and origin of the dignity and sanctity of all these mysteries, qualities and actions, and even of her person; that is to say, her love and charity, for love and charity are the measure of merit and the principle of all sanctity.

It was the love and charity of her Heart, so full of both that sanctified all the thoughts, words, actions and sufferings of our Saviour's most holy Mother; sanctified also her memory, understanding, will and all the faculties of both the superior and inferior parts of her soul. This love adorned her whole interior and exterior life with such marvelous holiness; containing in itself, to a sovereign degree, all the virtues, gifts and fruits of the Holy Spirit, which rendered her worthy to bear and nourish Him who supports the whole world, and Who is the life of all living things. It was the love and charity of Mary's Heart that exalted her to a place in heaven above all the Seraphim and established her on a throne of incomparable glory, grandeur, happiness and power in proportion to her unsurpassable dignity as Mother of God.

Add to this that our Lady's most gracious Heart is an inexhaustible source of gifts, graces, favors and blessings for all who love this Mother of Beautiful Love, and devoutly honor her most lovable Heart. In short, we have unspeakable obligations, both in number and quality, to the royal and maternal Heart of our great Queen and dearest Mother, on which account we can never sufficiently honor, praise and glorify her.

Ejaculatory prayer:

"Infinite, boundless, eternal thanks be to the most loving Heart of Mary."

Gratias infinitas, immensas, aeternas, amantissimo Cordi Mariae.

SIXTH MEDITATION

Fifth Day of the Octave

Further Reasons for Honoring the Holy Heart of Mary

The Holy Heart of Mary Is a Living Gospel

THE virginal Heart of the Mother of God is the faithful depository of all the mysteries and marvels of our Saviour's life, according to the testimony of St. Luke: "And his mother kept all these words in her heart" (Luke 2, 51). Her Heart is a living book, an eternal Gospel, in which the Holy Spirit has inscribed that wonderful life in letters of gold. It is this book of life we should incessantly study in order to understand perfectly and love ardently the beauty of all the Christian virtues, whose practice imparts true life. Above all, we ought to study the wondrous excellence of holy humility, as well as the way of practising it and ridding our hearts entirely of the accursed canker-worm of pride and vanity which works such terrible havoc, not only in the souls of the children of perdition, but even in the hearts of the children of God.

O Mother of Goodness, what obligations we have to honor thy most lovable Heart in which thou hast preserved such precious treasures, for which be thou blessed for all eternity. Cause our names to be written in that book of life, we beseech thee, and help us to study deeply the beauteous truths and holy maxims inscribed therein.

The Holy Heart of Mary Carefully Watched Over the Saviour of the World

Who can describe the burning love for her Son Jesus, which filled the incomparable Heart of the Mother of God? How studiously watchful she was in caring for Him whom she nurtured, clothed and tended in order to give Him to us as our Saviour, for which we owe her a debt of gratitude beyond all power to conceive!

THIRD POINT

The Holy Heart of Mary Suffered Intense Pains for Us

Who could enumerate the intense sorrow and cruel wounds that lacerated the maternal Heart of the Mother of Jesus throughout her whole life, especially at the time of her Son's Passion, and above all when, at the foot of the Cross, it was transpierced with a sword of sorrow? "In the Heart of the Blessed Virgin," says St. Lawrence Justinian, "was clearly mirrored the Passion of her Son Jesus, and a perfect representation of His death." "It was then," says Richard of St. Laurente, "that those inspired words were accomplished in this virginal Heart: 'The sadness of the heart is every plague'" (Ecclus. 25, 17), that is, there was no part of this afflicted Mother's Heart that was not pierced through and through with a thousand darts of anguish.

Now, it was we who brought upon her all these sorrows by our sins; therefore, we are obliged to render her all the honor and glory we possibly can, in order to repair in some measure the agony and grief we have caused her.

Ejaculatory prayer:

"O Jesus, by the most loving Heart of Thy holy Mother, transpierced with a sword of sorrow, have mercy on us."

Per Cor amantissimum sanctissimae Matris tuae doloris gladio transfixum, miserere nobis, Jesu.

SEVENTH MEDITATION

Sixth Day of the Octave

Other Reasons Which Bind Us to Have a Special Devotion to the Holy Heart of Mary

THE HOLY HEART OF MARY IS THE TRUE ALTAR OF HOLOCAUSTS

THE devout and learned Gerson likens the loving Heart of our Saviour's Mother to the bush seen by Moses, ever burning with the flames of most ardent charity but never consumed. Gerson says that it is the true altar of holocaust on which the sacred fire of divine love glows day and night. The sacrifice most pleasing to God and most beneficial to the human race, after the self-immolation of Our Lord on the Cross is the divine holocaust which the Blessed Virgin offered to the Eternal Father on the altar of her Heart, when she so frequently and with so much love offered to God in sacrifice that same Jesus, her Only Son so dearly beloved. We may add that He was sacrificed only once on the Cross, but was immolated a thousand upon a thousand times in the Heart of His holy Mother, that is, as many times as she offered Her Divine Son to the Eternal Father for us.

O holy Altar, what veneration is thy due, and what praises all creatures owe thee! Mother of Love, take our hearts and unite them with thy Well-beloved Son as a holocaust and sacrifice to Our Heavenly Father.

The Holy Heart of Mary Is the Principle of Jesus' Life

What veneration we owe to the august Heart of the Mother of God, which was the principle of the life humanly divine and divinely human of the Infant Jesus while He dwelt within her! At that time, the Heart of the Mother is as much the source of her child's life as of her own, the one depending on it as much as the other.

What praise and respect are therefore due to the loving Heart of Mary on which the Infant Jesus chose that His life should depend, to that Heart which was the principle of two lives both so holy, so precious, to that Heart on which the adorable Babe so often reposed when in His Mother's arms! That Heart, most noble and revered organ of that virginal body gave a Body to the Eternal Word to be for all eternity the object of the adoration and praise of all celestial and blessed spirits. The Heart of our Lady being the principle of the life of our Head and consequently of His members, and being the principle of life to Jesus and Mary, is also that of the lives of their children. "*Vitam datam per Virginem, Gentes redemptae plaudite.*"

O Mother of Goodness, may the hearts of all the faithful unceasingly bless and love thy maternal and devoted Heart! May it be the heart of my heart, the soul of my soul and the life of my life.

Ejaculatory prayer:

"O Mary, my life, my sweetness and my dearest hope!"
O Maria, vita, dulcedo, et spes mea carissima.

EIGHTH MEDITATION

Seventh Day of the Octave

Three Additional Reasons for Honoring the Holy Heart of Our Blessed Mother

FIRST POINT

THE HOLY HEART OF MARY IS THE TEMPLE OF
THE HOLY TRINITY

THE admirable Heart of Mary is the august temple of the Divinity, a temple built by the hand of the Almighty, a temple consecrated by the continual indwelling of the Divine Spirit, a temple dedicated to eternal love, a temple never profaned either by the smallest sin, or taint of the spirit of the world, or by love of self or any other creature. Our Lady's Heart is the temple in which, after the Divine Heart of Jesus, the Most Holy Trinity is more perfectly adored, loved and glorified than in any other temple, material or spiritual, in heaven or on earth. Within this temple, O glorious Virgin, thy spirit ever dwelt in seclusion and recollection, offering to God a continual sacrifice of praise, honor and fervent love. It is there that I desire unceasingly to adore, bless and love the Creator of all hearts who made and sanctified it for His glory, wherein He will be eternally glorified in a higher degree · than in all the empyrean heavens.

SECOND POINT

THE HOLY HEART OF MARY IS THE PARADISE OF DELIGHTS
OF THE NEW ADAM

This wondrous Heart is to the new Adam, that is, to Jesus Christ Our Lord, a veritable Paradise of delights, of which He is the real

249

Tree of life, planted in the midst of this Paradise where neither the serpent nor sin have ever entered, whose gates have always been carefully guarded, not by a Seraph only, but by the very King of the Cherubim and Seraphim.

What delight the Divine Son of Mary found in that motherly Heart which loved Him more ardently than He had ever been loved, even by the purest spirits in the heavenly Paradise! What a joy it was to thy Divine Babe, O Blessed Mother, when He reposed on thy virginal breast, and thou wast wholly filled, penetrated and possessed by His holy spirit and His divine love, which utterly transported and absorbed thy whole soul, spirit and heart.

O Mother of Fair Love, obtain for me that I may have no other Paradise or pleasure in this world to love, serve and honor Jesus, the Son of Mary, and Mary, the Mother of Jesus.

THIRD POINT

THE HOLY HEART OF MARY IS THE KING OF HEARTS

After the adorable Heart of Jesus, the Sovereign Monarch of heaven and earth, the august Heart of Mary, the Queen of Angels and the Mother of the King of kings, is the eternal King of all hearts which were created to adore and love God. Therefore, all men are bound to pay homage to the holy Heart of Mary as to their Sovereign.

O royal Heart of my loving Queen, I wish to honor and revere thee as the true king of my heart. Exercise thy power over my most unworthy heart that thou mayest destroy everything that displeases thee and establish in it the reign of thy love and of all thy virtues.

Ejaculatory prayer:

"May the Heart of Jesus and of Mary live and reign in my heart for ever."

Vivat et regnet Cor Jesu et Mariae in corde meo in aeternum.

NINTH MEDITATION

Octave Day of the Feast

The Holy Heart of Mary Is the Heart of the Mother of Fair Love and Charity

FIRST POINT

THE HOLY HEART OF MARY IS A FURNACE OF THE LOVE OF GOD

WE SHOULD contemplate and honor the most lovable Heart of our Lord's Mother as a furnace of the love of God.

It is a furnace of love because sin, worldly affection, self-love have never had part therein, because it has always been replete and aflame with the fire of Divine love.

It is a furnace of love because it has never loved aught but God, and His holy will, which it sought in Him and for His sake.

It is a furnace of love because our Blessed Lady always loved God with her whole Heart, with her whole soul and with her whole strength. All her actions were done from the purest love of God, nor had she ever any other intention in all her thoughts, words and sufferings but to please Him, doing everything *"Corde magno et animo volenti,"* with a great heart and all possible perfection, in order to give all possible pleasure to His divine majesty.

Mary's Heart is a furnace of love not only because it willed always exactly what God willed, and never deflected from His holy will, but because she ever placed all her happiness and joy in the most lovable Will of God.

It is a furnace of such burning love that not even the torrents and floods of bitter sorrows that deluged her soul were ever capable, I will not say of extinguishing, but of cooling in the smallest degree the glowing flames of that fire.

It is a furnace of love in which the Holy Spirit, who is a consuming fire, enkindled His divine flame in her virginal Heart at the first moment of its existence, and never ceased to increase it more and more, from moment to moment, up to the last breath of her life.

O sacred fire and flame of this holy furnace, come and consume our hearts.

SECOND POINT

THE HOLY HEART OF MARY IS BURNING WITH LOVE FOR JESUS

The Heart of the Mother of Fair Love is a furnace of love in which the Only Son of God, who is also the only Son of Mary, ever dwelt and will continue to dwell eternally, He who is the essence of love, called in Holy Scripture, "a consuming fire" (Deut. 4, 24). Judge from this what burning flames, what glowing heat He generated in His holy Mother's Heart, where He found no obstacle to His designs. It is as if the Beloved Son of Mary existed in the Heart of His holy Mother as an immense furnace of divine love in the centre of another furnace all on fire with that same love, and from it the flames reached to the inmost being of the Seraphim to inflame them more and more and even to the subject of the Eternal Father's infinite felicity, His Well-beloved Son, who, inspired by the love of Mary, was drawn from His Father's bosom down to her virginal breast.

O holy furnace, blessed are they who approach thy sacred fire! Still more happy they who are enkindled by thy heavenly flames, and happiest of all those who cast themselves into that divine brazier to be wholly consumed therein.

O furnace of love, spread thy flames throughout the entire universe so that my Saviour's desire may be accomplished which He expressed, saying that He came to cast fire on the earth, and desired that it might be enkindled in the hearts of all men (Luke 12, 49).

Whoever wishes to burn with this holy fire must strive to extinguish within himself the flames of love of the world and self. He must study to love God alone, with his whole heart and to perform each and all his actions for love of Our Lord and to do them well, having no other intention, at any time, except to please Him, and for love of

Him to place all his joy in the fulfilment of His holy will and in the acceptance of all possible crosses.

O Mother of Love, obtain by thy prayers that this transformation may be accomplished in us.

The Holy Heart of Mary Is a Furnace of Charity Towards Men

The pure Heart of the Mother of Jesus is a furnace of charity towards mankind; a furnace in which there has never been a single thought or sentiment contrary to virtue; a furnace of such burning charity for even the greatest enemies that she sacrificed for them her Only and Dearly Beloved Son at the very time they were cruelly putting Him to death, and piercing her maternal heart with a thousand darts of anguish.

It is a furnace of charity for her beloved children, whom she loves so ardently that if the love of all fathers and mothers past, present and future were united in one heart, it would be but a spark in comparison with the furnace of love burning in the Heart of our heavenly Mother.

It is a furnace on fire with such charity and zeal for souls, that she would have willingly suffered all the torments of hell to help to save a single soul. Moses, St. Paul, St. Catherine of Siena and several other saints have been ready and willing to do so, but how much more the Queen of all Saints, who was more filled with love for souls than all the saints together.

Return thanks, then, to the Divine Son of Mary for having so inflamed her Heart with that fire of divine charity for us, with which His own is burning. Thank her also for all she has accomplished in her charity for the human race. Desire earnestly to imitate your holy Mother in the practice of that virtue. Examine the faults you have committed against charity in the past, in order to humble yourself and beg pardon of God, offering Him the most lovable Heart of our Lady in reparation.

Also offer your own heart to the most holy Virgin, begging her to destroy in it all that is contrary to charity, and engrave instead a perfect image of her charity towards her enemies, her friends, and the souls of all mankind.

Ejaculatory prayer:

"O Heart of Jesus and of Mary, burning with love, may our heart be for ever immersed in you."

O Cor Jesu et Mariae, fornax amoris, in te cor nostrum demergatur in aeternum.

Eight Other Meditations on The Holy Heart of Mary

FIRST MEDITATION

The Holy Heart of Mary Is Our Sun, Our Treasure, and Our Refuge

FIRST POINT

THE HOLY HEART OF MARY IS OUR SUN

OUR loving Saviour has given us the very benign Heart of His Blessed Mother as a divine sun to clear the shadows of this earth, to warm us in the wintry cold of this mortal life, to gladden and to console us in earthly sadness and sorrows, and to vivify and fortify us in the lethargy and weakness of human fragility. Infinite thanksgiving be to the adorable Sun of eternity, Jesus Christ, for the gift of this sun!

O Mother of Fair Love, since your Well-beloved Son has given us your maternal heart to be our sun, enlighten our minds with your celestial radiance so that in knowing Jesus Christ, we may render the service, honor, and love that we owe Him. Illuminate our hearts so that in knowing the horror of sin we may have a hatred for it, in knowing the world we may detach ourselves from it, and in knowing ourselves we may have scorn for self. Make us participants in the celestial warmth of thy saintly charity so that we may love God above all things and our neighbor as ourself. Console us in our desolation, fortify us in our weakness. May thy shining Heart be the true sun of our hearts.

THE HOLY HEART OF MARY IS OUR TREASURE

Our benign Saviour has given us the Sacred Heart of His beloved Mother as the inestimable treasure of an infinity of good. If St. Chrysostom calls the very charitable heart of St. Paul, "a fountain of innumerable blessings" for the Christians who invoke the help of this divine apostle, what words must one use in speaking of the incomparable heart of the Queen of Apostles?

It is a treasury in which immense riches are locked, because the most blessed Virgin kept hidden in her Heart, while on this earth, and will continue to do so eternally in heaven, all the mysteries of the life of her Divine Son our Redeemer, mysteries which are the price of our redemption, the source of the sanctification of the Church Triumphant and the consolation of the Church Suffering.

Her Heart is a treasury which conserves in itself all the graces merited and acquired for us by our Saviour through His sufferings and death on earth. Therefore, our Lady is called by all the saints, "the admirable treasure of the Church," "the treasury of God's graces," "the most holy treasure of all sanctity," and "the treasure of salvation." Our Lord has enclosed in her breast and Heart all the treasures of His graces, which are given to us through her mediation; therefore, St. Bernard said that all God's gifts to mankind pass first through the hands of the Mother of Divine Grace: *Nihil nos Deus habere voluit, quod per Mariae manu non transiret.*

O what joy it is to possess so rich a treasure! O what profound gratitude we owe to our very benign Redeemer! But if we wish to enjoy the inconceivable blessings destined for us in this precious treasure, let us be careful to render to the Queen of heaven the honor and praise due her, and let us be careful to have respectful and confident recourse to her in all our needs. We shall find in this treasury the means to pay our spiritual debts, to satisfy all our obligations, to practise all Christian virtues, to live in a saintly manner, and to know and love God worthily.

THE HOLY HEART OF MARY IS OUR REFUGE

Our very loving Jesus has given us the divine Heart of His glorious Mary to be a tower of great strength, an impregnable fortress, an all-powerful refuge where we can take shelter against the enemies of our salvation. Have recourse to our Lady, tower of ivory, in all the temptations of the world, the flesh and the devil because her heart is so filled with goodness for all kinds of people that never has anyone in need implored her help in vain. Do not fear that her heart will fail you; retire with confidence into this most beautiful refuge, and you will feel the effects of its strong protection.

Ejaculatory prayer:

"O Heart of Mary, tower of strength, protect us."
O Cor Mariae, turris fortissima, protege nos semper!

SECOND MEDITATION

The Holy Heart of Mary Is Our Rule, Our Heart, a Fountain of Wine, Milk and Honey, and Our Oracle

FIRST POINT

THE HOLY HEART OF MARY IS OUR RULE

THE sovereign Legislator has given us the august Heart of His glorious Mother as a holy rule which, if faithfully kept, will make us saintly. The Heart of Mary is a rule of the celestial life which we must live, a rule with which we must be clothed. Her heart encloses all the maxims we must follow, the saintly dispositions with which we must perform all our actions. It is a rule for the sentiments and affections which must abide in our hearts, and a rule of all our thoughts, words and actions. In one word, it is a rule to guide both our interior and exterior life.

Let us render thanks to the adorable Legislator for having given us a rule so holy, amiable, sweet and easy, filled with love. Your joy and pleasure must be in keeping it since this rule is simply the all sweet and loving Heart of our adorable Mother, who will never cease to obtain for us from God the graces necessary to observe it faithfully. Therefore, you must often scrutinize this divine rule, studying it carefully so that you may follow it honestly and exactly.

SECOND POINT

THE HOLY HEART OF MARY WAS GIVEN TO US TO BE OUR HEART

The Son of God gave us the holy Heart of His most cherished Mother, which is none other than His own true Heart, so that His children have only one Heart with their Father and Mother, and all the members of His family have only the heart of their adorable chief.

Let us remember that we constantly serve, love and adore God with a heart worthy of its infinite grandeur: *Corde magno et animo volenti;* with a heart all pure and holy, singing His divine praises and performing all our actions with saintliness, love, humility and with all the other holy dispositions characteristic of this beautiful Heart of Mary.

To accomplish this, at the beginning of each action, we must completely renounce our own heart, which means our mind, self-love and will, and we give ourselves to our Lord, to be united with the love of His Heart and the Heart of His most Blessed Mother. Let us work, then, to become detached from our own earthly, wicked and depraved heart, so that we shall gain a Heart truly celestial, holy and divine.

THIRD POINT

The Holy Heart of Mary Is a Fountain of Wine, Milk and Honey

Our most sweet Jesus has given us the very benign Heart of His precious Mother as a fountain of wine, milk and honey, from which we draw the charity, gentleness and meekness which we must show to our neighbor. Our Lord has also given us her Heart as an oracle to be devoutly consulted in all our doubts and perplexities, so that we may know and follow faithfully His adorable will.

Oh Mother of Fair Love, bind our hearts so closely to yours that they may never be separated! Pray that the hearts of your children may have no other sentiments than those of the most Immaculate Heart of their all-perfect Mother.

Ejaculatory prayer:

> "Queen of our hearts, direct our hearts forever."
> *Regina cordis, dirige cor nostrum in aeternum.*

THIRD MEDITATION

The Holy Heart of Mary Is the Sanctuary
of the Human Passions

FIRST POINT

THE PASSIONS OF THE SACRED HEART OF JESUS ARE
DEIFIED THROUGH THE HYPOSTATIC UNION

ELEVEN passions are implanted in the human heart, namely: love, hate, desire and aversion, joy, sadness, hope, despair, boldness, fear and anger. Adore all these emotions in the divine Heart of our Saviour, where, according to the theologians, they have been exalted to divinity through the hypostatic union, and by sanctifying grace which reigns perfectly in the Son of God made man. Thank Him for the glory that He has rendered to His Heavenly Father, by His most holy use of His human body. Offer to the Adorable Father all the honor thus rendered to Him by His divine Son. Give your heart to Jesus, together with all its passions. Beg Him to unite your emotions with His, to bless and sanctify them through His and to grant you all the graces necessary to imitate Him in the holy use of these passions.

SECOND POINT

THE PASSIONS OF THE HOLY HEART OF MARY ARE
ENTIRELY SUBMISSIVE TO THE HOLY SPIRIT

These same passions existed in the amiable Heart of the Blessed Virgin, where they were so perfectly subjected to reason and to the spirit of God who possessed her entirely, that always her passions were under entire control. Her love was constantly for God above, and for the things God loves. She hated only the objects of God's hatred. She rejoiced in the things that were pleasing to His divine majesty. Nothing was capable of bringing sadness to her except those things which could sadden her Well-beloved Son.

Her only fear was the filial fear of saying, thinking or doing anything displeasing to God. She had no other desire but to accomplish wholly and entirely His most adorable will. Her entire hope rested in God alone. It is a certainty that her Heart was filled with a saintly boldness and a marvelous generosity to undertake and to do the acts pertaining to the service of God no matter how difficult. She understood that she could do nothing of herself, and remained continually in a state of humiliation and in great scorn of herself, never having hoped or believed herself able to do anything through her own strength alone for the glory of His divine majesty.

That is why we must honor the very august Heart of the Mother of God, as the sanctuary of all passions, which human emotions were sanctified so excellently that they have been actuated only by the Holy Spirit, who possessed and animated them much more perfectly than human mind can conceive. Let us offer to God all the honor accorded to His majesty by the Holy Virgin in her perfect use of these same passions, and beg her to obtain for us all the necessary and suitable graces to enable us, through a faithful imitation, to govern our emotions according to the example of our divine Mother.

THIRD POINT

We Must Make a Fitting Use of Our Passions

Let us make an exact and careful examination of all our passions, in order to perceive our mistakes and abuse of them; humiliate ourself and ask pardon of God, begging Our Lord and His holy Mother to correct our errors and to take complete possession of our heart and all its passions. Beg them to teach you how to use your emotions for the love and glory of the Most Holy Trinity.

Ejaculatory prayer:

"My soul doth magnify the admirable Heart of Jesus and Mary."
Magnificat anima mea Cor admirabile Jesu et Mariae!

FOURTH MEDITATION

The Holy Heart of Mary Is the Kingdom and Throne of All Virtues

FIRST POINT

THE HOLY HEART OF MARY POSSESSED PERFECTLY ALL CHRISTIAN VIRTUES

THE Holy Spirit, having considered the most sacred Virgin from the moment of her Immaculate Conception as the one chosen from all eternity to be the Mother of God, infused in her Heart the three theological virtues: faith, hope, and charity; the four cardinal virtues: prudence, justice, temperance and fortitude, and all the other virtues: religion, humility, obedience, patience, meekness, purity, etc. The Holy Spirit bestowed the excellence of the virtues, in her virginal Heart in a degree proportionate to the dignity and grace of the Mother of God. Therefore, this admirable Virgin possessed all these virtues from the first moment of her life, in such a high degree of perfection that the greatest saints never equalled her excellence even in the closing days of their heroic lives.

All these virtues flourished constantly in the Heart of the Mother of God, and from time to time during her life they were increased in merit. So much so that no mind can comprehend the degree of perfection attained when Mary left this world to be assumed into heaven.

O Queen of Virtue, what great joy my heart feels in beholding thee as Queen of all virtue, supreme over all the angels and saints of Paradise! Oh my Jesus, I render Thee infinite gratitude for having given to your holy Mother a Heart that is most saintly and wholly consecrated to Thy divine love.

The Reign of Christian Virtues in the Holy Heart of Mary

Not only did all virtue abide in the holy Heart of the Mother of our Saviour, but in addition it established its throne there from the earliest moment of her life and reigns in her Heart forever in a most special manner. It reigned in a sovereign degree over her thoughts, words, actions, and over all her most intimate feelings, both interior and exterior; consequently, these perfect virtues made God reign more perfectly and gloriously in her Heart than in the empyrean world.

The all-perfect power of the Eternal Father ruled there through the admirable effects continually produced in her Heart: "He hath done great things to me" (Luke 1, 49).

The infinite wisdom of the Son of God reigned in the Heart of Mary through the Christian virtues that communicated to her great knowledge and light. The love and goodness of the Holy Spirit reigned in the Heart of Mary through the Christian virtues that enkindled in her great love and enthusiasm.

Infinite glory be to the Father, Son and Holy Ghost for having established in the royal heart of the Queen of Heaven the throne of all the virtues and the sovereign kingdom of, their incomprehensible glory! Oh how very fitting it is to render all possible honor and praise to this incomparable Heart, where the Most Holy Trinity is infinitely more glorified than in all the hearts of heaven and earth.

We Must Practice All the Christian Virtues

The Blessed Virgin is our Mother; therefore, having the honor of being her children, although greatly unworthy, we must try to resemble her as closely as possible. Consequently we must imprint in our hearts a living image of the virtues that reign in her heart.

To accomplish this, let each one of us make a careful and honest examination of his heart, in order to know how far removed it is from the virtues and sanctity of the Heart of our divine Mother, and to humiliate ourselves before God and her. We must make a strong resolution to begin in earnest to engrave on our hearts the semblance of the perfections of the divine heart of the Queen of the Angels.

Ejaculatory prayer:

"O Heart of Mary, throne of all virtues, reign in our hearts forever."
O Cor Mariae, thronus omnium virtutum, regna super cor nostrum in aeternum!

FIFTH MEDITATION

The Holy Heart of Mary Is the Centre of Humility

FOUNDATIONS OF HUMILITY IN THE HOLY
HEART OF MARY

REFLECT on the fact that humility is the centre of the Heart of the most holy Virgin. Being the foundation stone of all virtue, it has occupied the first position in her Heart since her Immaculate Conception. Humility has always found in her breast complete rest and satisfaction, never having been attacked by its enemies, because it is established there on four solid foundations. The first is the perfect knowledge of humility possessed by this humble Virgin, so much so that she understood completely that being created by God from nothing as other creatures, she was nothing, had nothing, and would never be anything by herself. She knew very well that being the daughter of Adam she would have been conceived in original sin if God had not preserved her and, consequently, she would have been capable of all sins whose source is original sin.

The second foundation of her humility is her profound knowledge of all the gifts, graces and innumerable privileges which God showered upon her, and the infinite dignity of the Mother of God, with which God honored her. She knew well the rule that the Holy Spirit gave to all mankind in these words: *Quanto magnus est, humilia te in omnibus,* which point out, as St. Augustine says, that the humility of the creature must be proportionate to the favors that it receives from its Creator. That is why the infinite grace of the Mother of God obliged that most blessed Virgin to humiliate herself most profoundly.

The third foundation is her understanding that the sovereign and infinite grandeur of God demands deep humility on the part of the creature: *Summae celsitudini summa debetur humilitas.* Her ardent zeal for the honor and glory of God carried her to the point of consummate humility before His divine majesty.

The fourth foundation is that, beholding her Beloved Son plunged into the abyss of scorn, ignominy and shame, for the love of men, but much more for love of her than for all other children of Adam, she longed to abase herself below Him, thus her self-annihilation knew no end. It is thus that her Heart was the centre of humility.

O very humble Virgin, thou wast chosen to crush the head of the serpent which is pride. Crush it completely then in my heart and enlighten me with thy divine wisdom so that I may imitate thee in thy vast humility!

SECOND POINT

EFFECTS OF HUMILITY IN THE HOLY HEART OF MARY

Consider the five prodigious effects of this humility in the Heart of the holy Virgin.

The first effect is that because God elevated her to the highest honor that a pure creature can attain, she never had any self-esteem, but always humiliated herself.

The second effect is that having stood constant and firm amid all the ignominies and insults she suffered in the passion of her Divine Son, her soul, remaining quiet even when it was pierced by a sword of sorrow, was greatly troubled by the praise of St. Gabriel, more insupportable than all her trials and sorrows.

The third effect is that the praise and benediction of St. Elizabeth at the time of the Visitation inspired her to disclaim all honor and give all the glory to God in her divine Canticle, the "Magnificat."

The fourth effect of her boundless humility is that she concealed the extraordinary favor of the Divine Goodness so that God had to send an angel to St. Joseph to expressly communicate to him the mystery that his holy spouse was too humble to reveal.

The fifth effect is that she continually sought the company of the poor, sinners and other miserable people, and that after the Ascension of her Divine Son, she sought the lowest place in the gatherings of the faithful.

What immeasurable glory thou hast rendered to God, by thy very profound humility, O most humble Virgin! May eternal praise be thine! Oh how I long to imitate thee in this holy virtue! Obtain for me, I beseech thee, from thy Beloved Son, all the graces that I need for this purpose.

THIRD POINT

WAY TO ACQUIRE HUMILITY

Examine carefully all your faults against humility—in your thoughts, affections, words and actions. Ask pardon from God, make a strong resolution of amendment, and pray constantly to the most sacred Virgin to obtain the grace to practise humility.

Ejaculatory prayer:

"O Heart of Mary, centre of humility, intercede for us."

O Cor Mariae, centrum humilitatis, intercede pro nobis!

SIXTH MEDITATION

The Holy Heart of Mary Is the Treasure of the Gifts of the Holy Spirit

FIRST POINT

THE EFFECT OF THE GIFTS OF WISDOM, INTELLIGENCE, COUNSEL, AND FORTITUDE IN THE HOLY HEART OF MARY

AFTER considering and revering the august Heart of the Queen of Heaven as the highest throne of all virtue, we must contemplate and honor her Heart as the richest treasure of the Holy Spirit, where He deposited immense and inestimable riches, among them seven incomparable graces which are commonly called the seven gifts of the Holy Ghost: the gifts of wisdom and understanding, counsel and fortitude, knowledge and piety and fear of the Lord.

There is this difference between the moral virtues and the gifts of the Holy Ghost: the moral virtues are given to make our souls stronger, to help them to be docile and obedient to the light and commands of reason predisposed through grace, while the gifts of the Holy Ghost are qualities and perfections infused with sanctifying grace which they accompany everywhere, in order to dispose us to correspond promptly with all the divine inspiration, all the interior actions of the Holy Ghost, and to follow His guidance wherever He may call us. The gifts of the Holy Ghost are the saintly habits bestowed by God to raise our souls to a state of perfection higher than that which ordinarily proceeds from virtue alone, and to fortify us more strongly even than virtue into meeting the difficulties of life.

All these gifts of the Holy Ghost existed, with their Author, in the Heart of the Blessed Virgin from the moment of her Immaculate Conception, and to a degree, conformable to her destined dignity of becoming the Mother of God.

Let us consider the workings of these gifts in her virginal heart.

The gift of *wisdom* filled her Heart with such clear knowledge and engraved on it such a high esteem and love for God that all her contentment and joy were to contemplate His adorable perfection, to concern herself solely with divine and eternal things, whose contemplation gave her soul all possible delight. For this reason, she possessed a strong scorn for the foolish wisdom of the world and its terrestrial and temporal attributes.

Through the gift of *understanding* she gained the greatest knowledge of all the secrets and mysteries contained in the divine writings of the Old as well as of the New Testament; a greater knowledge than all the holy doctors of the Church ever had or ever will have.

The gift of *counsel* taught her to make fervent resolutions and to follow the inspiration of the Holy Ghost through His gifts of wisdom and understanding.

The gift of *fortitude* implanted in her heart great contempt of herself and attachment to God, in Whom she placed all her confidence and strength, in virtue of which she surmounted all the difficulties and obstacles she encountered and bore patiently all her many persecutions and trials.

Offer to God all the glory that this divine Virgin has rendered to Him, through her most saintly exercise of these four gifts and beg her to make you a participant in them.

SECOND POINT

THE RESULTS PRODUCED IN THE HOLY HEART OF MARY BY
THE GIFTS OF WISDOM, PIETY, AND FEAR

Let us consider the effects of the operation of the gifts of wisdom, piety, and fear of the Lord in the heart of the most Blessed Virgin.

The gift of *wisdom* endowed her with the knowledge of created things and inspired in her the correct use of them. Through this gift she realized the inestimable value of souls, created to the image and likeness of God, which made her most zealous for our salvation.

The gift of *piety* engraved in her Heart the love and tenderness of a real mother for her children and filled her with a compassion for all our miseries and afflictions, so great that she offered to His divine majesty everything she could do and suffer to assuage and help mankind.

The gift of *fear* of the Lord filled her filial Heart with a great apprehension to do only what was agreeable to God and to accomplish His most holy will at all times, in all places, and for His glory and satisfaction alone.

O adorable Spirit, may eternal thanks be rendered to Thee for having thus enriched the very perfect Heart of Thy divine Spouse with all the treasures of Thy most infinite goodness.

THIRD POINT

Means of Participation in the Gifts of the Holy Spirit

The Holy Spirit desires ardently to engulf your heart with a share of all the gifts with which He filled the heart of your divine Mother. Humiliate yourself and ask pardon for all the impediments that you have placed there; make a strong resolution of amendment, and ask the Blessed Virgin to acquaint you with the holy dispositions of her heart towards the sublime gifts of the Holy Ghost.

Ejaculatory prayer:

"O Heart of Mary, treasure of holiness, intercede for us."
O Cor Mariae, thesaure sanctitatis, intercede pro nobis!

SEVENTH MEDITATION

The Holy Heart of Mary Is the Sanctified Garden
of the Fruits of the Holy Spirit

FIRST POINT

THE SIX FIRST FRUITS IN THE HOLY HEART
OF MARY

LET us consider that the amiable Heart of the Blessed Mother of God is the enclosed garden that is mentioned in the fourth chapter of the Canticle of Canticles, *Hortus conclusus,* a garden locked against the serpent and to everything displeasing to God, a garden open only to the Holy Ghost who produces in it innumerable fruits, among which are twelve principal fruits which differ from the gifts of the Holy Ghost. The seven gifts are holy and virtuous habits which dispose souls to follow promptly the inspiration of the Holy Spirit, while the fruits are actions produced by the gifts and by virtue which we practise happily and joyfully with true love of God, under the direction of the Holy Ghost. The twelve fruits of the Holy Ghost are: charity, joy, peace, patience, longanimity, goodness, benignity, meekness, faith, modesty, continence and chastity. Let us consider the effects of the first six fruits in the Heart of the glorious Virgin.

Her Heart, because of *charity* and *love,* was wholly detached from all that was not God and was intimately and uniquely bound up in His divine majesty. *Joy* filled her with great happiness in all the things accomplished by the Mother of love in the service of God's glory. *Peace* maintained a profound tranquillity in her very generous heart in the midst of all the tempests and storms which so often assailed her. *Patience* sustained her in her many trials. *Longanimity* made her await courageously the great things she expected from divine liberality. The incomparable *goodness* with which her soul was filled made her incapable of the slightest unkind thought towards any man, even her cruelest enemies, and urged her continually to wish good for all.

Let us rejoice upon seeing so great and marvelous perfection in the heart of our inviolate Mother. Let us be deeply grateful to the Holy Ghost for lavishing these gifts upon her Heart and beg Him to make us a sharer in them.

SECOND POINT

The Six Other Fruits of the Holy Spirit in the Holy Heart of Mary

Let us consider the effects of the six other fruits of the Holy Spirit in the heart of the Queen of Angels. *Benignity* rendered her sweet, affable, capable of doing good to all. *Meekness* kept all thoughts of sharpness and impatience from her, to soften her being with milk and honey. *Faith,* or rather, fidelity, filled her with truth, naïveté, and frankness and made her scrupulous in accomplishing her promises. *Modesty* forbade anyone to see in her the slightest shadow of worldly vanity and pomp; this holy virtue was reflected in her countenance with such true perfection that she could have been taken for an angel and even a divine being according to St. Denys if the rules of faith were not opposed to it. *Continence* reigned in her heart and actions so that never did she experience any instinct other than the inspiration of the Holy Spirit. *Chastity* clothed her with a purity so admirable that it made her worthy to be the Mother of the Saint of saints and the Queen of Seraphim.

O Mother of my God, my heart is delighted to behold thy Heart filled with all perfection so that it is infinitely more worthy of honor and praise than the hearts of all angels and saints. Eternal praise to the King of all hearts!

THIRD POINT

Ways to Enjoy the Fruits of the Holy Spirit

Let us adore the infinite desire of the Holy Spirit to imprint in our heart an image of all the fruits nurtured in the heart of His divine

Spouse. Let us ask pardon for all the obstacles we have interposed. Let us make a firm resolution to correspond to His great graces by a careful imitation of the adorable Heart of our amiable and loving Mother.

Ejaculatory prayer:

"O Heart of Jesus and Mary, rule of our hearts, reign in our hearts forever."

O Cor Jesu et Mariae, cordis fidelis regula, regna super cor nostrum in aeternum!

EIGHTH MEDITATION

The Holy Heart of Mary Is the Paradise of the Eight Beatitudes

The First Four Beatitudes in the Holy Heart of Mary

LET us consider how the blessed heart of the Mother of our Saviour is the rich paradise of the eight evangelical beatitudes which are similar to the fruits of the Holy Spirit, in so much as both are acts springing from virtuous habits infused into our souls with sanctifying grace, but they differ in that the beatitudes are perfect and eminent acts of several virtues through which the Holy Spirit elevates souls to a state of perfection higher than that of the fruits.

The Holy Ghost infused all the beatitudes into the Heart of Mary from the moment of her Immaculate Conception, more perfectly than they ever existed in the hearts of even the greatest saints. Let us consider and honor in this marvelous Heart the beatitudes:

First, "Blessed are the poor in spirit: for theirs is the kingdom of heaven" (Matt. 5, 3). This beatitude contains two things: humility and love of poverty, which were deeply implanted in Mary's Heart, the most humble of all hearts except the Heart of Jesus, the Heart that had made a vow of poverty because of great love, as the Blessed Virgin revealed to St. Bridget. Consequently, our Lady gave all to the poor; she earned her daily living by her hands; she only wore a colorless woolen cape, according to Nicephore and Cedrenus; the presents she received from the Magi were given away as alms, St. Bonaventure says. Our Lady told St. Bridget that often Jesus, her Son, St. Joseph, her spouse and she herself lacked the necessities of daily life. This is easy to believe when we recall the words of the Son of God: "The foxes have holes and the birds of the air nests, but the son of man hath not where to lay his head" (Matt. 8, 20); because He would not have said that if His holy Mother had enjoyed some comforts, no matter how small.

The second beatitude is "Blessed are the meek." Who could express the sweetness and gentleness of this meekest of Hearts?

The third beatitude is "Blessed are they that mourn." O blessed Virgin, who could count the many swords of sorrow that pierced thy loving heart? O what torrents of tears poured from thy sorrowful eyes, tears even, so say the Saints, of blood!

The fourth beatitude is "Blessed are they that hunger and thirst after justice." Justice here means all Christian virtues, all the holy acts by which God is honored and served. To know the insatiable hunger and thirst of the Blessed Mother, to know the ways and means of best serving and honoring God, would also require a comprehension of her all-consuming love and ardor for His divine majesty and glory.

O my all-good and sweet Mother, I give thee my heart; unite it, I beseech thee, to thine, even though it be most unworthy. Engrave on my heart a perfect picture of thy charity, humility, love for the poor and thy most intense yearning and thirst for all virtue.

SECOND POINT

THE REMAINING BEATITUDES IN THE
HOLY HEART OF MARY

Contemplate and honor the other beatitudes in the Heart of the Blessed Virgin. The fifth is "Blessed are the merciful." Two types of people are included in this beatitude. First, those who, for the love of God, readily forget the injuries done them. Secondly, those who, filled with compassion for the corporal and spiritual sorrows of their neighbor, try to give them all possible aid and help. O Mother of Mercy, throughout thy life thou didst show mercy more perfectly than ever will be shown on earth even by the greatest saints; it is what thou art constantly doing, because all creatures on this earth have experienced the help of thy mercy.

The sixth beatitude is "Blessed are the clean of heart." O what purity,

Queen of Virgins, in thy Heart inviolate, undefiled by any trace of sin, either original or actual, thy Heart filled to overflowing from the moment of the Immaculate Conception with a purity greater than that of all the angels and saints in heaven.

The seventh beatitude is "Blessed are the peacemakers." It is through thee, O Queen of Peace, that the God of peace and love was given to us, the God who brought peace from heaven to the world. It is through thy help that the schisms and heresies which tear the holy robe of thy Divine Son are crushed. It is because of thy powerful intercession that true peace is imparted to men of good will, given to those who willingly renounce their own desires and seek only the things of God.

The eighth beatitude is "Blessed are they that suffer persecution for justice' sake." To know all the persecutions endured by the Mother of the Saviour, we would have to understand the innumerable and countless sufferings of her Well-beloved Son. Because of us, O incomparable Mother, thou and thy Dear Son Jesus Christ have become the target and butt of an infinity of insults, opprobrium, outrages, calumnies, scorn and unspeakable cruelties. Because of our great love for thee, we gladly embrace all the afflictions and persecutions that may ever beset us.

Infinite thanks to the Holy Ghost for having enshrined these beatitudes in thy pure heart. Let us ask the Holy Ghost, O sweet Virgin, to make us participants in thy grace, to teach us and give us the grace to find all our joy, our paradise, and our pleasure even as thou didst during life, that is, in serving, glorifying and loving the divine majesty.

Ejaculatory prayer:

"O Heart of Jesus and Mary, joy of our hearts."
O Cor Jesu et Mariae, cordis nostri gaudium!

VIII

MEDITATIONS
ON
THE SACRED HEART OF JESUS

VIII

MEDITATIONS ON THE SACRED HEART OF JESUS[1]

MEDITATIONS FOR THE FEAST OF THE SACRED HEART OF JESUS

FIRST MEDITATION

The Vigil of the Feast

Dispositions for the Worthy Celebrations of This Feast

FIRST POINT

THE FIRST DISPOSITION FOR THE FEAST OF THE SACRED HEART
OF JESUS IS A BURNING DESIRE TO CELEBRATE IT DEVOUTLY

THE adorable Heart of Jesus is the principle and source of His Incarnation, Birth, Circumcision, Presentation in the Temple, and of all
the other mysteries and states of His life, as well as of all His thoughts,
words, deeds, and sufferings for our salvation. His Heart burning with

---

[1] "Meditations on the Sacred Heart of Jesus" were first published in the twelfth book
of *The Admirable Heart of Mary*. Like the "Meditations on The Holy Heart of Mary"
they are divided into two series, one for the Feast of the Sacred Heart on the excellence
of the Feast and our duties to the Sacred Heart, and the other for any occasion on the
perfections of the Sacred Heart of Jesus. Historically, these meditations are most important because they are the first ever written on the subject. They contain the substance
of St. John Eudes's doctrine of the devotion to the Sacred Heart of Jesus. Cf. *The Sacred
Heart of Jesus* (New York 1946), pp. 85-135.

love prompted Him to perform all these things for us. Thus it is that we owe honor and love to this most amiable Heart for countless reasons, and to show our affection we must celebrate this Feast with all possible devotion.

Let us offer our hearts to the Holy Ghost, and earnestly beg Him to enkindle us with a burning desire to celebrate the Feast of the Sacred Heart with as much devotion as though we were to celebrate it only once on earth. This great desire constitutes the first requisite in preparation for this solemn Feast.

SECOND POINT

THE SECOND DISPOSITION IS HUMILITY

The second disposition is one of deep humility. We must acknowledge our infinite unworthiness to participate in the celebration of such a holy solemnity:

1. Because it belongs to heaven rather than to earth, for the Feast of the Sacred Heart of Jesus is a feast of the Seraphim rather than of sinful men.

2. Because, through our negligence, God's blessings have not borne adequate fruit in our soul, although we have celebrated this Feast many times.

The divine Heart is the source of every grace that we have received from heaven throughout our lives; yet our ingratitude and infidelity have rendered these precious gifts fruitless and ineffectual.

May these thoughts inspire us to profound humility. Let us enter again and again into a true spirit of penance, which will prompt us to detest our sins, to excite genuine contrition in our souls, and to make a good confession to purify our hearts so that we may become worthy recipients of the light and grace necessary for a holy celebration of this Feast.

THIRD POINT

THE THIRD DISPOSITION IS UNION WITH THE THREE DIVINE PERSONS OF THE BLESSED TRINITY, THE BLESSED VIRGIN MARY, THE ANGELS AND THE SAINTS

To excite the third disposition, we must offer ourselves to the Father, Son and Holy Ghost, to the Blessed Virgin Mary, to all the angels and saints, especially to our guardian angels and our patron saints. We must implore them to prepare our hearts and to invite the heavenly court to celebrate this Feast with us. Let us ask them to make us associates and participants in their ardent love for the most adorable Heart of Jesus.

Ejaculatory prayer:

"Thanks be to Thee, Lord Jesus, for the ineffable gift of Thy Sacred Heart."
Gratias tibi, Domine Jesu, super inenarrabili dono Cordis tui.

SECOND MEDITATION

The Day of the Feast

The Gift of the Sacred Heart of Jesus

FIRST POINT

JESUS HAS GIVEN US HIS SACRED HEART

ADORE and consider our most lovable Saviour in the excess of His goodness and in the generosity of His love towards us. Consider attentively His boundless beneficence. He has given us life and all the benefits that spring from the gift of life. He has given us His Eternal Father to be Our True Father, His most holy Mother to be our dear Mother, His angels to be our protectors and His saints to be our advocates and intercessors. He has given us His Church, our second Mother, together with all the sacraments of His Church for our salvation and sanctification. He has given us all His thoughts, words, actions and mysteries, all His sufferings and His very life which He spent' and sacrificed for us, even to the last drop of His Precious Blood.

Moreover, He has given us His most lovable Heart, the principle and source of all other gifts. The charity of His divine Heart impelled Him to emanate from the adorable bosom of His Father, and come upon earth so that He might give us all these priceless favors. This Heart, humanly divine and divinely human, merited these graces by His sufferings, endured for us on earth.

SECOND POINT

WE SHOULD GIVE OUR HEARTS TO JESUS

How shall we repay our loving Redeemer for so much love? We must render love for love. In return for the gift of His Sacred Heart, we must give Him our hearts without reserve. To return Our Lord love for love, we must offer our love wholly and completely to Him. He has given us His Heart for all eternity; we must give Him ours forever. He has given us His Heart with infinite love; let us give Him ours in union with His infinite love. He is not satisfied with giving us His own Heart, He has also given us the Heart of His Eternal Father, the Heart of His most holy Mother and the hearts of all His angels and saints. He even gives the hearts of all mankind who are commanded under pain of eternal damnation to love us as He has loved us: "This is my commandment, that you love one another, as I have loved you" (John 15, 12).

Let us also offer Him in thanksgiving the Heart of His Eternal Father, the Heart of His holy Mother, the hearts of all the angels and saints and of all men; these are ours to give as though they belonged to us. St. Paul assures us that with the gift of His Son the Eternal Father has given us all things: "Hath he not also, with him, given us all things?" (Rom. 8, 32), and that all things are ours: "For all are yours" (1 Cor. 3, 22). Above all, let us offer Him His own Heart; He has given it to us; therefore, it is ours and is the most acceptable offering we could make to Him. It is His own Heart and at the same time the Heart of His Eternal Father, one by unity of essence. It is also the Heart of His most Holy Mother, whose heart is one with His by unity of will and affection.

Ejaculatory prayer:

"Let us give thanks to the Sacred Heart of Jesus for His ineffable gifts."
Gratias infinitas super inenarrabilibus donis ejus.

THIRD MEDITATION

The Gift of This Feast Is a Great
Favor Bestowed by Our Lord

FIRST POINT

EXCELLENCE OF THE FEAST OF THE
SACRED HEART OF JESUS

LET us adore the incomprehensible goodness of our most loving Redeemer in giving us this holy Feast. It is, indeed, most extraordinary grace.

To understand it at all adequately, we must remember that the feasts celebrated by Holy Church during the course of the year are fountains of sanctification and blessings, but this Feast is a veritable sea of grace and holiness. The Feast of the most Sacred Heart of Jesus constitutes an immense ocean of feasts because it commemorates the principle of all the other feasts celebrated by Holy Church. It also is the festival of the prime source of everything that is great, holy and venerable in each of the other feasts.

It is our duty, then, to render infinite thanks to our Saviour for His goodness, and to invite the Blessed Virgin, all the angels and saints and all creatures to unite with us to praise, bless and glorify Him for this ineffable favor.

We should also dispose our souls to receive the graces Our Divine Lord wills to communicate to us during the solemnity of this wonderful Feast. We must make a strong resolution to do everything in our power and to employ all our affections and every means possible to continue to celebrate it appropriately and devoutly during the Octave.

OUR DUTIES TO THE SACRED HEART OF JESUS

Why has the King of all hearts given us this Feast of His most lovable Heart? Solely that we may discharge our obligations to Him. We have four principal duties to fulfil.

The first duty is adoration. Let us adore the Heart of Jesus with all our heart and all our strength. It is infinitely worthy of adoration because it is the Heart of God, the Heart of the Only-begotten Son of the Eternal Father and of God made man. Let us adore this precious Heart, offering It all the adoration ever accorded to It in heaven and on earth. O my Saviour, may the whole universe unite in adoration of Thy divine Heart! I willingly consent to be reduced to nothingness now and forever, by means of Thy grace, so that the Sacred Heart of Jesus may be incessantly adored by the whole universe.

Our second duty is to praise, bless, glorify and thank His infinitely generous Heart for Its tremendous love for the Eternal Father, His most holy Mother, all the angels, all the saints, and all creatures, especially ourselves. Let us also thank Him for all the gifts, favors and blessings poured out from this immense sea of graces upon all things created, particularly upon us. O most sublime Heart, I offer Thee all the praise, glory and thanksgiving rendered Thee in heaven and on earth, in time and eternity. May all hearts praise and bless Thee forever!

The third duty is to ask pardon of His kind Heart for all the sorrow and suffering endured for our sins, and to offer in reparation all the satisfaction and joys given to Our Lord by His Eternal Father, by His Blessed Mother and by all ardent and faithful hearts. Let us accept out of love for the Sacred Heart all the trials, sorrow and affliction which may come upon us.

The fourth duty is to love this divine Heart with all possible affection and fervor in the name of those who do not love It and to offer It the entire love of all hearts that belong to It. O Heart all-lovable and all-loving, when shall I begin to love Thee as I should? I am under countless obligations to love Thee; yet, alas, I realize that I have not even commenced. Grant me the grace to begin straightway to love Thee. Destroy in my heart whatever is displeasing to Thee and establish instead the reign of Thy holy love.

Ejaculatory prayer:

> "O God of my heart, O Jesus, my portion forever."
> *Deus cordis mei, pars mea, Jesus in aeternum.*

FOURTH MEDITATION

The Sacred Heart of Jesus Is Our Refuge, Our Oracle and Our Treasure

FIRST POINT

THE SACRED HEART OF JESUS IS OUR REFUGE

IN THE Feast we are celebrating, our most loving Saviour has given us His Heart not only as the object of our homage and adoration, but also as our refuge and our shelter. Let us have recourse to this haven in all our undertakings, and seek therein our consolation in our sorrows and afflictions. Let us place ourselves in the shadow of its protection against the malice of the world, against our own passions and the snares of the devil; let us retire to this shelter of goodness and mercy to shield ourselves from all the perils and miseries of life. Let us seek refuge in the Sacred Heart, in the tower of strength, where we may escape the vengeance of divine justice for our sins which caused the death of the very Author of life. May this most benign and generous Heart be our shelter and our refuge in all our necessities!

SECOND POINT

THE SACRED HEART OF JESUS IS OUR ORACLE

Our Divine Lord has given us His Heart also to be our oracle. How much more valuable is this gift than the first oracle which was placed in the tabernacle of Moses and afterwards in the temple of Solomon! The first oracle was confined to one place, but ours is to be found wherever our Saviour is present. The former remained in existence but a few centuries; ours will last until the end of time. The oracle of Old Law spoke by the voice of an angel, but the oracle of the New Law is the very voice of Christ Himself. O Jesus, Thou dost speak heart to heart, teaching us Thy will, resolving our doubts, smoothing our difficulties when we have recourse to Thy Sacred heart with faith, humility and confidence.

If we wish to know what God asks of us upon different occasions, if we have a difficult task to undertake, if we are in doubt or perplexity, let us have recourse to the Heart of Our Lord, celebrating Holy Mass in His honor or else receiving Holy Communion. Thus, we shall experience the consoling effects of His goodness.

THIRD POINT

THE SACRED HEART OF JESUS IS OUR TREASURE

Our most lovable Redeemer has also given us His most loving Heart to be our treasure. It is an immense and inexhaustible treasure which enriches heaven and earth with infinite blessings. Let us draw from this treasure whatever we need to pay our infinite debts to divine justice for our failings. Let us offer the Most Sacred Heart in satisfaction for our numberless sins, offenses and negligences.

If we lack a particular virtue, we must draw upon the treasure house of all virtues, the Sacred Heart of Jesus. If we need humility, let us beg Him to impart to us a share in His profound humility. If we need charity, let us implore Him by His most ardent charity to give us perfect charity. Likewise we may develop each virtue in turn.

When we need a special grace to meet certain circumstances, let us ask our Lord through His most benign Heart to grant it to us from His Sacred Heart, our treasure house.

If we desire to help the souls in purgatory, let us offer God our precious treasure that He Himself may take from it the price due His justice.

When the poor beg for alms, we should ask the Sacred Heart for the grace to respond to their appeal and give them a share in our heavenly treasure by saying this prayer: "O most benign and generous Heart of Jesus, have mercy upon all those who suffer."

When people ask to be remembered in our prayers, or make any request of us, we should lift up our hearts to Christ, our treasure, saying with true confidence and with deep humility: "O loving Saviour, arouse in me the feelings of Thy charitable Heart toward all who come to me for help."

The heart of every man is attached to whatever is his treasure. Let us so direct our life that all the affections of our heart may be concentrated on the greatest of all treasures, the most amiable Heart of Jesus.

Ejaculatory prayer:

> "O God of my heart, O Jesus, my love forever."
> *Deus cordis mei, amor meus, Jesus in aeternum.*

FIFTH MEDITATION

The Sacred Heart of Jesus Is the Perfect Model and Rule of Our Lives

THE SACRED HEART OF JESUS IS OUR PERFECT MODEL

WE SHALL never be able to understand adequately and esteem at its full value the inconceivable grace our Lord has granted us through the gift of His Divine Heart. Let us picture a man who was such a favorite of a king that he could truthfully say: "The king's heart belongs to me." What happiness and joy to be so favored! But we have infinitely more than the heart of an earthly king. We have the Heart of the King of Kings, who loves us so ardently that each one of us can truly say: "The Heart of Jesus belongs to me."

Yes, this admirable Heart is mine. It is mine because the Eternal Father has given it to me; it is mine because the Blessed Virgin has given it to me; it is mine because He Himself has given it to me, not only to be my refuge and shelter in my needs, to be my oracle and my treasure, but also to be the model and rule of my life and of my actions. I wish to study this rule constantly so as to follow it faithfully.

I must consider what the Heart of Jesus hates and what it loves, in order to hate only what it hates and love only what it loves. The only thing it hates or ever shall hate is sin. Did the gentle Heart of Our Lord feel any hatred for the miserable Jews who persecuted Him so unjustly, or for the executioners who treated Him so cruelly? No, He never experienced the emotion of hatred. On the contrary, He besought His Eternal Father to pardon His executioners and even excused the most outrageous of all crimes.

I wish to follow the Divine Rule for love of Thee, my Saviour. I will hate nothing but sin; I will love all that Thou lovest, even my enemies. With the help of Thy grace I will do all the good I can to those who seek to harm me.

SECOND POINT

SENTIMENTS THAT SHOULD FILL OUR HEARTS IN
IMITATION OF THE SACRED HEART OF JESUS

My rule tells me that I must have in my heart what is in the Heart of Our Lord: "For let this mind be in you, which was also in Christ Jesus" (Phil. 2, 5). These sentiments are:

1. His affection for the person and will of His Eternal Father. He so loves His Father that He has sacrificed Himself and is still prepared to sacrifice Himself a hundred thousand times for the glory of God the Father. His love for the divine will is so great that never once in the course of His life did He prefer His own will and found His entire satisfaction in doing His Father's will: "My meat is to do the will of him that sent me" (John 4, 34).

2. Another sentiment of His Heart is horror of sin. He hates evil to such a degree that He delivered Himself to the wrath of His enemies and to the torments of the Cross to crush the infernal monster.

3. A third sentiment is His esteem for the Cross and for suffering, which He loves so tenderly that the Holy Ghost, speaking of His Passion, called it the day of His Heart's joy: "In the day of the joy of his heart" (Can. 3, 11).

4. His love for His Mother is the fourth sentiment of His divine Heart. He loves her alone more than all His angels and saints together.

5. There is also a sentiment of charity for us. Our Saviour so devotedly loves us that "it seems," says St. Bonaventure, "that He hates Himself for us." *In tantum me diligis, ut te pro me odisse videaris.*

6. Lastly, there is the attitude of His Heart towards the world. He regards it as something accursed and outcast, openly declaring that it has no part in His prayers: "I pray not for the world" (John 17, 9), and that His children are not of the world: "They are not of the world, as I also am not of the world" (John 17, 16).

Such are the divine principles I wish to observe for love of Thee, my Saviour. I long to love God with all my heart, with all my soul and with all my strength. I long also to find my satisfaction in following in all things and everywhere His most adorable will. I long so to abominate all kinds of sin, that by means of Thy holy grace I may rather die than ever consent to it. O my Jesus, make me love crosses and afflictions that I may seek all my joy in them for the love of Thee, and that I may say with St. Paul: "I am filled with comfort: I exceedingly abound with joy in all our tribulation" (2 Cor. 7, 4).

Grant me a share in Thy very great love for Thy holy Mother that she after Thyself may be the centre of my veneration and fervent devotion. Impress upon my heart the hatred Thou hast for the world. Make me detest it as a veritable antichrist which is always opposed to Thee and has crucified Thee so relentlessly. Grant, I beseech Thee, O God of my heart, the grace, that for the love of Thee I may always preserve in my soul an entire and perfect charity for my neighbor. This is the rule of rules: "And whosoever shall follow this rule, peace on them" (Gal. 6, 16).

Ejaculatory prayer:

> "O Sacred Heart of Jesus, law and rule of our heart."
> *O Cor Jesu, lex et regula cordis nostri.*

SIXTH MEDITATION

Jesus Gave Us His Sacred Heart to Be Our Heart

THE SACRED HEART OF JESUS IS GIVEN TO US TO BE OUR HEART

THE Son of God gives us His Heart not only to be the model and rule of our life, but also to be our heart, so that by the gift of this Heart, immense, infinite and eternal, we may fulfil all our duties to God in a manner worthy of His infinite perfections. We have three obligations towards God:

1. To adore His divine grandeur.

2. To render Him thanks for His unspeakable gifts.

3. To implore Him to grant through His divine generosity all the necessities of soul and body.

How are we able to discharge these duties in a manner worthy of God? We are utterly unable to do so. Even if we had the mind, the heart and the strength of all angels and men united, and if we were to use them to adore, thank and love God and to satisfy His divine justice, we could accomplish absolutely nothing to discharge our obligations as creatures of God. We have, however, received from our divine Saviour the gift of His adorable Heart which is the perfect means of fulfilling all these duties. We should employ the Sacred Heart as if It were our own heart, to adore God fittingly, to love Him perfectly, and to satisfy all our obligations adequately so that our homage and love may be worthy of His supreme majesty. Eternal and infinite thanks be rendered Thee, O good Jesus, for the infinitely precious gift of Thy divine Heart. May all the angels, saints and all creatures bless Thee forever.

How We Should Make Use of the Sacred Heart of Jesus

What happiness and what wealth to possess the divine Heart of Jesus! What a treasure to have at our disposal! How great is our obligation, O my Saviour, because of Thy incomprehensible goodness! Thou dost ask the Eternal Father to make us one with Him and with Thee, as Thou and He are but one. Consequently Thou dost wish to be one in heart with Thee and with Thy Adorable Father. Thou hast willed to be our Head, and hast willed us to be Thy members and to have but one heart and one spirit with Thee. Thou hast made us children of Thy Heavenly Father; Thou hast given us Thy divine Heart, so that we may love the Father with Thy very own heart.

Thou hast assured us that the Adorable Father loves us even as He loves Thee. "Thou hast loved them, as thou hast also loved me" (John 17, 23). Thou dost love us with the same Heart with which the Father loves Thee: "As the Father hath loved me, I also have loved you" (John 15, 9). Thus, Thou dost give us Thy Heart that we may love the Father and Thyself with the same heart and with the same love with which Thou lovest us. We should, therefore, employ Thy Sacred Heart to offer Thee our adoration, praise, thanksgiving and all our other duties with a reverence and a love worthy of Thy infinite greatness.

What must we do to employ the great Heart that God has given us? We must do two things. First, whenever we adore, praise, thank and love God, or practise acts of some virtue, or accomplish some deed in His service, we must renounce our own heart which is poisoned with the venom of sin and of self-love. Secondly, we must unite ourselves to the love, charity, humility and all the holy dispositions of His Sacred Heart, so that we may be worthy to adore, love, praise, serve and glorify God with the Heart of God.

O my Saviour, extend the power of Thy eternal arm to separate me from myself and unite me to Thee. Pluck out my miserable heart and replace it with Thine own, enabling me to say: "I will give praise to

thee, O Lord, with my whole heart" (Ps. 9, 2). I will praise Thee and
love Thee, my Lord, with my whole heart—with the great Heart of
Jesus, which is my own heart.

O all lovable and all loving Heart of my Saviour, be Thou the Heart
of my heart, the soul of my soul, the spirit of my spirit, the life of my
life and the sole principle of all my thoughts, words and actions, of all
the faculties of my soul, and of all my senses, both interior and exterior.

Ejaculatory prayer:

"O Heart all mine, I possess all things in possessing Thee!"
O Cor meum, Cor unicum, in te mihi sunt omnia!

SEVENTH MEDITATION

Profound Humility of the Sacred Heart of Jesus

SELF-ABASEMENT OF THE SACRED HEART OF JESUS

Humility is a virtue including an infinity of degrees because there are innumerable sources of humiliation. There are, however, three fundamentals. The first is our nothingness, which is a bottomless abyss of abjection and humiliation. The second is the infinite grandeur of God for all greatness necessarily involves lowliness in 'those who are inferior to it, and the greater the elevation, the greater is the demand of humiliation on the part of the inferior. That is why the supreme greatness of the majesty of God should impress on created beings an abasement infinite in itself. The third principal humiliation is sin. The least of our sins is an infinite abyss of abasement, and God could justly annihilate us for our smallest fault.

Self-abasement is the first effect that humility should produce in our heart. It operated prodigiously in the Heart of our Divine Saviour because Jesus, as man, understood very clearly that He Himself was nothing and of Himself had only nothingness.

Secondly, His very clear perception of the immense grandeur of God held our Lord continually in a state of incomprehensible lowliness.

Thirdly, the God-Man realized that He was a son of Adam, and that original sin is an immense ocean of sin. It is the very fountainhead of all the sins past, present and future in the whole world, even if it should last for thousands of years more. Jesus understood that if He had been merely man and had been born of an ordinary mother, and if He had not been preserved at the moment of His conception, He would have been as capable as the other children of Adam of committing sin. This realization held Him in a state of profound humiliation. Beyond this,

He saw Himself charged with all the crimes of the world as if they had been His own. *Peccata nostra sua esse voluit*, says St. Augustine, and He saw Himself obliged to bear before God the humiliation of a number of sins as great as the drops of water and grains of sand in the sea.

O Jesus, who could understand all the humiliations Thou didst bear on earth to destroy my pride? How is it possible that, after all this, my heart can tolerate for one single instant this frightful monster?

SECOND POINT

HATRED OF THE HEART OF JESUS FOR THE GLORY AND ESTEEM OF THE WORLD

To know the second effect of humility in the Heart of our Redeemer, let us study His continual hatred for the esteem and glory of this world during the whole course of His life here below. He is the Only Son of God and is God equal to His Father. He is the King of glory, the sovereign Monarch of heaven and earth, who merits the homage and adoration of all creatures. If He were to display the palest ray of His majesty, the whole universe would fall prostrate at His feet to adore Him. But He permits none of His grandeur to appear, either at His birth or in the course of His life, not even after the Resurrection, nor in the most adorable Sacrament where He is glorious and immortal. He fled when the Jews wished to make Him king, and declared that His kingdom is not of this world, so much did He detest the glories and honors of the world.

O Jesus, impress these sentiments upon my heart and grant that I may learn ever to esteem the praises of the world as poison from hell.

THIRD POINT

LOVE OF THE HEART OF JESUS FOR HUMILIATION

Recall to your mind all the humiliations, all the confusion, contempt, abjection, opprobrium and ignominies that our most adorable Saviour bore in His Incarnation, in His Birth, in His Circumcision, in His Flight into Egypt, and in all the mysteries of His Passion. All these humiliations constitute a magnificent feast that His divine love ·has prepared and all the ignominies are as delicious viands, upon which He has feasted and satisfied His extreme hunger for abasement.

Whence did this insatiable hunger proceed if not from His infinite love for His Heavenly Father and for us? This love gave Him the incredible desire to be humiliated and considered as nothing, to atone for the infinite injury and the inconceivable dishonor the sinner had shown to God. The sinner tears God from His throne so that he may put himself in His Creator's place, preferring his own satisfactions to God's good pleasure, his own honor to that of God and his own will to the Divine Will. This injury only a God can perfectly repair by his own abasement.

That is why the incomprehensible love of the Son of God for His Father not only obliged Him to suffer so many humiliations, but also brought Him to the abyss of ignominies to seek his joys and delights, to repair more perfectly the dishonor shown to His Father. His love compelled Him also to deliver us from the eternal pains of hell, to acquire for us everlasting bliss in heaven, to destroy our pride, the source of all our sins, and to establish in our souls that humility which is the true foundation of all virtues.

Infinite thanks, O my Jesus, be to Thy holy humility! Everlasting praise to the Eternal Father who exalted Thee as highly as Thou hast been humiliated and has given Thee a name above all other names! May every knee in heaven, on earth and in hell bend to adore and glorify Jesus Christ, and may every tongue confess my Saviour, rejoicing in the immense and eternal glory of His Father!

Ejaculatory prayer:

> "Jesus, meek and humble of Heart, have mercy on us."
> *Jesu, mitis et humilis corde, miserere nobis.*

EIGHTH MEDITATION

The Sacred Heart of Jesus Is the King of Martyrs

FIRST POINT

SUFFERINGS OF THE SACRED HEART OF JESUS
BECAUSE OF OUR SINS

ALL the sufferings of the Holy Martyrs pale into insignificance in comparison with the infinite sufferings of the adorable Heart of the King of Martyrs. If we could number all the sins of the universe, we would count the myriad sharp arrows that pierced the divine Heart of our Saviour with so many wounds. These wounds caused the Sacred Heart to burn with love for His Eternal Father, whom He beheld outraged and dishonored by innumerable crimes. O my Saviour, I hate all my sins because they are the detestable executioners that brought Thy most gentle Heart to martyrdom.

Again, let us picture to ourselves a countless number of miserable souls for whom our Saviour had an incredible love. He foresaw that, notwithstanding all His sufferings for their salvation, they would by their own fault be lost forever. This vision of the damned inflicted unutterable sorrow on the most charitable Heart of Jesus. O unhappy souls, why have you not loved Him, who has loved you more than Himself, since He has given His very life and blood for your salvation! O dearest Jesus, give me all the hearts of these unfortunate souls, that I may love and praise Thee for them eternally.

SUFFERINGS OF THE SACRED HEART OF JESUS BECAUSE OF THE TRIALS AND TORMENTS OF THE MARTYRS AND CHRISTIANS

Let us recall to our minds all the sufferings, the agony, the trials and the torments of so many thousands of martyrs and of all true Christians. All these afflictions are so many bleeding wounds for the most Sacred Heart of Jesus. His most benign Heart could suffer more than the tenderest of hearts because it was filled with an infinite charity for His beloved children. He retained before His eyes the sight of all their crosses and sufferings. In the hour of affliction each one sought consolation from His adorable Heart.

No human mind can understand the agonizing martyrdom suffered by the all-paternal heart of our Saviour in union with His heroic martyrs. This is expressed most remarkably in the words of the Prophet Isaias: "Surely he hath borne our infirmities and carried our sorrows" Isa. 53, 4), and also in the words of St. Matthew: "He took our infirmities, and bore our diseases" (Matt. 8, 17). Truly we can call the Sacred Heart the King of Martyrs and the Glory of the Cross! How consoling it is for the afflicted to know that all their pain and sorrow have already been suffered by the most benign Heart of Jesus!. He has borne all sufferings first out of love for His martyrs! Let us give ourselves also to Him to bear all our afflictions in union with immeasurable love with which He first suffered them.

SUFFERINGS OF THE SACRED HEART OF JESUS ON THE CROSS

All the other sufferings of our Saviour seem to diminish .when compared to those endured by His divine Heart on the cross. The sufferings of Calvary were so excruciating that the perfect body of our Saviour was broken with pain and sorrow and His soul He commended into the hands of His Father. O my Saviour, what made Thee suffer so many torments if it was not Thine infinite love for Thy Father and for us? Indeed, we can say that Thou hast died of loving sorrow and that Thy Heart has been torn and broken by sorrowing love for the glory of Thy Father and for our redemption. O most adorable Heart of Jesus, how shall I thank Thee for the excess of Thy bounty? O that I could possess all the hearts of heaven and earth to sacrifice them in the flames of Thy love!

O Most Holy Father, how canst Thou refuse any petition asked of Thee through the amiable Heart of Thy Son, broken with sorrow for love of Thee and for love of us? No, it is impossible. Rather wouldst Thou allow heaven and earth to disappear. It is, then, through this divine Heart overcome by love and sorrow for me that I implore Thee, O Adorable Father, to take full and entire possession of my heart and to establish there perfectly and forever the reign of the holy love of Jesus and Mary.

Ejaculatory prayer:

Hail! Victim of all woes enthroned
Upon the Cross, the Martyrs' King!
Make Thou the Cross a joy intoned,
The crown and glory that we sing.
Ave, dolorum victima,
Centrum crucis, Rex Martyrum,
Fac nostra sit Crux gloria,
Amor, corona, gaudium.

NINTH MEDITATION

The Sacred Heart of Jesus Is the Heart of Mary

FIRST POINT

MUTUAL LOVE OF THE SACRED HEARTS OF JESUS AND MARY

THE virginal Heart of the Blessed Mother of Jesus contains more love for her Dear Son than all the angels and saints together; thus, the Sacred Heart of the Only Son of Mary is so full of love for His most loving Mother that He is more to her than all created things together.

Let us offer to Jesus the heart and love of His Blessed Mother in reparation for all our want of love and service towards Him. Let us offer to His most worthy Mother, who is also our Mother, the Heart and love of her Son in satisfaction for our ingratitude and infidelity towards her.

SECOND POINT

THE THREE DIVINE PERSONS GAVE THE HEART OF JESUS TO MARY, AND THROUGH HER TO US

Not only is the Blessed Virgin the first object, after God, of the ardent love of the Sacred Heart of Jesus, but the Sacred Heart is really the Heart of Mary for five principal reasons. The first three reasons are: 1. Because the Eternal Father has given her the Heart of His Only-begotten Son as a Father gives the heart of a son to his mother; 2. because the Son has given His most loving Heart to the most admirable of mothers; 3. because the Holy Ghost has imparted to Mary the very spirit of love which unites the Blessed Trinity in the Sacred Heart of her Son. These Three Divine Persons continually and eternally give Mary the adorable Heart of the God-Man, so that she may give us her most precious gift, the Sacred Heart of her Divine Son.

Incessant and everlasting praise be to the Father, to the Son and to the Holy Ghost for this infinitely precious gift that They have given to our Blessed Mother and through her to us. O Most Holy Trinity, I offer Thee the most adorable Heart of Jesus and the most loving Heart of His Mother in thanksgiving for Thy infinite goodness in my regard. I also offer Thee, in union with those two most ardent Hearts, my own unworthy heart, with the hearts of all my brethren, humbly beseeching Thee to take full possession of them forever.

THIRD POINT

OTHER REASONS WHY THE SACRED HEART OF JESUS IS THE HOLY HEART OF MARY

The fourth reason why the Sacred Heart is truly the Heart of Mary is that the Eternal Father, having considered the Blessed Virgin from the very instant of her conception as the one chosen to be the Mother of God, gave her from the first moment of her life a love similar to His love for His Divine Son. According to many theologians, Mary had more love for Jesus at that moment than all the Seraphim will ever have. Therefore, Mary's incomparable love for Jesus drew Him into her sacred womb and into her Heart to rest there eternally as the Heart of her Heart and as a divine Sun that sheds its celestial light into her soul and inflames it with divine fire.

The fifth reason why the Sacred Heart of Jesus is the Heart of Mary is that, at the moment of the Incarnation, she cooperated with the Blessed Trinity to form the human Heart of Jesus, which was formed of her virginal blood. The blood of her holy Heart passed into the Heart of Jesus and received the perfection that was needed to form the Heart of the God-Man. This divinely human and humanly divine Heart dwelt in the sacred womb of Mary as a furnace of divine love, a furnace which transformed the Heart of Mary into the Heart of Jesus and made these two Hearts but one and the same Heart in a unity of spirit, affection and will.

The holy Heart of Mary was, therefore, always closely united to the Sacred Heart of her Divine Son. She always willed what He willed and also consented to act and to suffer so that the work of our salvation might be accomplished. Hence, the Fathers of the Church plainly assert that the Mother of the Saviour cooperated with Him in a very special way in the redemption of mankind. That is why our holy Redeemer told St. Bridget of Sweden, whose revelations have been approved by the Church, that He and His holy Mother worked in perfect harmony, *uno corde,* for our salvation.

Thus, the Sacred Heart of Jesus is the Heart of Mary. These two Hearts are actually only a single Heart, which was given to us by the Blessed Trinity and by our Blessed Mother, so that we, the children of Jesus and Mary, might have but one heart with our Heavenly Father and our holy Mother and that we might love and glorify God with the same heart, a heart worthy of the infinite grandeur of His divine majesty.

Ejaculatory prayer:

O Heart of Jesus and Mary, my most loving Heart!
O Cor Jesu et Mariae, Cor meum amantissimum!

Eight Other Meditations on
The Sacred Heart of Jesus

FIRST MEDITATION

The Blessed Trinity Lives and Reigns
in the Sacred Heart of Jesus

THE ETERNAL FATHER DWELLS IN THE SACRED HEART OF JESUS

CONSIDER that the Eternal Father is in the Sacred Heart of Jesus, bringing to birth His Well-beloved Son and causing Him to dwell there the same all-holy and divine life that He lives in His own adorable bosom from all eternity. He imprints there a perfect image of His own divine fatherhood, so that this humanly divine and divinely human Heart shall be Father to all the hearts of the children of God. Therefore, we should look upon Him, love and honor Him as Our Loving Father, and endeavor to imprint upon our own hearts a perfect likeness of His life and virtues.

O good Jesus, engrave the image of Thy most holy Heart upon our hearts and make us live only by love for Thy Heavenly Father. Would that we might die of love for Thee, as Thou didst die of love for Thy Eternal Father!

SECOND POINT

THE DIVINE WORD LIVES AND REIGNS IN THE
SACRED HEART OF JESUS

Consider that the eternal Word exists in that royal Heart, united with it in the most intimate union imaginable, the hypostatic union,

305

which causes that Heart to be worshipped with the adoration that is due to God. He is there with a life that is somehow more helpful, if one may so speak, than His life in the Heart and bosom of His Father. The Word lives, but does not rule in the Heart and bosom of the Heavenly Father; whereas He lives and rules in the Heart of the God-Man, ruling over all human passions which are centered in the heart so absolutely that they do not stir except by His order.

O Jesus, King of my heart, live and rule over my passions, uniting them with Thine, never allowing them to be used except under Thy guidance and for Thy glory alone.

THE HOLY GHOST LIVES AND REIGNS IN THE SACRED HEART OF JESUS

Consider that the Holy Ghost lives and reigns ineffably in the Heart of Jesus, where He conceals the infinite treasures of the knowledge and the wisdom of God. He fills the Sacred Heart with all His gifts to a preeminent degree, according to His divine words:

"And the spirit of the Lord shall rest upon him: the spirit of wisdom, and of understanding, the spirit of counsel, and of fortitude, the spirit of knowledge, and of godliness. And he shall be filled with the spirit of the fear of the Lord" (Isa. 11, 2-3).

Consider, finally, that these Three Divine Persons live and reign in the Heart of the Saviour, as if they were seated on the most high throne of their love, in the primal heaven of their glory, in the paradise of their dearest delights. They there shed abroad, with inexplicable abundance and profusion, wonderful lights, and the burning fires and flames of their eternal love.

O Most Holy Trinity, infinite praise be to Thee forever for all the wonders of love that Thou dost work in the Heart of my Jesus! I offer Thee my heart, with the hearts of all my brethren, begging Thee most humbly to take entire possession of them, to destroy in them everything displeasing to Thee, and to establish there the sovereign rule of Thy divine love.

Ejaculatory prayer:

O most Holy Trinity, Eternal Life of Hearts, reign in all hearts forever!

O sacrosancta Trinitas, aeterna vita cordium, in corde regnes omnium!

SECOND MEDITATION

The Sacred Heart of Jesus Is the Sanctuary and the Image of the Divine Perfections

FIRST POINT

THE DIVINE PERFECTIONS SUBSIST AND REIGN IN THE SACRED HEART OF JESUS

LET us adore and contemplate all the perfections of the divine nature, subsisting and reigning in the Sacred Heart of Jesus: that is to say, the eternity of God, the infinity of God, His love, charity, justice, mercy, power, immortality, wisdom, goodness, glory, felicity, patience, holiness and all other perfections.

Let us adore these divine perfections in all the wonderful effects they produce in the divine Heart of the Son of God. Let us give wholehearted thanks for these manifestations, and offer them all the worship, glory and love which have been and shall be rendered to them eternally by that same Heart.

SECOND POINT

THE DIVINE PERFECTIONS STAMP THEIR ETERNAL IMPRESS ON THE SACRED HEART OF JESUS

Let us consider that those adorable perfections imprint their image and likeness on the divine Heart of Our Lord, in a manner infinitely more excellent than the most gifted human or angelic minds can conceive or express. The adorable Heart of Jesus bears within itself the image of eternity by its perfect detachment forever from things fleeting and temporal and by its exceeding great affection for things divine and eternal. The Sacred Heart bears the image of immortality by Its infinite love for the Heavenly Father and for us, a love whose immensity reaches everywhere, in heaven, on earth and under the earth. If we consider the nature of that incomparable Heart, we shall see without difficulty that it bears within itself a living likeness of all the other perfections of the Godhead.

O wonderful Heart of Jesus, we offer Thee our hearts; impress upon them, we beseech Thee, some reflection of that divine likeness, so that in us may be accomplished the commandment of our divine Master: "Be you therefore perfect, as also your heavenly Father is perfect" (Matt. 5, 48).

THIRD POINT

The Divine Mercy Should Be the Object of a Very Special Devotion

Of all the divine perfections mirrored in the Sacred Heart of our Saviour we should have a very special devotion to divine mercy and we should endeavor to engrave its image on our heart. To this end three things may be done. The first is to pardon with all our heart and promptly forget the offenses done against us by our neighbor. The second is to have compassion on his bodily sufferings, and to relieve and succor him. The third is to compassionate the spiritual misfortunes of our brethren, which are much more deserving of sympathy than the corporal ills. For this reason, we ought to have great pity on the numbers of wretched souls who have no pity on themselves, using our prayers, our example and our teaching to safeguard them from the eternal torments of hell.

O most gracious and merciful Heart of Jesus, imprint on our hearts a perfect image of Thy great perfections, so that we may fulfil the commandment Thou hast given us: "Be ye therefore merciful, as your Father also is merciful" (Luke 6, 36).

Ejaculatory prayer:

"O Holy God, O Strong God, O Immortal God, have mercy on us."
Sanctus, Deus, sanctus fortis, sanctus immortalis, miserere nobis!

THIRD MEDITATION

The Sacred Heart of Jesus Is the Temple, the Altar and the Censer of Divine Love

FIRST POINT

THE SACRED HEART OF JESUS IS THE TEMPLE OF DIVINE LOVE

THE Holy Ghost, love uncreated and eternal, built this magnificent temple and fashioned it of the virginal blood of the Mother of love. It is dedicated to eternal love. It is infinitely more sacred, more noble, and more venerable than all the temples material and spiritual in heaven and on earth. In this temple, God receives worship, praise and glory worthy of His infinite greatness. In this temple, the supreme Preacher continually teaches us most eloquently. It is an everlasting temple that shall have no end. It is the centre of all holiness, incapable of any profanation. It is adorned with all the Christian virtues in the highest degree, and with all the perfections of the divine nature, as with so many living images of the Eternal Godhead.

Let us rejoice in the vision of all the splendors of this wonderful temple and all the glories there rendered to the divine majesty.

SECOND POINT

THE SACRED HEART OF JESUS THE ALTAR OF DIVINE LOVE

The Heart of Jesus is not only the temple, but it is also the altar of divine love. On this altar, the sacred flame of omnipotent love burns night and day. On this altar, the great High Priest Jesus continually offers to the Most Holy Trinity manifold sacrifices and supreme oblation.

First, He offers Himself as a sacrifice and victim of love, the most holy and precious victim that ever was or can be. He sacrifices utterly and entirely His body, His blood, His soul, His whole life, all His thoughts, all His words, all His actions and all that He suffered on earth. Moreover, He makes that sacrifice perpetually, with a love that is boundless and infinite.

Secondly, He sacrifices everything the Heavenly Father has given Him, namely, all rational and irrational creatures, animate and inanimate beings, which He immolates as so many victims in praise of His Father; but, above all, He sacrifices human beings, the good and the wicked, the blessed and the reprobate. The good He offers as victims of love to His divine goodness. The evil He immolates as victims of the wrath of God, to His awful justice: "Every victim shall be salted with salt" (Mark 9, 48). Thus, the great High Priest sacrifices all things to the glory of His Father on the altar of His Heart. Therefore, He alone may rightly say: "I have joyfully offered all these things" (1 Par. 29, 17).

Let us offer ourselves to Him and beg Him to rank us with the victims of His love, to consume us as holocausts in the divine flames burning incessantly on the altar of His Sacred Heart.

THIRD POINT

THE SACRED HEART OF JESUS IS THE CENSER OF DIVINE LOVE

The Sacred Heart of Jesus is not only the temple and the altar, but also the censer of divine love. It is the golden thurible described in the eighth chapter of the Apocalypse, which St. Augustine interprets as the loving Heart of Jesus. In that precious censer all the worship, praise, prayers, desires and affections of all the saints are placed, like so many grains of incense to be offered to God in the Heart of His Well-beloved Son, ascending as a most pleasing odor to His divine majesty. There we also must place all our prayers, all our desires, all our devotions, and all the pious affections of our hearts, yes, our very hearts themselves, with all that we do and all that we are, beseeching the King of all hearts to purify and sanctify all these things, and to offer them to His Father as a heavenly incense of sweet fragrance.

Thus, the Sacred Heart of our divine Lord is the temple, the altar, the censer, the priest, the victim of divine love, all for our sake, performing on our behalf the functions of those divine offices. O love so abundant! O my Saviour, how wonderful are Thy loving kindnesses! Ah, what reverence and praise I should give to Thy loving Heart in return! O most blessed Heart of my Jesus, let me be naught but heart and love towards Thee and let all hearts on heaven and earth be immolated to Thy praise and glory!

Ejaculatory prayer:

> Hail, priest of hearts and victim, hail!
> Alone Thou equal art to God.
> Most worthy Temple, Holy Grail,
> And Altar, holiest to laud.
> *Ave, Sacerdos cordium,*
> *Ave, Deo par Victima,*
> *Templum Deo dignissimum,*
> *Et Ara sacratissima.*

FOURTH MEDITATION

The Sacred Heart of Jesus Loves Us with an Everlasting and a Boundless Love

FIRST POINT

THE SACRED HEART OF JESUS LOVES US WITH AN EVERLASTING LOVE

THE divine Heart of our Saviour is filled with eternal love for us. To realize this truth, one should understand two truths about eternity: first, that it has neither beginning nor end: secondly that it comprised in itself all ages, past, present and future; all the years, months, weeks, days, hours and moments of the past, present and future, and that it comprises them in a fixed and permanent manner, holding all those things united and joined together in one indivisible point. That is how eternity differs from time. Time runs on incessantly; as one moment arrives, another elapses and is left behind, and so one never sees two moments of time together. But in eternity everything is permanent; whatever is eternal always remains of the same extension.

That is why the eternal love of the Sacred Heart of Jesus for us comprises two elements. First, this incomparable Heart has loved us from all eternity, before we were and could have known and loved it, even in spite of the vision and knowledge that it had of all our offenses which were present to its vision as they are now. Secondly, the amiable Heart of Jesus loves us at every moment with all the love wherewith it has ever loved us and shall love us throughout all eternity. Thus, we can see the difference between God's love and ours. Our love is a passing act; the love of God is constant. The love that God has exercised towards us for a hundred thousand years remains in His Heart together with that which He will dispense a hundred thousand years from now. Eternity implies that in God there is nothing past nor future, but all is present, so that God loves us now with all the love wherewith He has loved us from all eternity and wherewith He will love us forever.

O eternity of love! O eternal love! If I had existed from all eternity, I should have been bound to love Thee from all eternity; and yet, my God, I have not begun to love Thee as I should. At least, let me begin now, O my Saviour, to love Thee as Thou wouldst be loved. O God of my heart, I give myself to Thee to be united to Thy ceaseless love for me from all eternity. I surrender myself to Thee to be united to the love wherewith Thou lovest Thy Father before all centuries, so as to love the Father and the Son with an eternal love.

SECOND POINT

THE SACRED HEART OF JESUS LOVES US WITH
A BOUNDLESS LOVE

The loving Heart of Jesus loves us with a boundless love. The divine and uncreated love which possesses that adorable Heart, is nothing else but God Himself. Now, since God is unlimited, His love is also unlimited. Since God is everywhere, His love is everywhere, in all places and in all things. Therefore, the Sacred Heart of Jesus loves us not only in heaven, but He also loves us on earth. He loves us in the sun, in the stars and in all created things. He loves us in the hearts of all the denizens of heaven and in the hearts of all persons that have some measure of charity for us on earth. All love for ourselves existing in the hearts in heaven and on earth is a participation in the love of the Sacred Heart of Jesus. Moreover, He loves us even in the hearts of our enemies despite the hatred they bear us. I even make bold to say that He loves us in hell, in the hearts of the devils and the damned, in spite of all their wrath and hatred, since the divine love is everywhere, filling heaven and earth like the presence of God.

O boundless love, I plunge myself into thy fires and flames that fill all created beings, in order to love my God and my Saviour in all places and in all things. O Jesus, I offer Thee all the boundless love of Thy Heart, of the adorable Heart of Thy Divine Father, the lovable Heart of Thy holy Mother, and of all the hearts that love Thee in heaven and on earth. I ardently desire that all creatures of the universe be transformed into flaming fires of love towards Thee.

Ejaculatory prayer:

"How late have I loved Thee, O Goodness so ancient and yet so new,
  how late have I loved Thee."
 Sero te amavi, bonitas tam antiqua et tam nova, sero te amavi.

FIFTH MEDITATION

The Sacred Heart of Jesus Is the Source of the Life of the God-man, of the Mother of God and of the Children of God

THE SACRED HEART OF JESUS IS THE SOURCE OF THE LIFE OF THE GOD-MAN

THE adorable Heart of our Saviour is the source of the life of the God-man, and consequently is the source of all the thoughts and feelings of the Son of God on earth, of all the words He pronounced, of all the actions He performed, of all the sufferings He endured, and of the incomprehensible love wherewith He did and suffered all things for our salvation. Therefore, it is to Thy loving Heart, O my Jesus, that our obligation is due. What shall we do to thank Thee? We can do nothing more pleasing to Thee than to offer Thee Thy most· divine Heart. I offer it then to Thee, my Saviour, in union with the infinite love wherewith it hath accomplished so many wonderful things for our Redemption.

SECOND POINT

THE SACRED HEART OF JESUS IS THE SOURCE OF THE LIFE OF THE MOTHER OF GOD

The Sacred Heart of Jesus is the source of the life of Mary, the Mother of God. When that admirable Mother was carrying her Beloved Son in her blessed womb, her virginal Heart was the source of the natural bodily life of her divine Child, but the Heart of that adorable Child was, at the same time, the source of the spiritual and supernatural life of His most worthy Mother. Hence the divine Heart of the Only Son of Mary was the source of all the pious thoughts and

316

feelings of His Blessed Mother, of all the sacred words she spoke, of all the good deeds she performed, of all the virtues she practised, and of all the pains and sorrows she suffered in order to cooperate with her Beloved Son in the work of our salvation.

Praise eternal, O my Jesus, to Thy divine Heart! O my Redeemer, I offer Thee also in thanksgiving for the great wonders of grace that Thy filial Heart hath wrought in Thy glorious Mother, I offer her maternal Heart flaming with love for Thee.

THIRD POINT

THE SACRED HEART OF JESUS IS SOURCE OF LIFE
OF THE CHILDREN OF GOD

The Sacred Heart of Jesus is the source of life of all the children of God. Since it is the source of the life of the Head, it is also the source of life of the members; and since it is the source of life of the Father and the Mother, it is the source of life of the children. That is why we should regard and honor that benign Heart as the source and origin of all the good thoughts in the minds of all Christians, of all the holy words that have issued from their lips, of all the virtues that they have practised, and of all the toil they have borne for their sanctification as Christians.

O my Saviour, may all these things be transmuted into immortal praise to Thy Most Sacred Heart! O Jesus, since Thou hast given me that very Heart to be the source of my life, let it be, I beseech Thee, the sole source of all my feelings and affections, of all the faculties and functions of my soul, and of all the use I make of my interior and exterior senses! In fine, let it be the soul of my soul, the spirit of my spirit, and the Heart of my heart!

Ejaculatory prayer:

"O Heart of Jesus, source of all good, to Thee be praise and glory for ever."
O Cor Jesu, Principium omnium bonorum, tibi laus, tibi gloria in aeternum!

SIXTH MEDITATION

Three Hearts of Jesus Which Are But One Heart

THE DIVINE HEART OF JESUS

WE HAVE three Hearts to adore in our Saviour which, nevertheless, are but one single Heart by virtue of the hypostatic union.

The first is His divine Heart existing from all eternity in the bosom of His Adorable Father, which is but one Heart and one love with the love and Heart of His Father, and which, with the Heart and love of His Father, is the source of the Holy Spirit. Therefore, when He gave us His Heart, He also gave us the Heart of His Father and of His adorable Spirit, hence His marvelous words: "As the Father hath loved me, I also have loved you" (John 15, 9).

He simply means: "I love you with the same Heart and the same love wherewith I love my Father. My Father loves Me with an eternal, boundless and infinite love; I love you also with a love that is eternal, boundless and infinite. My Father causes Me to be what I am, God like unto Himself and Only Son of God; and I make you to be by grace and participation what I am by nature and essence, that is to say, gods and children of God, seeing that you have but one and the same Father as I, a Father who loves you with the same Heart and the same love wherewith He loves Me: 'Thou hast loved them, as thou hast also loved me' (John 17, 23). My Eternal Father has constituted Me universal heir of all His goods: 'He hath appointed him heir of all things' (Heb. 1, 2); and I make you My co-heirs: 'Heirs indeed of God and joint heirs with Christ' (Rom. 8, 17); I promise to give you possession of all My treasures: 'He shall place him over all his goods' (Matt. 24, 47). My Father finds all His pleasure and delight in Me; and I take My delight and pleasure in you: 'My delights were to be with the children of men'" (Prov. 8, 31).

O goodness! O love! O God of love, how is it possible for the hearts of men to be so hard and cold towards Thee who art all aflame with the fire of love towards them? O, let all my joy and delight be in thinking of Thee, in speaking of Thee, in serving and loving Thee! O my All, let me be wholly Thine, and do Thou alone possess all that is in me.

SECOND POINT

The Spiritual Heart of Jesus

The second Heart of Jesus is His spiritual Heart, which 'is the will of His holy soul, a purely spiritual faculty, whose function is to love what is lovable and to hate what is hateful. But the divine Saviour so perfectly sacrificed His human will to His Divine Father that He never exercised it while on earth and will never exercise it even in heaven, but He sought uniquely and solely His Father's will, according to those words of His: "I seek not my own will, but the will of him that sent me" (John 5, 30). "I came down from heaven, not to do my own will, but the will of him that sent me" (John 6, 38). Now, it is out of love for us that Our Lord renounced His own will, in order to perform the work of our salvation solely by the will of His Father, in particular when He prayed to Him in the Garden of Olives: "Father, not my will, but thine be done!" (Luke 22, 42).

O God of my heart, if for love of me Thou didst sacrifice Thy utterly holy and divine will, how much more should I renounce my own will for love of Thee, wholly depraved and corrupted as it is by sin! Ah, let me renounce it with all my heart forever, imploring Thee most humbly, O my adorable Redeemer, to crush it like a serpent full of venom and to establish in its place the rule of Thy divine will.

THIRD POINT

The Corporeal Heart of Jesus

The third Heart of Jesus is the Sacred Heart of His deified body, a furnace of love divine and of incomparable love for us. Since the corporeal Heart is hypostatically united to the Person of the Word,

It is enkindled with flames of infinite love for us. Its love is so intense that it constrains the Son of God to bear us continually in His Heart; to fix His eyes ever upon us; to take such a great interest in the smallest details concerning us that He verily numbers all the hairs of our head, allowing not one of them to perish; to ask His Father that we might make our eternal abode within His bosom: "Father, I will that where I am, they also whom thou hast given me may be with me" (John 17, 24); and to assure us that, if we vanquish the enemies of His glory and of our salvation, He will make us sit with Him on His own throne, and will let us enter into possession of the same kingdom and the same glory that His Eternal Father has given Him.

Oh, how abundant and rapturous is the love of Jesus for such faithless and ungrateful men as we! O Jesus, my love, either take away my life or let me live only to love Thee, to praise and glorify Thee unceasingly. Let me die a thousand deaths rather than willingly do anything to grieve Thee! Thou hast three Hearts which are but one and the same Heart, a Heart wholly devoted to loving me continually. Would that I possessed all the hearts in the universe that I might consume them in Thy holy love!

Ejaculatory prayer:

"I love Thee, O most loving Jesus, I love Thee, O infinite goodness, I love Thee with my whole heart and I wish to love Thee more and more."

Amo te, amantissime Jesu, amo te, bonitas infinita, amo te ex toto corde meo, et magis atque amare volo.

SEVENTH MEDITATION

The Miracles of the Sacred Heart of Jesus

MIRACLES OF THE SACRED HEART OF JESUS
IN THE REALM OF NATURE

PICTURE to yourself the realm of nature, the great universe comprising so many wonderful things, namely, the heavens, the sun, the moon, the stars and comets, the four elements, of which the air is peopled by such a great variety of birds; the earth, replete with its marvelous abundance of animals, trees, plants, flowers, fruits, metals, stones; the sea, filled with such a prodigious multitude of fishes. Add to that the creatures of reason, men and angels; consider them in the natural state of their creation. What a miracle to have made this amazing universe out of nothing! It is not only a miracle, it is a world of miracles without number.

Count all the creatures made by God and you will count so many miracles that God has performed in drawing them from the abyss of nothingness. Number all the moments that have elapsed since the creation of the world and you will number so many miracles since preservation is a continuous creation. There are also innumerable other wonders perpetually wrought in the governance of this universe. Now, who is the author of those innumerable miracles? It is the inconceivable goodness and the incomprehensible love of the divine Heart of that adorable Word, mentioned by St. John the Evangelist in the first words of his Gospel: "All things were made by him" (John 1, 3). It is because of His love for us that our divine Lord has made all things, even though He had always before His eyes the ingratitudes, the offenses and the crimes without limit which He was obliged to suffer and still endures every day from us.

That is why all those things which He created are so many tongues and voices preaching to us unceasingly the ineffable charity of His most gracious Heart, and exhorting us to adore Him, to love Him and to glorify Him in every possible manner.

Heaven and earth, says St. Augustine, and all things contained therein, cease not to tell me that I should love my God: *Caelum et terra et omnia quae in eis sunt, non cessant mihi dicere ut amem Deum meum.*

SECOND POINT

MIRACLES OF THE SACRED HEART OF JESUS
IN THE REALM OF GRACE

Picture the realm of grace, which comprises innumerable wonders incomparably surpassing those of the world of nature. It encompasses all the miracles of sanctity that have been wrought on the earth by the Holy of Holies; all the wonders that transpired in the Mother of grace; the entire Church Militant; all the Sacraments, with all the marvelous effects which they produce; all the wonderful things that divine grace has effected and will effect in the lives of all the saints that have been and that shall be in this world. What is the source of all those wonders? Is it not the inconceivable charity of the blessed Heart of our Redeemer, who has established and constantly preserves this amazing world of grace on earth, for love of us?

O my Jesus, let all these wonders of Thy most loving Heart and all the powers of Thy divinity and Thy humanity be employed to bless Thee and praise Thee unceasingly and eternally: "O all ye powers of the Lord, bless the Lord" (Dan. 3, 61).

THIRD POINT

MIRACLES OF THE SACRED HEART OF JESUS
IN THE REALM OF GLORY

Let us raise our mind and our heart to heaven, to contemplate the realm of glory, the fair, great and glorious city of heaven, of which all the citizens are forever freed from tribulation and showered with countless blessings. Let us behold that innumerable army of the blessed: "Which no man could number" (Apoc. 7, 9), who are more dazzling than the sun, who possess incalculable riches, joys unspeakable and glories indescribable. Consider the inconceivable happiness which awaits you in that heavenly Jerusalem, since the Holy Ghost declares to us that never hath eye seen, nor ear heard, nor human heart understood nor can ever understand the infinite treasures that God has prepared there for them that love Him. Now, what has made heaven and who is the author of all the miracles contained therein? It is the intense love of the Sacred Heart of the Son of God, who has merited it by His blood, who has filled it with an ocean of unutterable delights, to give us the full and perfect possession of it eternally.

O my Saviour, graciously let me offer Thee, I beg Thee, as an act of thanksgiving, all the glories and wonders of paradise! If I were possessed of a hundred thousand paradises, how gladly would I, by the help of Thy grace, divest myself of them so as to sacrifice them to Thy eternal praise!

Ejaculatory prayer:

"Let the mercies of the Lord give glory to him: and his wonderful works to the children of man."
Confiteantur Domino misericordiae ejus, et mirabilia ejus filiis hominum.

EIGHTH MEDITATION

The Sacred Heart of Jesus Is a Furnace of Love, Purifying, Illuminating, Sanctifying, Transforming and Deifying

FIRST POINT

THE SACRED HEART OF JESUS A FURNACE OF LOVE FOR US

THE most loving Heart of our benign Saviour is a burning furnace of most pure love for us; a furnace of purifying love, of illuminating love, of sanctifying love, of transforming love and of deifying love. His love is a purifying love, in which the hearts of holy souls are purified more perfectly than gold in the furnace; an illuminating love, which scatters the darkness of hell with which the earth is covered and lets us into the wonderful brilliance of heaven: "Who hath called you out of darkness into his marvellous light" (1 Pet. 2, 9); a sanctifying love, which destroys sin in our souls in order to establish there the kingdom of grace; a transforming love, which transforms serpents into doves, wolves into lambs, beasts into angels, children of the devil into children of God, children of wrath and malediction into children of grace and blessing; a deifying love, which makes gods of men: "I have said: you are gods" (Ps. 81, 6), letting them share in the holiness of God, His mercy, His patience, His goodness, His love, His charity and His other divine perfections: "Partakers of the divine nature" (2 Pet. 1, 4).

O divine love of my Jesus, I give myself wholly to Thee; purify me, enlighten me, sanctify me, transform me into Thee, that I may be naught but love for my God.

SECOND POINT

THE FURNACE OF THE SACRED HEART OF JESUS
RADIATES LOVE TO ALL BEINGS

The august Heart of Jesus is a furnace of love which spreads its fiery flames in all directions, in heaven, on earth and throughout the whole universe. Its fiery flames would have consumed the hearts of the Seraphim and would have enkindled all the hearts on earth if the terrible chill of sin had not set in. Those divine fires transform all the hearts of heavenly lovers into so many furnaces of love for Him who is all love for them.

All creatures on earth, even senseless, inanimate and irrational beings, feel the effects of the incredible goodness of that magnificent Heart since He loves all things that are and hates nothing that He has made, sin being the only thing that He did not make, the only object of His hatred: "For thou lovest all things that are, and hatest none of the things which thou hast made" (Wisd. 11, 25).

Jesus Christ possesses an extraordinary love for men, as well for the good as the wicked, for His friends as for His enemies, for whom He has such intense charity that even the overwhelming torrents and floods of their innumerable sins are not able to extinguish it: "Many waters cannot quench charity" (Cant. 8, 7). Not a moment elapses that He does not grant to men manifold natural and supernatural favors, corporal and spiritual, even while they are offending Him and dishonoring Him by their misdeeds.

The divine fires of the precious Heart of the Son of God reach even into hell, to the devils and the damned, preserving their being, life and the natural perfections which He gave them at creation, and not punishing them as much as they have deserved for their sins, for which His divine justice might very justly chastise them much more severely than it does: "There is no one that can hide himself from his heat" (Ps. 18, 7).

O sacred fires and flames of the Heart of my Saviour, rush in upon my heart and the hearts of all my brethren, and kindle them into as many furnaces of love for my most loving Jesus!

THIRD POINT

INTENSITY OF THE LOVE OF THE SACRED HEART OF JESUS

Imagine all the charity, all the affections, all the tender and intimate feelings of all the hearts that the omnipotent hand of God might fashion as being collected and united in one heart large enough to contain them. Would they not all be capable of forming one unimaginable furnace of love? But, realize that all the fires and flames of such a furnace would not make one tiny spark of the immense love with which the infinitely loving Heart of Jesus is inflamed towards you, O Christian soul.

O furnace infinitely to be desired! Who will grant me to be plunged into that burning fire? O Mother of Jesus, O all ye angels, O all ye holy saints of Jesus, I give myself to you all and to each in particular, and I give you also all my brothers and sisters, and all the inhabitants of earth, that you may plunge us all into the abyss of that sacred furnace! Attend and hear, O vast furnace of love! A tiny straw asks most humbly and earnestly to be plunged, buried, lost, devoured and consumed wholly in thy sacred flames and thy holy fires forever and ever!

Ejaculatory prayer:

"O fire which ever burnest and is never extinguished. O love which is ever fervent and never grows tepid, inflame me wholly that I may love Thee wholly."

O ignis qui semper ardes et nunquam extingueris. O amor qui semper ferves et nunquam tepescis, accende me totum, ut totus diligam te!

IX

MEDITATIONS
FOR
SPECIAL DAYS OF THE YEAR

IX

MEDITATIONS FOR SPECIAL DAYS
OF THE YEAR[1]

Meditation for New Year's Day

FIRST POINT

LET US ADORE JESUS AT THE BEGINNING
OF HIS LIFE ON EARTH

O JESUS, my Lord, I adore, bless and love Thee with all the powers of
my soul, at the first moment of Thy life of suffering on earth.

I adore all the holy thoughts, sentiments and dispositions of Thy
divine soul, and all that took place within Thee in that first moment.

O Admirable Jesus, from the very first moment of Thy mortal life,
Thou didst turn towards the Eternal Father to adore, love and glorify
Him, to refer to His omnipotence Thy being, Thy life and all its consequences. Thou didst give Thyself to Him to do and suffer everything
He pleased, for His glory and for love of us. I behold that, at the same
instant, Thou didst turn Thy spirit and heart towards me, to think of
me, to love me, to make great plans for my soul and to prepare very
special graces for me.

Blessed be Thou, O Good Jesus, and may all the creatures of heaven
and earth, and all the powers of Thy divinity and Thy humanity
eternally bless Thee for these divine operations.

[1] The first and last of these meditations are taken from "Part Six" of *The Kingdom of
Jesus*. The others are to be found in the *Manual of Piety* which St. John Eudes compiled
for his order of priests, the Congregation of Jesus and Mary.

Let Us Give Ourselves to Jesus to Begin the Year as He Began His Life Upon Earth

O Jesus, I give myself to Thee, that I may commence this year as Thou didst begin Thy life on earth, and share in Thy most holy dispositions. I beg Thee, by Thy great mercy, to implant these dispositions in my heart.

O Most Adorable Jesus, in honor of and in union with the humility, love and other holy dispositions with which Thou didst adore and love the Eternal Father, giving Thyself to Him at the first moment of Thy life, I adore, love and glorify Thee, as my God and my Saviour, as the Creator of time, the King of years and of centuries, and as the divine Redeemer who purchased for me, at the cost of Thy Precious Blood, all the time that is allotted to me on earth.

O Jesus, I consecrate to Thee all my minutes, hours, days and years, my being and my life, and all that goes with them. I desire to employ everything for Thy pure glory alone. I desire all my thoughts and acts, every beat of my heart, every breath I draw, and all else that shall take place in me this year, and during my whole life, to become so many acts of praise and love for Thee. May it please Thee, my dear Jesus, to grant that this may be so, through Thy most great power and goodness.

I also offer Thee, O Jesus, all the love and glory that shall be given to Thy majesty. I unite myself with all the honor and praises that shall be given Thee this year and forever, by the Eternal Father, the Holy Spirit, Thy Blessed Mother, the angels and saints and all Thy creatures.

O Most Amiable Jesus, I adore all the designs Thou dost shape for me during this year. Do not permit me to put obstacles in their way. I give myself to Thee to do and suffer everything Thou dost please, for the accomplishment of these eternal designs. In honor of, and in union with the love with which Thou didst accept, at the first moment of Thy Incarnation, all the sufferings Thou hadst to bear in life, I now accept and embrace, for Thy love, all the sufferings of body and spirit I shall have to undergo this year and during my whole life.

O my Saviour, a year will come that will be the last in my life. Perhaps this very year now unfolding is to be my last. If I knew with certainty that this was to be my last year on earth, with what care and fervor would I spend it in Thy service! Nevertheless, I wish to spend this year as if I had no more time to love and glorify Thee in this world, and to make up for the occasions in the past, when I have fallen away from my love of Thee. Grant me, O Good Jesus, all the graces that I need for this constancy.

THIRD POINT

Let Us Offer the Beginning of the Year to
the Blessed Virgin in Honor of the
First Moment of Her Life

O Blessed Virgin, Mother of my God and Saviour, I honor and reverence thee in the first moment of thy life. I honor and reverence the dispositions of thy holy soul, and all that took place in thee at that time.

Thou didst begin immediately, O holy Virgin, to love and glorify God most perfectly, and from that first moment to the last of thy life, thou didst ever love and glorify Him more and more. As for me, in spite of all the years I have been in this world, I have not yet begun to love and serve Him as I should.

O Mother of mercy, beg thy Divine Son to have mercy on me. Atone for my failings, offering Him on my behalf all the love and glory thou didst ever give Him, to satisfy for my neglect in loving and glorifying Him. Grant that I may share in thy surpassing love for Him, and in the fidelity of that great maternal love. Pray for me, that He may give me the grace to begin, at least now, to love Him perfectly, and that all that shall take place during this year, and all my life, may be consecrated to His glory and thy honor.

O angels, and saints of Jesus Christ, pray for me, that our loving Saviour may give me new grace and new love for Him, to devote this year and my whole life, purely and solely to the service of His glory and love.

Ejaculatory prayer:

"Behold I make all things new."
Ecce nova facio omnia (Apoc. 21, 5).

Meditation for Ash Wednesday
The Holy Season of Lent

LENT IS A SEASON OF GRACE AND BLESSING

O JESUS, King of ages and Sanctifier of time, I adore Thee as the Author of the holy season of Lent, and as the source of all its holiness. O my God, I adore Thy providential designs towards the Church, towards our own Community and myself in particular, during this penitential time of special grace and benediction, in which, O my Saviour, Thou dost indeed desire to grant me many very special graces if I interpose no obstacles. Do not permit any obstruction, but destroy in me whatever may be contrary to Thy benevolent designs, and grant me the dispositions to accomplish perfectly Thy most holy will. O my dearest Lord, I testify that with all my strength I detest my sins for love of Thee, I renounce my self-love, my own will and all that pertains to "the old man," and I give myself to Thy Providence to do and suffer all that Thou dost please on my behalf throughout my life, and especially during this holy season of Lent.

O my God, I wish to consider and spend this Lent, as it were to be the last Lent of my life. To that end, I dedicate and consecrate to Thee all my actions, promising that I wish to do or think nothing save for Thy supreme glory, and to fulfil my obligations with all the perfection possible to me, with the help of Thy bountiful grace, which I implore with my whole heart for this intention.

SECOND POINT

HOW TO SPEND THE SEASON OF LENT PROFITABLY

O my Jesus, I desire to spend this holy season in company with Thee and Thy most holy Mother and, so far as I can with the assistance of Thy grace, to keep it as Thou and she would have done. I see that Lent was spent by Thee in solitude, apart from the society of men, apart even from the sweet company of Thy most holy Mother, in unbroken silence, in ceaseless prayer, in extremely rigorous penance, fasting stretched on the ground, suffering in the desert a multitude of pains both bodily and mental.

I adore Thee, O my God, in all these achievements and in all the interior dispositions of Thy holy soul. I give myself to Thee for the accomplishment and imitation of Thy Lent, inasmuch as Thou shalt desire of me. I wish to love with Thee, and for love of Thee, solitude, silence, prayer and penance. I beseech Thee to grant me the grace to dissociate myself from vain and useless conversations, to abstain from all wrong and idle words, to perform all my acts in spirit of prayer and recollection, and to practise, for love of Thee, some measure of penance and mortification.

O my Saviour, I offer Thee the abstinence and fast of this Lenten season, together with all the fasts and other mortifications of Holy Church, of all the Saints, of Thy Blessed Mother, in honor of and in union with Thy most exemplary fast and penance, in atonement for my sins and in fulfilment of Thy divine designs for Holy Church, for our Community and for my own soul in particular.

O Mother of Jesus, I offer myself to thee. Make me, I beseech thee, a participant in the holy dispositions with which thou didst spend this penitential season.

O angels of Jesus Christ, O saints of God, pray for me. Obtain for me the grace to employ this Lent and the remainder of my life in faithful service of my God, according to His most holy will.

Ejaculatory prayer:

"The world shall rejoice: and you shall be made sorrowful."
Mundus gaudebit, vos autem contristabimini (John 16, 20).

Meditation for Good Friday

DUTIES TO OUR DYING SAVIOUR

THIS is the last hour of the temporal and passible life of our Lord Jesus Christ on earth. Our God, Our Saviour, Our Father is agonizing and dying on the Cross. Let us render Him, with all possible devotion, our final homage and service.

Our first duty is to adore Jesus, and to invite all the angels and saints to adore Him with us, in the dreadful manifestation and awesome mysteries of His mortal life, especially of His last day, last hour, last moment, last thoughts, last words, actions and sufferings, in the last disposition of His holy soul and in His last breath.

The second duty is to bless and thank Him, begging all the angels, saints and His most holy Mother to help us to offer Him thanksgiving for everything He spoke, did and suffered for the glory of His Heavenly Father and for our salvation.

The third duty is to beg our Saviour's forgiveness and make reparation in the name of all men for the multiple offenses and outrages He suffered on earth on our account. We must offer Him, in atonement, all the love and honor which were, are and shall always be given Him in heaven and on earth by His Eternal Father, by the Holy Spirit, by His Blessed Mother, by all His angels and His saints, also to offer and yield ourselves to Him to do and suffer whatever shall please His holy will.

The fourth duty is to prostrate ourselves at the feet of Jesus, agonizing and dying on the Cross, beseeching Him to give us His benediction before leaving mortal life, and, by the virtue of this benediction, to destroy in us all kinds of malediction, that is, every trace of sin and inclination to evil, to bless our body and our soul, our eyes, our ears, our mouth, our tongue, our hands, our feet, our memory, our mind and our will, all our senses interior or exterior, so that henceforth we employ them only for His greater glory.

The fifth duty is to tell God the Son, dying for us on the Cross, that we wish to die with Him and for Him; to die to sin, to the world, to ourselves, to all that displeases Him. We should offer ourselves to Him for this purpose, begging Him very earnestly to impress on our minds a perfect image of His most holy death, and to make us die the precious and desirable death of the saints, that we may henceforth live only in Him and for Him.

SECOND POINT

Duties to Mary, Mother of Jesus

After having fulfilled our obligations towards the Son of God, we have still three duties to His holy Mother.

The first is to prostrate ourselves in heart and in spirit at her feet asking her pardon for the cruel death of her Son, and for the most bitter sufferings of her pure heart which we have caused. In reparation, we must offer her all the honor, glory and praise which have been, are and will be forever rendered to her in heaven as well as on earth by the Most Holy Trinity, by the sacred humanity of her Son, by all the angels and all the saints. We must also give ourselves to our Lady as her slaves, promising that we wish to serve and honor her all our lives in every way possible to us.

The second thing we must do for the Blessed Virgin is to remember that Our Lord Jesus Christ, dying on the Cross, gave her to us as our Mother, and gave us to her as her children, when, addressing her, He said: "Behold thy Son"; and speaking to each of us in the person of St. John: "Behold thy mother." We ought to thank Our Lord with our whole heart for having given us His Mother to be our Mother; we ought to give thanks to the most holy Virgin for having received us as her children, and to beg our Saviour that inasmuch as He has associated us with Him as the Beloved Son of Mary, He also make us share His perfect filial devotion to His admirable Mother.

Our third debt to the Mother of Jesus is to acknowledge and salute

her as our Mother, declaring that we desire to serve, love and honor
her as our Mother, obey her as a Mother and study to make ourselves
like unto her as children should resemble their mother; and, consequently, to imitate her humility, her patience, her obedience, her
purity, her mildness and docility, her charity and all her other virtues.
We must beseech our Lady to look upon us, her unworthy children,
to protect and to guide us in all things and to be a mother to us both
in life and in death.

Ejaculatory prayer:

"He loved me and delivered himself for me."
Dilexit me et tradidit semetipsum pro me (Gal. 2, 20).

Meditation

The Vigil of the Ascension of Our Lord

ADORATION AND THANKSGIVING

BEFORE Our Lord ascends to return to the bosom of His Heavenly Father we must render to Him four final tributes.

Our first duty is to adore our Saviour in all the states and mysteries of His life on earth, to ask His pardon for our failure to honor Him and for the little fruit we have derived from His all-meritorious life, and to offer Him in reparation the admirable glory which has been accorded our divine Redeemer by His Blessed Mother, the angels, the saints and by His whole Church.

Our second duty is to bless and thank Our Lord on the eve of His glorious ascension, begging the choirs of angels, the holy company of saints and His most holy Mother, to praise and glorify Him with us, in the name of the whole human race, for all that He thought, said, did and suffered while on earth out of love for us, affirming that we wish to do, say, think and suffer everything only for love of Him alone.

SECOND POINT

REPARATION

Our third duty is to prostrate ourselves at the feet of our Risen Saviour in a spirit of repentance and contrition and, in the name of all mankind, to make worthy reparation, begging His divine pardon for the countless injuries, offenses and outrages we have heaped upon Him which He endured on our behalf while He was on earth. In satisfaction we must offer Him all the honor and glory that He received, and that He will ever receive on earth and in heaven, as also to offer ourselves to Him to do and to suffer for this intention, whatever may be His august and holy will.

THIRD POINT

UNION IN SPIRIT AND HEART

Our fourth duty is to give ourselves to Him, begging Him to prepare us to leave this earth on the great feast of tomorrow, to ascend to heaven with Him in heart and spirit. We must implore Him to accomplish this by breaking all our bonds and detaching us entirely from everything in this world and in ourselves. We must beg our Saviour to tie and bind us so closely to Himself that He may transport upwards into heaven our minds, our thoughts, our hearts, our desires and our affections, that for the future we may be able to say with the first Christians: "Our conversation is in heaven" (Phil. 3, 20).

Ejaculatory prayer:

> "Our conversation is in heaven."
> *Conversatio nostra in caelo est* (Phil. 3, 20).

Meditation

The Vigil of the Assumption of Our Lady

HOMAGE AND THANKSGIVING

BEFORE the Blessed Virgin Mary leaves this earth to enter heaven, let us fulfil our final obligations to her.

The first duty is to prostrate ourselves at her feet, in the name of the whole human race, asking the angels and the saints to prostrate themselves with us to salute and honor her in all the states and mysteries of her life; to beg her pardon for the inadequate honor we have rendered during the course of the year, and for the little fruit we have gathered from her shining example. We must offer her, in place of our ingratitude and negligence, all the honor and all the praise accorded to her by the choirs of angels and by the vast company of saints in heaven and on earth.

The second duty is to give our Lady thanks from ourselves and from all men, begging also all the citizens of heaven to bless and thank her with us, for all that she thought, said, did and suffered in this world to cooperate with her Divine Son in the salvation of mankind.

SECOND POINT

REPARATION

Our third duty is to implore her pardon in the name of the whole world, for the countless injuries and offenses that she has received, and for all the pain, sorrow and anguish she has borne on account of our sins, on our behalf offering her in satisfaction and reparation the Adorable Heart of her Divine Son, together with all the service,

340

praise and honor which have been and will ever be tendered to her by the whole Church, Triumphant and Militant. We must also offer her ourselves to do and suffer anything she pleases, affirming that we wish to do all that is possible to us to serve and honor her throughout our lifetime, and to cause her to be served and honored by everyone else.

THIRD POINT

ACT OF OBLATION TO MARY

The fourth duty is to present her with a gift, before she leaves the earth to go to heaven, as she is our sovereign Lady and our Queen. What gift shall we offer her? What can we give her when everything is already hers? It is true that all creation belongs to her, but it is, nevertheless, very pleasing to her to receive from us what is already hers, provided we offer our gift with the same affection with which we would make our offering if we could give our Queen something that is not already hers. Let us give her our hearts. Our Lady wants most of all the gift of each human heart that she may give it to her Divine Son. Let us each give his heart to her entirely and irrevocably, beseeching her to destroy anything in it displeasing to her, to detach it completely from all creatures and to unite it closely to her own most admirable Heart in order to enrapture our hearts and bear them upward with her own into highest heaven.

Ejaculatory prayer:

"We offer thee our hearts."
Tibi cor nostrum offerimus.

Meditation
for
The Feast of the Holy Relics[2]

OBLIGATION TO HONOR THE RELICS
OF THE SAINTS

THERE are several reasons which oblige us to honor the precious relics of the saints, especially those enshrined in this place.

First, we should honor all that God honors. Almighty God honors to such a degree everything belonging to His saints that He counts the hairs of their heads and performs miracles by their bones and ashes, so that they become venerated by all men, even by kings and princes, who think themselves privileged to be allowed to touch and honor saintly relics.

Secondly, we should honor all creatures by which God is honored. Almighty God is greatly honored by the relics of the saints because the bodies of the saints have cooperated with their souls in the heroic virtue they performed for the glory of God; thus, all honor given to the saints and their relics proceeds to God, the Saint of saints and the fount of all sanctity.

Thirdly, we must venerate saintly relics because St. Paul testifies that the bodies of the faithful are the members of Jesus Christ, who is their Head, and members of the mystical body of Jesus, namely, His Church.

Fourthly, St. Paul also affirms that the bodies of true Christians are temples of the Holy Ghost, and that Jesus Christ will raise them up because the Holy Ghost has taken up His dwelling in them: "He

[2] Some religious communities celebrate this feast on November 5, during the Octave of the Feast of All Saints.

shall quicken also your mortal bodies, because of his Spirit that dwelleth in you" (Rom. 8, 11). This is why the Church, in the funeral ceremonies of a Christian, blesses the grave and asks God that His Holy Spirit may descend into it with the body to be placed there, in order to raise it up on the day of General Judgment.

Finally, Holy Mother Church, animated and guided by the Holy Ghost, has always held the relics of the saints in such veneration that St. Gregory Nazianzen, quoted by the great Cardinal Baronius in his *Ecclesiastical Annals,* says that the bodies of the holy martyrs have the same power as their souls if we touch or venerate them; and that drops of their blood and small tokens of their sufferings have the same power as their bodies. St. Gregory says, furthermore, that the veneration of the Saints was so widespread, that a little dust of the remains of a bone were honored as equivalent to the whole body, and that even the name of a saint, without the presence of any relics at all, was enshrined in the place of the martyr's body and possessed equal power. With good reason he exclaimed: "O prodigious thing! Their very memory alone gives life."

SECOND POINT

Dispositions with Which We Should Honor Holy Relics

The first disposition is deep humility, acknowledging to ourselves that, as sinners, we are unworthy not only to touch but even to gaze upon the holy relics of the saints.

The second disposition is the purification of our souls from all sin and from all affection to sin by means of true contrition; because holy things should be treated in a holy manner.

The third disposition is thanksgiving to our Lord Jesus Christ for all the glory He has rendered His Father by the saints whose relics are here present, for the countless favors He has bestowed upon them and for the rich graces He has given us through their intercession. We must also return thanks to the saints themselves for the wealth of honor they have rendered unto God and for the great assistance they have given us by their prayers and merits.

The fourth disposition is to give ourselves to Jesus Christ, the Saint of saints, and to ask Him to make us sharers in the spirit, in the love, in the charity, humility and other virtues of His saints and to unite us to all the love and all the glory that they have rendered and will eternally render with Him to the Most Holy Trinity. We must likewise offer ourselves to the saints and implore them to give us to Jesus and His most holy Mother, and to employ the God-given power to destroy in us anything that is displeasing to them. We must beg the saints to make us sharers in their ardent love and in all their magnificent virtues, to make us their associates in the praise which they send up and will forever send up before the throne of the most High, and to obtain for us the grace to imitate the holy life they lived while on earth.

Ejaculatory prayer:

> "God is wonderful in his saints."
> *Mirabilis Deus in sanctis suis* (Ps. 67, 36).

Meditation
for
Christmas Day

Our Duties to the Child Jesus

ADORATION, PRAISE AND THANKSGIVING

O DIVINE and adorable Child Jesus, prostrate at Thy feet, I adore Thee, praise Thee and thank Thee with Thy Blessed Mother, with St. Joseph, with the whole Church and in the name of all creatures. I adore, praise and thank the Blessed Trinity through Thee and in Thee. May everything in me and in the universe offer adoration, praise and thanks to the Blessed Trinity that reigns so perfectly in Thee.

SECOND POINT

HUMILIATION AND SATISFACTION

O Divine Child Jesus, Thou art the joy of the angels in heaven. The glory and the happiness of Thy Eternal Father are Thine from the very first moment of Thy mortal existence. Nevertheless, I now behold Thee lying in a stable, suffering the humiliation and pains of childhood. O Infant Jesus, my sins are the cause of Thy suffering. I hate and detest them with all my heart and in satisfaction I offer Thee all the tears and pains of Thy Holy Childhood, and I give myself to Thee to suffer in union with Thee whatsoever suffering it may please Thee to send me.

THIRD POINT

LOVE AND OBLATION

O Loving Child Jesus, Thou art all love for me and I wish to be all love for Thee. I give Thee my heart with all my affection, in union with the Eternal Father, the Holy Spirit, Thy Blessed Mother, and all Thine angels and saints. Take full possession of my soul forever.

O Most Sweet Jesus, Thou dost give Thyself to me with infinite love. In union with the same love, I give, consecrate and sacrifice myself entirely to Thee with every created being. If I had an infinity of worlds, I would gladly sacrifice them an infinite number of times if it were possible. O Almighty Child, use Thine infinite power to take full possession of me, to annihilate in me everything that is contrary to the spirit of Thy Holy Childhood, and to sacrifice me wholly with Thee to the glory of Thy Father.

Ejaculatory prayer:

"We adore Thee, O dear Child Jesus."
Adoramus Te, Domine Jesu Infans.

Meditation
for
The Last Day of the Year

LET US ADORE JESUS ON THE LAST DAY AND
LAST MOMENT OF HIS LIFE ON EARTH

O JESUS, my Lord, I adore, love and glorify Thee in the last day, the last hour and last minute of Thy mortal life on earth. I adore all that happened both inwardly and outwardly on that last day, meaning Thy last thoughts, acts, words and sufferings, Thy final use of the senses of Thy sacred body, and the last dispositions of Thy holy soul, to which I desire to unite myself now, with a view to the closing moment of my own life.

O Divine Jesus, by the light of faith I behold Thee on that last day of Thy life, adoring and loving the Eternal Father infinitely. Thou dost give Him fitting thanks for all the graces imparted to Thee and, through Thee, to the whole world during the time of Thy sojourn on earth. Thou dost ask His pardon for all the sins of men, offering Thyself to Him to suffer the penance due to them. Thou dost think of me with love exceedingly great, with a most ardent desire to draw me to Thyself. Finally, Thou dost sacrifice Thy Precious Blood and Thy most noble life, for the glory of the Heavenly Father and for love of us. Blessed be Thou infinitely for all these inestimable graces.

O Good Jesus, in honor of and in union with the love, humility and other holy dispositions with which Thou didst perform all the last actions of Thy life, I give Thee thanks for all the glory Thou didst render to the Eternal Father during Thy life on earth, for all the graces Thou hast bestowed upon me and all men this year and always, as well as for the graces Thou wouldst have lavished on me if I had not stood in Thy way.

I most humbly beg Thy forgiveness for all the outrages and in-dignities Thou didst suffer on earth because of me, and for all the offenses I have committed against Thee this year. In satisfaction, I offer Thee all the honor and glory rendered to Thee, during Thy time on earth and during the past year, by Thy Eternal Father, the Holy Spirit, Thy Holy Mother, and by all the angels and saints. So, too, I offer myself to Thee to bear all the penance Thou mayest ordain for me in this world and in the next.

O Jesus, most worthy of love, I adore Thy infinite thoughts and designs for me on the last day of Thy most precious life; and I give myself to Thee to do and suffer all Thou dost desire of me, for the fulfilment of these unfathomable designs. Grant that I may die a thousand times rather than hinder the operation of Thy loving Providence.

SECOND POINT

Let Us Offer Jesus the Last Day and Last Moment of Our Life

O Good Jesus, I offer to Thee the last day, the last hour and the last moment of my life and everything that may happen to me then out-wardly and inwardly. I mean, my last thoughts, words, actions and sufferings, as well as the last use of my bodily senses and of the powers of my soul.

May it please Thee to grant that all these things may be consecrated to the honor of the last day, the last hour and last moment of Thy perfect life. May I die loving Thee with Thy holy love. May my being and my life be sacrificed and consumed for Thy glory, and may my last breath be an act of pure love of Thee. This is my intention, my desire, my expectation. O my Dear Jesus, relying as I do upon the excess of Thine infinite love, may it please Thee to grant, by Thy great mercy, that this may be so.

THIRD POINT

LET US OFFER TO THE BLESSED VIRGIN THE LAST DAY OF OUR LIFE IN HONOR OF THE LAST DAY OF HER LIFE ON EARTH

O Mother of Jesus, Mother of the Eternal and Immortal God made Man, I honor and venerate thee in the last hour and moment of thy life. I honor thy last thoughts, words and acts, and the last use made of the senses of thine immaculate body and of the powers of thy glorious soul. Especially I wish to honor the last act of love made by thy mother's heart for thy Most Beloved Son.

With all my heart I bless and thank thee, O holy Virgin, for all the glory thou didst render to God during thy spotless life, and for all the graces thou didst ever obtain from His bounty for me and for all men, especially during this year.

I beg thy forgiveness, O Mother of Mercy, for all the offenses thou didst suffer on earth, as well as for those I have committed this year against thee. To make satisfaction for these, I offer thee all the honor that has ever been accorded thee in heaven and on earth.

O Mother of Fair Love, I offer thee the last day, the last hour and moment of my life, and all that shall take place in me at that last moment, in honor of the last moment, hour and day of thy life, and of all that occurred in thee on that day. Unite me, I beseech thee, with all the holy and divine dispositions of thy maternal heart and thy pure soul. Grant that, by thy merit and prayers, my last thoughts, words, acts and breaths may be consecrated to the honor of the last thought, words, acts and breaths, both of thy Son and of thyself. Grant that I may die loving Him with His holy love, and that I may be utterly consumed and sacrificed to His glory, and that my life may end with a last act of most pure love for Him.

O angels and saints of Christ, pray that He may consummate this final grace for me, by His exceedingly great mercy and for love of Him.

Ejaculatory prayer:

"Blessed are the dead who die in the Lord."
Beati mortui qui in Domino moriuntur (Apoc. 14, 13).

CPSIA information can be obtained
at www.ICGtesting.com
Printed in the USA
BVHW07s0818030618
518066BV00017B/221/P